Praise for *Trust-Based Selling*

Charles Green will tell you he's not a salesperson. So how has he written a book brimming with such practical selling wisdom? The answer lies in his long history as advisor to some of the best consulting firms in the world. He has distilled this experience and applied it to sales. I learned a lot from this book.

> Neil Rackham, Author *SPIN Selling*

At last, a sales book based on how adult, intelligent people actually buy. An important contribution that challenges the effectiveness of much of current sales practice, and shows how to do it better.

> David Maister, Author
> *Managing the Professional Services Firm*,
> coauthor *The Trusted Advisor*

Charles Green can be trusted — and so can his book. Trust is something that is earned, not just given. If you want to earn the trust of your customers, I suggest you read this book and heed its wisdom.

> Jeffrey Gitomer, Author *The Sales Bible*
> and *The Little Red Book of Selling*

Green has written a rarity—a practical book which talks about the critical role of trust in selling, and how to be honest and successful at the same time.

> Ken Roller, Director
> Strategic Relations, Intel Corp.

Trust-based Selling reminds us that long-term value creation is driven by putting the client first. It takes courage to put short-term financial goals aside to build long-term value through trusting relationships. Disciplined execution of the principles outlined in this book will reward the courageous.

> James McSherry, EVP
> Commercial Banking, CIBC

Charles Green's *Trust-based Selling* is the break-through book I have been searching for. It provides effective concepts and examples of how to build lasting relationships in businesses dealing with intangible products and services. It is timeless in its teachings, and will become the foundation for our professional development training.

> Jack Snyder,
> Managing Director Business Development, Guy Carpenter & Company

TRUST-BASED SELLING

TRUST-BASED SELLING

Using Customer Focus and Collaboration to Build Long-term Relationships

Charles H. Green

McGRAW-HILL

New York Chicago San Francisco Lisbon London
Madrid Mexico City Milan New Delhi
San Juan Seoul Singapore
Sydney Toronto

CONTENTS

ACKNOWLEDGMENTS

Thanks to my father, Thomas Green, for showing me that one could write books. Thanks to Bill Leigh and Wes Neff for helping me think boldly and wisely about what books to write. Thanks to David Maister for helping make this book the best it could be.

This book benefited from my earlier collaboration with David Maister and Rob Galford on *The Trusted Advisor*. Renee Wingo and Laverne Berry were keen sources of inspiration and insight. I'm grateful for the ideas gained by working with John Barch, Patricia Fripp, Kathy Hammond, Stewart Hirsch, Tom Howe, John Malitoris, Tom Neilssen, Scott Parker, Mark Petruzzi, Howard Schwartz, and Sims Wyeth. I benefited from the willingness of people to read earlier drafts and offer me their comments: Kathy Hammond, Barbara Hendra, Ford Harding, David Maister, and Scott Parker. The book also benefited editorially from the good people at McGraw-Hill.

Special thanks to Ken Roller at Intel for his help in developing these ideas to practical fruition.

Thanks to those who agreed to be interviewed, including Karl Almstead, Stephen Bommarito, Dwight Davies, Joseph Duane, Michael Fabiano, Mike Heal, Woody Heller, Steve Keller, Judy Lutzy, Maurie Mader, Kathie Magness, Priscilla Myers, Jennifer Nelson, and Howard Schwartz.

Above all, thanks to my consulting clients and participants in seminars and workshops who bore with me and helped me to articulate and communicate the ideas in this book.

INTRODUCTION

The words *sales* and *trust* are seldom used in the same sentence. Customers are skeptical, even cynical, about being "sold," often with good cause. The reason is simple—buyers don't trust sellers, fearing that sellers have only their own interests at heart.

Salespeople are well aware of the dilemma. On the one hand, we want to do right by our customers. On the other hand, we want to get the sale. It feels conflicting.

Can sellers really help buyers and, at the same time, serve their own bottom line without conflict? Or is this conflict the essence of a commercial relationship?

Trust-based Selling® is not an oxymoron. The gains of trust-based relationships can and do accrue to both parties. People prefer to buy what they have to buy anyway from those they have come to trust. It is possible for selling to be a genuinely value-adding, beneficial process for buyer and seller alike.

But in order for the relationship to work, we as sellers have to care—honestly and deeply—about our customer. If our primary objective is to help the customer, then we can become trusted and, among other things, make lots of money. But if our primary objective is just to make lots of money or become competitively successful by trying to become trusted—it will not work. The trick is—you have to care. The solution, simple to state, is hard to live.

"Fake it till you make it," a saying in the corporate training business, means to practice behaviors that feel alien to you until they become more comfortable. It works well for practicing golf swings, learning French, or improving public speaking.

But when it comes to trust, and to selling complex goods and intangible services, it's a recipe for failure. If you fake it, you break it. With sophisticated buyers, long selling cycles, and intense interpersonal contact it is virtually impossible for a seller to fake trust. The only way to make it is *not* to fake it. Ask any customer.

Trust-based Selling is no more an oxymoron than is a parent "selling" a child on experiencing something new, or someone "selling" good advice to a friend in need. Rather than simply focusing on getting the buyer to meet the needs of the seller, the interests of buyer and seller can be aligned. The only reason it sounds radical is because it's uncommon. This book aims to make it more common.

Who Should Read This Book

Trust-based Selling tries to serve all people in sales and all customer-facing roles, and is particularly aimed at complex products and intangible services businesses.

Today, that's every business with ticket prices of more than $1,000, buying processes that last longer than a few days, or relationships that involve more than a few phone calls. There are no pure product or hardware companies anymore. Buyers don't just buy boxes; they buy such intangibles as interoperability, access, plug-compatibility, scalability, multiple redundancy, and service contracts.

Companies in private banking, accounting, construction, commercial real estate, reinsurance all provide complex intangible services. And companies selling routers or automotive components know their business is less about selling hardware than it is about selling an ongoing network of services, capabilities, and personal relationships. "Stuff" isn't the issue anymore; managing relationships is.

If you are in the law, consulting, accounting, public relations, advertising, or actuarial businesses, this book is for you. If you are in the enterprise of expensive PC software or related services, this book is for you. If you are in the commercial banking, brokerage, insurance, financial planning, or private banking business, or you sell telecom or technology equipment or services, this book is for you. If you sell almost anything to OEM accounts in amounts of more than $10,000 per transaction, or your sales are relatively concentrated in a proportionally small number of key accounts, this book is for you. If you are a sales manager in almost any business, this book is for you. But most importantly, if you believe your business could benefit from creating greater trust between your customers and the salespeople with whom they interact, this book is for you.

A Note about Terms in This Book

I use the terms *client* and *customer* interchangeably in this book. Historically, "client" is used by those selling professional services to distinguish their services from "mere" product sales. But when all products come wrapped in services, customers are becoming clients. Or is it the other way round? I use both terms to reflect the truth about selling today—differentiating between a customer and a client is increasingly a distinction without a difference.

I have duplicated all the lists in the book in the Appendix. Some of you might want to start there just to get a feel for the book, in addition to the table of contents. Or, you may want to use it to identify particular topics of interest for which you can "drill down" quickly. Finally, you may want to use it after reading the book as a convenient reference point.

TRUST-
BASED
SELLING

PART I

UNDERSTANDING BUYING AND SELLING

HOW BUYERS BUY

This Chapter at a Glance

Buyers of complex products and services buy in a two-step process: screening and selection. Screening is largely rational; selection is heavily nonrational. In the screening phase, buyers look at the firm; in the selection phase, they look at the seller.

Trust-building, in spite of its importance, is often neglected in the selling process. When it is there, buyers prefer to buy what they have to buy anyway from the one they have come to trust. Trust goes beyond loyalty to affirm that the seller has the buyer's best interests at heart.

The acid test of selling from trust is whether or not you're willing in principle to ever recommend a key competitor to a significant client. If you can never envision such a situation, then you always put your own interests ahead of the customer's.

Imagine that you have recently moved to a new city and must find a pediatrician for your two-year old child. You have a list of six doctors—referrals from a combination of health plans, coworkers, and neighbors. Four of them seem fine, though not really distinguishable. One of the four has a slight edge in reputation of medical school; another has the most years' experience; two others are on staff at a teaching hospital and have written several articles.

The fifth pediatrician impresses you by describing in detail the four most common childhood health issues, and his response to them, as reflected in all aspects of his practice. The sixth, however, hits it off immediately with your two-year-old. She connects with you and seems genuinely focused on your interests as a parent and on those of your child, rather than on getting you as a new patient. She talks half the time with the child; the other half with you, about neighborhoods in your new city, about parenting issues, and about your line of work. In technical respects, this physician is in the top half, though she's not number one in any category.

Which doctor would you choose? Most people will opt for the pediatrician who seems to care as long as he or she is within an acceptable range of expertise. And, they will frequently use the word *trust* to describe their decision.

There are exceptions, of course; a few people always buy purely on the basis of technical specifications, a few more buy only on price, and occasionally one seller is overwhelmingly superior in the technical realm.

The pediatrician selection process is not unlike the decision faced by a corporate buyer charged with selecting a law firm, an enterprise software vendor, a reinsurance company, a construction firm, an automotive die-cast supplier, a tax accountant, an audit firm, a telecommunications network, or a financial advisor.

In such cases, trust plays a key role. Specifically, trust is used to "cut through" otherwise enormously complex issues. Given the luxury of choice, such buyers strongly prefer to buy whatever it is they have to buy anyway from someone they trust

Check the above statement against your own experience. Is this how you behave when faced with making decisions about complex intangible kinds of services? If so, then perhaps it is the way your customers make such decisions as well.

What Do Buyers Really Want?

The head of marketing for a major East Coast law firm was asked by three partners to help rehearse and prepare them for a key sales meeting with a major potential new client. "If only we can convince them that we are absolutely the best in this area, which we are," the senior partner said, "then they'll have to go with us."

This point of view seemed so self-evident to the senior partner that it didn't feel like an opinion; it seemed like an obvious truth. But it's not.

Lawyers, accountants, bankers, engineers, software designers, actuaries, systems developers, consultants, outsourcers—all behave more often than not as if the key to selling lies in a powerful display of expertise. Most complex goods and services are sold with the implicit, if not explicit, belief that expertise is the issue. But it's not. Three questions to be raised are:

- What do buyers really want?
- Why don't they say so?
- Why, if selling expertise isn't the best approach, is it the dominant one?

The answers lie in the psychology of the buyer and the seller of complex goods and services as well as in trust—which is what really lies at the heart of the successful selling of complex intangibles.

Ironically, people whose job it is to sell complex products and services are the *most* likely to have a simple view of the product. What does a client want when he or she hires a patent lawyer? Ask a lawyer and the answer is probably "someone who is an expert in patent law." Ask a construction company what a real estate manager wants and the answer is often "someone who can bring in the building on time, on spec, and on budget." But these answers only begin to touch on our real motivations as buyers.

As buyers, we tend to give at least four levels of answers to the question of motivation in buying:

1. The product and its characteristics or features
2. A solution to a problem
3. A good business partner
4. A person we can trust

Buyers will usually say they want the first or second; occasionally, the third. Most modern corporate sales training programs tend to focus on levels two and three—identifying buyers' needs through consultative approaches to selling.

But the first three levels of answers are purely rational and impersonal—and they assume a relationship with the seller that is somewhat at arm's length. The fourth level—a person we can trust—is far more powerful. This level is personal, *not* purely rational, complex, involved with the seller, sometimes even messy—in short, human.

How People Really Buy: The Two-Step Process

Buyers of complex products and intangible services generally buy in a two-step process (Figure 1.1).

The first step is rational and linear. It involves listing all the possible solution providers for a given problem. Buyers then apply a screening process—based on past experience, scope, technology, reputation—to narrow down the possible list of providers.

The screening process is similar to that of an employer looking to hire someone; the employer screens résumés to decide whom to invite to interview. The screening would probably look at past experience, credentials, and background.

If you are the one doing the job-hunting, then the purpose of your résumé is simple: *to get an interview*. Once you get the interview, the résumé has done its job. That part of the process is at an end.

Selling is the same. The buyer uses rational criteria to sort out the possible sellers; then buyer meets seller and everything changes.

In step two—the selection process—the buyer switches from using a largely linear, rational process to one that's much more complex.[1]

In the job-hunting analogy, once you get the interview you should leave your résumé at home—because what the employer wants to see in a job interview is how you handle yourself in real time. Are you interested in the employer? In the job? How do you respond to questions? Can you react on the spot? These are questions that can only be answered in an interview.

Similarly, in the seller selection process, the interaction becomes personal. Suddenly, the client is no longer interested in hearing dry statistical information—*even if he or she says otherwise*. The client is much more

Figure 1.1 The Two-Step Buying Process

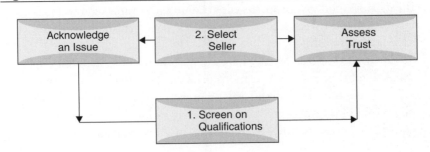

interested in things like whether you seem to understand his or her problem; whether you can demonstrate the value of your expertise, rather than just talk about it; and whether you seem to appreciate the client's specific personal situation, including his or her personal situation.

Here a paradox arises. You sell yourself best not by talking about yourself, but by talking about the client.

Years ago I heard about a job within my firm that would be just right for me. I really wanted the job, but at least two other applicants were more qualified than I was. They got in to see the president, to whom the job would report. In both cases, the president decided after a week or so not to hire them; each time, I let it be known again that I was interested.

Finally, I got my interview with the president. I blurted out all the things I would do with the job, and to my surprise, after five minutes he told me I had the job. "Why so fast?" I asked, "Not that I'm complaining!" "Because," he said, "the others all wanted to sell me on their credentials and to talk about compensation and promotion paths. You were the only one who talked about what you'd actually do."

I didn't know it at the time, but I had stumbled upon the old idea of selling by giving away samples. The best way to sell ice cream or perfume is to give samples. In intangible services businesses, it's called "selling by doing, not selling by telling," discussed at length in Chapter 7. People come to trust you by seeing you in action, by giving them samples of your work. This is what wins in selection.

Samples selling is focused on the customer—it demonstrates the benefits of your expertise on the customer's terms, not the seller's terms. The favorite subject of most of us is—ourselves. Samples selling allows the buyer to experience the benefits personally, rather than just hear about the seller's advantages. It's personal, and it's much more persuasive than purely rational discussion of features, needs, or even benefits.

Exceptions to the Two-Step Buying Process Rule

As buyers, when we have a strong existing relationship with a provider and we see the need for a new job, we almost unconsciously think first, "Can my existing provider handle this matter?" If so, we cut short the two-step process and give the business to the existing firm. For most clients, the inclination is "don't fix what ain't broke." This is one exception to the two-stop buying process rule—an important one, since it includes trust-based relationships.

Other exceptions to the rule include:

- Clients for whom corporate policy dictates multiple vendor relationships
- Customers who are extremely averse to relying on personal "feel" in the selection process and who therefore treat selection like screening
- Clients for whom preexisting external relationships exist (and for whom sham processes are therefore constructed to give the appearance of objectivity and hide "wired" decisions)

But these exceptions are relatively uncommon.

In general, sellers are well advised, in phase one, to market the firm in ways that help clients *screen;* and in phase two, to sell the individual in ways that help customers make *selections*.

Why Trust Usually Isn't Developed

It's my experience that the general public throughout the industrialized world tends to have a negative perception of "sales." Many of us salespeople share that negative view of sales. We want to be trusted, but we are not the most trusting of people. Some of us still see sales as being about getting the customer to do something not in his or her best interests, as being manipulative, and as being focused on the needs of the seller, not the buyer.

Some of us more than others accept this oppositional role; our biggest fear is that we may not get the sale. So we focus excessively on process execution, closing techniques, and other "tips and tricks." Ironically, fear of losing the sale is likely to cause you to behave in nontrustworthy ways and thus to increase the odds of losing the sale.

Others among us feel deeply troubled by this oppositional role; our biggest fear is that we may *get* the sale through some form of manipulation. So we compensate by not asking for the sale (thus sabotaging ourselves) or by giving away too much (with the same result). Ironically, this form of internal self-conflict signals a warning to customers: watch out, this person can't be trusted.

In both cases, as a result of the conflict about the buyer-seller relationship, we become perceived as untrustworthy—*even if* our motives were relatively clean to begin with.

We know that when we are the buyers, we are afraid of being manipulated or taken advantage of; of looking stupid or silly in the eyes of our peers or bosses or subordinates; or of risks only dimly perceived. In all cases, our inclination is to revert to features and price, away from the relationship—and away from the risks and opportunities of trust.

The Power of Trust in Selling

Woody Heller is an Executive Managing Director and head of the Capital Transaction Group at Studley Commercial Real Estate. Studley primarily represents tenants, but Woody's group also represents owners looking to sell their properties. Woody tells this story:

"We were selling a large tower in Manhattan a few years ago. We had three bidders who had all stretched through numerous rounds of bidding to the same price. The seller realized that they could not be pushed further on pricing, and we needed a means other than price to distinguish between them. So I said to the seller, 'Let's make it their problem to solve.'

"We asked each bidder, 'What can you tell us or do for us to convince us to choose you?' Two of them came back with variations on the themes of reputation, track record, bank references, deep pockets, and so forth. But the third one surprised me.

"He said, 'If you tell me that I can rely on the projections in your marketing materials, then I'll commit right now to making $250,000 of my deposit nonrefundable, before even starting due diligence review of the financials. I want to convince the seller of how serious I am.'

"I was taken aback. He had upped the ante on trust. He was saying, 'If you look me in the eye and tell me I can trust you, I will.' And I respected that. I said, 'Let me check with my people first,' because I didn't do the numbers personally. And if I'm going to put my personal reputation on the line, I want to be certain that I can rely on them myself.

"I checked, and the numbers were clean; I called him back, and he made the $250K 'hard' on the spot. And we did the deal. What's interesting is that up until then he was very careful about revealing his feelings; he was the hardest-to-read buyer I had ever dealt with. But, in this brief phone call, we both accelerated our level of trust. Since then, he treats me like an insider and a partner, not as a potential adversary. He clearly trusted me; and I felt challenged and honored by that trust."

Trust is not the same as loyalty—at least not as that term has often come to be used. Customers who trust you tend to stay with you—but not all customers who stay with you trust you. Some customers stay with you just because they don't have a better alternative. Others are behaviorally loyal. They stay because the relationship is a narrow, economically good deal for them—but their trust is wafer-thin. All these kinds of buyers show up as retained customers, and customer retention has become a commonly used proxy for customer loyalty.

But a rich trust relationship—or for that matter, loyalty worth the name—is much more than just repeat buying. If I have a choice between two service stations to change the oil in my car, I may go to one or the other depending on ease of access, or scheduling, or price. If I do so repeatedly, that produces high customer retention rates. But if I really trust the mechanic at one station, I am much more likely to go to that station even if it is farther away, less convenient, and more expensive. That can produce the same customer retention rate—but a very different qualitative driver behind the numbers.

The term "loyalty" has a rich emotional connotation—think "semper fi" or "'til death do us part." But in practice in the business world, it has become synonymous with customer retention, whether obtained through trust or through promotional pricing. The very term *loyalty* has become commoditized, devalued.[2]

Trust relationships are related to deeper personal and psychological connections. Buyers "need" things, but they "want" feelings. In the category of "needs" are things like toothpaste, automobiles, chip sets. But in the category of "wants" are aspirational feelings like respect, peace of mind, excitement, or security.

Much of selling talks about meeting buyers' needs. But connecting on the basis of their wants is much more powerful.

When we as buyers feel our wants and aspirations are heard, understood, valued, and appreciated, we feel that the other person cares. And if we sense that the seller cares, we are inclined to trust that person—and in turn to buy from him or her.

In one study of 2,514 buyers by Bill Brooks and Tom Travesano,[3] 94 percent of buyers who bought on the basis of needs nonetheless said they would "certainly" consider buying from another provider. And 91 percent of buyers who bought on the basis of benefits (a deeper connection than needs) still said they would "probably" do so. But in stark contrast, *99 percent* of those who bought on the basis of *wants* said they would "absolutely *not*" consider buying elsewhere. That's a dramatic difference.

And here's the punch line—the authors of this study found that, to achieve this level of sales success, you do *not even have to deliver* on their wants and aspirations; after all, customers don't expect you to perform miracles. It is enough that you understand and appreciate them for who they are. That is the power of the human need for connection, understanding, caring, and trust at work.

What Brooks and Travesano point out is the highly emotional, nonrational aspect of trust. A lot of it rests on the buyer's sense that the seller actually cares. Caring is indicated by things like paying attention to, showing interest in, and exhibiting curiosity about the things that customers themselves care about. If you do, people tend to trust you, and to buy from you when they need what you are selling.

Can you fake caring? Not for very long; not in the kinds of businesses we're talking about, with sophisticated (and suspicious) customers. No, you have to care for real.

The Acid Test of Trust in Selling

The acid test of trust in selling arises when there are conflicts between our interests and our customers' interests. What do you do when you can make a short-term sale that might not be the best thing for the customer? What do you do when you can design in all-your-company specs, but the customer might benefit from a diverse supplier network? And the real acid test—can you ever refer a competitor?

Howard Schwartz was a senior partner at a general management consulting firm and cochair of the firm's financial services practice. He describes the actions of a McKinsey partner with a West Coast banking client that had a 20-year McKinsey relationship. One day, the McKinsey partner called Howard. He and the McKinsey man had been friendly rivals at a major New York bank for a decade and had developed considerable respect for each other's work and reputation.

"I've hit a brick wall with my client," the McKinsey consultant said. "I'm not finding people available in the firm to satisfy the client; I've tried two of our best, and the chemistry isn't working; my client is very upset. So I'm calling you, Howard, my competitor, to see if you can send your best person in to work this assignment. The client needs the work done."

Howard couldn't believe his ears. A chance to gain entrée to a competitor's long-standing client, through the front door, with his best consultant, doesn't come every day. He sent in Lucy, one of his firm's best. And Lucy did a terrific job. The client was very satisfied.

"But at the end of the day," says Howard, "when we tried to say 'we think there's a lot more we could do for you,' the client said 'thanks very much but no thanks—we'll stay with the firm that was devoted enough to us to recommend a competitor when they believed that was the best way to help us.' You can't buy that kind of relationship." "And," Howard says, "I had to agree with them. Giving their competitor access to their client actually increased their client's trust. I had to hand it to them."

We trust most those people who do not always put *their* interests ahead of our own. There's a paradox here: by being willing to put others' interests ahead of our own, we usually end up doing even better than if we always put our interests ahead of others.

The right way to deal with these kinds of conflicts is to ask yourself: "What's the right long-term answer; what's the best solution for the customer; and what creates the most value for the seller-customer combined relationship?" If your answer would never put the customer's interests ahead of your own to the extent of recommending a competitor, then frankly you cannot be trusted. You're in it only for yourself. That's the acid test.

This doesn't mean you should always put the customer's needs ahead of yours. That's a recipe for going out of business. But if you're *never* willing to do it, you'll never build a trusting relationship.

Notes

1 For a much richer discussion of how clients choose between professional services firms, see David Maister, *Managing the Professional
   Services Firm*, Free Press, 1993, Chapter 10, "How Clients Choose."
2 Much of the original work on customer loyalty was done by
   Frederick Reichheld at Bain & Company. See *The Loyalty Effect*,
   Frederich Reichheld with Thomas Teal, Harvard Business School
   Press, 1996. Reichheld clearly defined loyalty as more than just
   continued purchasing behavior; he sees it as a human response by
   customers and employees to principled behaviors of management.
   But the term has come to be used more narrowly in business.
   Hence we hear about "loyalty schemes," and about programs
   based largely on price-shopping that claim to "create loyalty,"
   which in turn is measured by simple customer retention metrics.
   Reichheld likely feels dismayed.
3 Bill Brooks and Tom Travesano, *You're Working Too Hard to Make
   the Sale*, Irwin Professional Publishing, 1995.

TRUST-BASED SELLING

This Chapter at a Glance

Trust-based Selling works because people would rather buy what they need to buy anyway from those they have come to trust. To be trusted, you must be trustworthy, which means being, among other things, buyer-centric. Adding trust to selling goes beyond rational needs-based selling; it's a myth that corporate buying is done only with the brain.

The paradox of Trust-based Selling is that, if you can give up trying to control or maximize profit from customers, you increase your influence and profit.

We don't need trust in sales all the time; but it is powerful in complex product and intangible services businesses. Buyers as well as sellers benefit from a sales relationship built on trust. In Trust-based Selling, the relationship is the customer. Trust-based Selling uses the same principles underlying other critical relationships in life.

Trust-based Selling works because of a simple but powerful human dynamic that I will repeat several times:

People greatly prefer to buy what they have to buy anyway from those they have come to trust.

If you establish truly caring, trust-based relationships with your customers, then when they need to buy what it is you are selling, they are likely to buy it from you. That rule has implications for the economic model of sales, for how salespeople should spend their time, and for even the most basic objectives of selling.

What is Trust-based Selling?

1. Trust-based Selling means *doing business in such a way that you are worthy of the customer's trust.* That means you must be *trustworthy* as a salesperson. Telling people "trust me" won't make you trustworthy (in fact, it's a fast way to make people distrust you). And if the salesperson is perceived as personally untrustworthy, the buyer will not trust the company. There's no way around it—you must *be trustworthy.*

2. Trust-based Selling is *personal.* Trust is mainly personal, not institutional, and buying is heavily personal as well. Buying decisions are more than just rational and calculating. Buyers are feeling human beings, not just centers of enlightened economic self-interest. Trust-based Selling sells to the person as well as to the institution and to the heart as well as to the brain.

3. Trust-based Selling at its core is not seller-centric—it's *buyer-based.* The objective of most approaches to selling is to get the buyer to buy. The objective of Trust-based Selling is to help the buyer do the right thing—for the buyer. Period.

4. Trust-based Selling rests on a paradox. If you gain your customers' trust, you will sell a lot and be very profitable—more profitable than you will be through seller-centric approaches. But if your overriding objective is to sell a lot and be very profitable— if you try to turn trust into a tactic—it will not work. People smell hypocrisy and recoil from it. *You can't fake it.* Your overriding objective must be to help your customer. In other words, you have to care.

5. Trust-based Selling is *samples selling.* Trust is earned by example, not by declaration or logic. We as people trust our own experience above all else, and buyers are people. In complex intangible services, it's the seller people are buying, not just the product. You need to give them a sample of you, and you do that best by letting them experience you.

Selling based on trust goes beyond needs-based selling, consultative selling, or problem-solving selling. It is not about getting the transaction—it is about establishing a relationship. And it is not about getting the sale—it is about making sure your customer succeeds.

It requires two perspectives not common to sales: selling beyond the brain, and selling without being seller-centric.

Selling Outside the Brain

One of the leading books on large-company sales says, "Buying is a special case of decision-making. Every time one of your customers makes a buying decision, he does so in a series of predictable and logical steps."[1] Is that your experience? Do your clients treat buying as a category of decision making, in predictable and logical steps? Or do they do something else?

Much of corporate sales training is based on what seems like a self-evident proposition—customers will buy from you if you can rationally and logically convince them you have the product/service/solution/system that best meets their needs. But that's only *partly* accurate.

True, buyers do try to analyze things rationally, and they certainly prefer to describe their own buying behavior as rational—especially after the fact.

But it's far from the whole picture. Very few people buy in a purely rational way. Here's how best-selling author Jeffrey Gitomer puts it: "The sale is emotionally driven and emotionally decided. Then it is justified logically."[2]

This is not just about retail consumer behavior. Consider the experience of Dwight Davies.

Dwight Davies sells complex consulting assignments to the telecommunications sector for Deloitte Consulting. During the recent recession, he was asked to bid on a multimillion dollar RFP (request for proposal) from one of the world's major telecomm firms.

"We hate to bid on RFPs," said Dwight, "but the recession was looming, everything was going out to bid that way, and we had mouths to feed. So we bid on it.

"When they showed us the RFP, my first thought was 'I didn't know they made binders that big.' The whole process took several months—presentations, submissions, more submissions.

"Near the end, I finally got a call from the main purchasing contact. 'Congratulations,' he told me, 'you folks won the technical competition.'

"And I said 'uh-oh—if you're telling me we won the technical competition, then that means we lost the whole deal, doesn't it? Is that right?'

"And the client said, 'Yes, I'm afraid you did lose the deal.'

"'Why?' I asked. "We did great work on that RFP; we have the best team, the most experience, and no one had better systems. And you just said we won the technical competition. Why, then, did you give the bid to someone else?

"And the client told me—'the problem was, you don't use our phone service in your offices.'

"I was shocked. This was a contract for many millions of dollars. No one had ever mentioned the issue of whose phone service we used. It made no earthly difference to what the client had insisted was important, or to the effectiveness of the work itself. Yet at the end of the day, it made all the difference to the buying decision. I don't even think they noticed the irony."

Buying is a whole lot more than just "decision making." And it's not all rational and logical. Of course, nonrational decision making isn't the monopoly of the corporate world.

In 1986, Stephen Keller was a Lieutenant Commander in the U.S. Navy and Executive Officer (second in command) of a San Diego-based guided missile frigate that was unexpectedly deployed to the Arabian Gulf for six months. Steve had spent the majority of his career in the Navy's Atlantic Fleet. The Captain had spent his entire career in the Pacific Fleet.

The Arabian Gulf was 90 miles short of being exactly halfway around the world. Having gone to the Gulf via the Pacific, Keller and the Captain saw a unique opportunity to provide the crew with experiences in waters that many of them had never sailed. The ship proposed to return via the Mediterranean and the Atlantic, transiting the Suez and Panama canals—completing an around the world deployment.

The Captain and crew would benefit greatly by sailing the Atlantic, as had Steve in his assignment to a Pacific-based ship. The Navy could greatly improve the return on its training investment, at zero added cost.

But the Navy budgets operations on a regional basis. The fuel oil for the original trip had been budgeted out of the Pacific command's budget. Funding for such an operation had not been anticipated by the Atlantic Fleet, and a clearly established, timely means to transfer funding between fleets wasn't in place either.

And so the ship sailed the same route back it had taken out. A chance to develop personnel at no cost was squandered due to the inertia of a budgeting process.

Most human decision making is not linear, sequential, logical, or rational. Yet that is how most sales models describe the buying process.

It's not that buyers behave irrationally—most decisions make a lot of sense. It's that they are often based on things like fear, politics, friendship, risk profiles, and other largely emotional factors. Pure economic logic is far from the whole story.

Rational selling provides rational answers to rational business problems. Trust-based Selling creates relationships, and takes into account buyers' emotions as well.

Rational selling focuses on solving the business problem at hand. That's important, and it's often all that customers ask from you. Certainly we all need to be good at it; and most of our time will be spent doing the tasks required by rational selling.

But that doesn't mean buyers don't want something more. *What buyers really want—even when they don't say so—is a seller they can trust.*

Buyers—including you and me—are human beings. They (and we) do much more than calculate features and design solutions to business problems. They also must make decisions as humans—take risks, make assumptions, worry about consequences, and wonder who is with them and who is not.

You or I may become convinced that a particular solution is the best solution to a problem. But we may still lie awake at night worrying—

did I do enough research? Too much? How will I explain my decision? What will my boss think? Did I pay too much? And so on.

Rational problem solving can't help with those issues; yet those issues are vital to long-term, ongoing, customer relationships. Solving problems can be done rationally; sleeping through the night comes from trusting the seller.

Trust-based Selling requires solid levels of competence, credibility, and reliability. But it critically requires a sense on the part of the buyer that the seller actually cares about what is good for the buyer.

Selling without Being Seller-Centric

Selling happens at four different levels—three of them are all about the seller. Here's what the first three levels look like (see Figure 2.1).

- *Level 1—selling based on products and features.* This works when needs are simple and well-understood. If you want to buy milk, you only want to know about features—size of container, milk-fat content, price. *At its best, product-based selling helps buyers get what they ask for.*

Figure 2.1   Levels of Buying

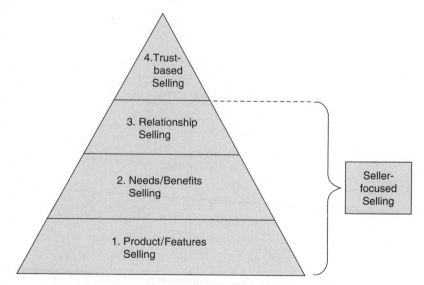

- *Level 2—selling based on needs and benefits.* The difference between product- or feature-based and needs- or benefit-based selling is the difference between starting with solutions and starting with problems. *At its best, needs-based selling identifies and solves customers' problems—it gives them what they need, not just what they asked for.*
- *Level 3—selling based on relationships.* This recognizes that transactions don't exist in a vacuum. Repeated experiences make the seller more able to meet buyer needs. The lifetime value of a customer exceeds the value of any one transaction. *At its best, relationship selling meets buyers' needs efficiently and over time.*

Levels 1 through 3 are all seller-focused at root. All three of them have the seller's increased sales as their goal. Any technique, any insight, any attention paid to customer needs, is all done with one goal in mind— to increase the sales of the seller.

After all, the objective of seller-focused selling is to convince the buyer to buy the seller's product or service. The point is to sell.

But put yourself in the buyer's shoes—how likely are you to trust people whose primary, ultimate, overriding goal is to get you to buy what they have to sell?

You may be saying, "Wait a minute. Everyone's in it for themselves, that's nothing new; of course the other guy's got to make a buck, and I don't hold it against him. That doesn't mean we don't trust each other."

Actually, that's *just* what it means. You don't blame a shark for being sharklike; you can respect a shark for being a good shark. You just don't do stupid things around it. But you surely don't *trust* a shark—at least, not to do anything but be a shark.

Seller-focused selling simply cannot be Trust-based Selling. Trust requires that the one being trusted cares about the one doing the trusting. To put it simply—You must care about *them!*

Selling Based on Trust

Why would a buyer ever trust a seller? For one reason above all others: A buyer will trust a seller *if the buyer is convinced—legitimately—that the seller has the buyer's best interests at heart.*

In Trust-based Selling, the phrase *customer focus* means that you care about the customer for the customer's sake, as an end in itself not simply as a vehicle for your own enrichment. (If this sounds too noble to be realistic, ask yourself: how do *you* respond when you meet a seller who sees you as a means to his ends versus a seller who you feel is trying to help you?)

> • The objective of seller-focused selling is to convince the buyer to buy the seller's product or service. The point is to get the sale.
> • The objective of Trust-based Selling is to help the buyer do the right thing. The point is to *help the buyer.*

Selling based on trust means the relationship *itself* is valued over the transaction—even over the lifetime value of the transactions—because it's the relationship of trust that lets us help the buyer. It means we have the buyer's best interests at heart. It means, above all, that we as sellers care. If you're a good salesperson, you probably have a customer relationship that works this way. You know how this relationship works. And if so, then you already know the paradox.

> *The paradox:* If you put the customer's interests ahead of yours—if you care—you will get more than your fair share of sales. But *only* if you give up *trying* to get them. You can't fake trust.

What Trust Does for Buyers

When we are buyers, some of us focus on features because of fear—fear of being taken advantage of, fear of missing something, or fear of appearing ignorant.

Some of us may overemphasize benefits, because we think it is our job to solve our business problems rationally. Not fully trusting the seller, we feel we must emphasize problem solutions in order to feel comfortable about a decision.

Still others among us will focus on relationship issues: discounts, contracts, and contingency clauses, perhaps because we fear losing control and not getting a good deal.

But when we as buyers encounter a seller we can trust—truly, legitimately, with reason—these behaviors change. We put less emphasis on technical mastery, because we can trust the seller's intentions. *We never really wanted technical expertise; all along, we just wanted a technical expert we could trust.*

Trusting buyers put less emphasis on contracts. We value the handshake behind the legal contract more than the contract itself, because we know the former can be stronger. We know that we are all working on the same team.

Imagine how much money your customers could save if they really, honestly, believed they could trust you. The need for multiple vendors "in principle"; RFPs; lengthy contract negotiations; legal advice; required multistage processes; and cumbersome purchasing regulations would all be significantly reduced. Their transaction costs are greatly reduced.

And the value of trust to a buyer goes well beyond lowered costs. It allows him or her to be more open to ideas, to explore options, and to be faster to market.

Trust radically changes the buyer-seller dynamic. The end result of seller-centric selling is a transaction or a series of transactions. The end result of Trust-based Selling is another step forward in an evolving mutual relationship.

The concept is not new. The iconic sales trainer and speaker Zig Ziglar says, "You can get whatever you want, if you help enough people get what they want." Going back even further, Dale Carnegie said, "The only way to influence someone is to find out what they want, and show them how to get it." But both have been misinterpreted.

Because, if your whole purpose in helping someone is just to get what *you* want, then you may strike a bargain with someone—but that person won't trust you.

By contrast, if you conduct your business life to maximize the help you provide to potential and real customers—then people *will* trust you. And coincidentally—as a byproduct, as a second-order outcome—they will overwhelmingly want to buy from you as well. But only if your motives are clean.

Maurie Mader, of Vernon Sales Promotions, sells promotional items, from customized shirts to pens to anything with a logo on it.

"Early in my career," Maurie says, "a sales manager told me, 'Anyone can sell a rush order—they're desperate! The hard work is selling someone who isn't in a hurry.'

"But I've learned he was wrong. A rush order means I have a customer who trusts me enough to put themselves in my hands. A rush order isn't easy to sell; in fact, a rush order is the hardest to sell because of all the hard work and effort that goes into creating a relationship like that. If you get a rush order, it means you've done a lot of things right; and you never take it for granted."

Who Needs Trust-based Selling?

We don't need trust in all our sales all the time. When we go into a store to buy toothpaste or a fast-food chain to buy a hamburger and fries, we are not interested in developing a personal relationship with the people behind the counter. Nor do we want their opinion about our dental or dietary problems. In these cases, we only want fast, efficient, rational problem solving. What does this product do, how does that compare with others, how much is it, and how fast can I get out of here are our concerns.

But there are other times when we really do want a trust-based approach. As consumers, we often have to purchase complex products or services—automobiles, insurance products, health care—about which we know very little.

Think about how you react in situations when you have to buy something and the seller knows far more than you ever will. Your reactions are probably a mix of several factors. First, you want some information about the product, so you don't feel at risk. Second, you don't want to appear ignorant. Third, you try to assess whether you can trust the salesperson.

In these situations, a salesperson who can offer true trustworthiness is often more powerful than one who simply has great technical expertise. *As buyers we don't just want right solutions; we want to feel confident in those solutions—and that confidence often comes to us from the seller.*

The Relationship Is the Customer

"The medium is the message," said Marshall McLuhan in the 1960s. Those five words made us see the limitations of our old way of thinking.

After McLuhan, we could no longer look at content isolated from the way it was delivered.

Sun Microsystems, only a decade ago, said, "The network is the computer," shifting our ideas of technology to a new paradigm in which everything is connected.

In the same way, Trust-based Selling reframes selling so that *the relationship is the customer.*

We hear a lot these days about customer focus, customer relationships, and customer-centric processes. Consider initiatives like customer relationship management (CRM), customer loyalty, one-to-one marketing, and mass customization. Customer focus is the current business equivalent of political correctness. But the phrase has been co-opted by those with a seller-centric mindset.

In seller-centric selling, the underlying focus remains on the seller's sustainable competitive advantage. The overriding goal is to beat the competition. Customers are like poker chips. He who collects the most chips, or the most profitable chips, wins. Customers become means, not ends. In that paradigm, customer focus is still a tactic, not a goal.[3]

In Trust-based Selling, customer focus is instead about the customer—not the seller. The point is not to win competitive battles, but to improve constantly the collaborative relationship with customers themselves. The customer relationship is the *point itself.*

Relationships nurture transactions; but focusing on transactions alone destroys relationships.

The relationship itself—an interlocking web of personal commitments, existing over time, conducted with transparency, and founded on respect for each other as ends in themselves—is the source of value. In Trust-based Selling, "customer focus" means *the relationship is the customer.*

You Get Paid for the Relationship, Not the Product or Service

If I buy a product or service from a traditional seller, we would both say that the object of my purchase was the product or service and that I paid a certain monetary price for it.

But if I buy a product or service from someone I trust, I am doing something different. What I really value, what I am really buying, is the

TRUST-BASED SELLING   25

trust-based relationship itself, and all it does for me; the good or service becomes a means of payment.

If I'm a small businessman with a trust-based relationship with my commercial banker, I will call her about various topics. We might talk about more than just cash management and lines of credit. We talk about new inventory management tools, trends in interest rates, the stock market, pension plans, the local real estate market, or references to other specialists.

In return for this valuable relationship, the natural quid pro quo or rule of engagement is that I will do my core commercial banking business with her.

For the seller, that means two things: First, your value added lies not in the product, but in the relationship. And, the purchase of the product or service is really just the means of repaying the seller, pegged to the line of business she happens to be in.

In other words, *in Trust-based Selling, people buy the relationship and pay for it in product.*

Real Customer Relationships

None of this is revolutionary in any other form of human relationship—spousal, parent-child, friend. Relationships founded on naked self-interest—unless consistently backed up by abusive power—are only as good as the other options available to both parties.

We do not talk about the "sustainable competitive advantage" that one spouse has over another. A true friend doesn't operate from a "customer focus" that is aimed only at maximizing his or her value from the friendship. Parents do things all the time that are motivated by holding the best interests of the child at heart—even when doing so may not seem to serve their own interests.

When other relationships fail to value the relationship itself, we call them dysfunctional. Business relationships are no different. Behaving from pure self-interest is a way to kill any kind of a relationship. Ask any jilted lover, neglected child, or rejected grandparent. Or just ask yourself—how do you feel about that guy who still hasn't paid back the $50 he borrowed last year?

In a world increasingly based on relationships—networking, outsourcing, alliances, joint ventures, modular business units—it is increasingly dysfunctional to behave from purely self-aggrandizing motives. You may or may not think such actions in business are immoral, or wrong, or unidealistic. I'm not trying to argue one side or the other. I'm simply pointing out that they don't work as well as trust.

What should a business do vis-à-vis its would-be trust-based customers? The business should nurture its relationships with:

an eye to understanding the customers' perspectives
a medium-to-long-term view
a habit of collaboration
an approach of transparency

If we behave as if *the relationship is the customer*, all parties to the relationship benefit. And that's the key definition of Trust-based Selling that you should think of as you finish reading this book.

Notes

1   Robert Miller, Stephen Heiman, *Conceptual Selling*, Warner Books, 1989.
2   Jeffrey Gitomer, *Little Red Book of Selling: 12.5 Principles of Sales Greatness*, Bard Press, Austin, 2004.
3   Financial language is increasingly being applied to issues of relationships, particularly customer relationships. Consider "relationship capital," "lifetime customer value," and "return on human capital." The language takes topics that are, of their essence, personal and depersonalizes them. There's nothing wrong per se with analyzing relationships, or with seller-centric selling—unless we infer that such "customer focus" actually has something in it for the customer!

CHAPTER 3

THE BUSINESS CASE FOR TRUST

This Chapter at a Glance

The best proof of the benefits of Trust-based Selling lies in your own experience. The economic benefits to the seller include those of high customer loyalty, lower transaction costs, and higher revenues, as well as enhanced creativity and shortened purchase cycle times.

The chief barriers to Trust-based Selling are our overemphasis on competition, our view of selling as seller-centric, and plain old fear. Trust-based Selling requires higher-order relationship skills on the part of both seller and buyer.

High-trust selling is profitable for seller and buyer alike. As a seller, which would you rather have: (a) the best product line in your industry, or (b) the strongest trust-based relationship with the number-one customer in your industry?

Most of us would rather have the strongest customer relationship. It is generally easier to develop new products than new relationships. Look at the box below for some more examples of the value of trust-based customer relationships.

THE MORE YOUR CUSTOMERS TRUST YOU, THE LESS THEY WILL

- Challenge your ideas indiscriminately
- Use multiple vendors

- Second-guess your advice
- Rely solely on narrowly written RFPs (requests for proposal)
- Challenge you on pricing
- Double-check on things you do or say
- Force you to adhere to a rigid purchasing process where unjustified

THE MORE YOUR CUSTOMERS TRUST YOU, THE MORE THEY WILL

- Be willing to listen to you
- Share information that might be useful to you
- Take your phone calls
- Make exceptions to standard procedures as appropriate
- Expedite, fast-track, and move things quickly
- Sole-source business to you
- Allow you to influence or interpret RFP specs
- Give you preferred status
- Forgive you the occasional mistake
- Share important information with you
- Seek out and take your advice

The first list centers on reducing your costs. The second list is primarily about margin, revenue, and profit enhancement.

What would it be worth to *you* to have your key customer rely less on RFPs; sole-source some business to you; or seek you out for advice?

The benefits of trust-based relationships don't just accrue to the seller. Trust is a bilateral affair. Look at the box below for 22 benefits that trust-based relationships bring to buyers.

22 BENEFITS OF TRUST-BASED RELATIONSHIPS FOR BUYERS

1. Lower cost of purchasing
2. Lowered risk exposure to the good or service being purchased
3. Shorter time to market
4. Availability of expertise
5. Advance warnings of problems with goods or services
6. Input early on in product design and development decisions

7. Early access to relevant market information
8. Economies of information sharing
9. Ability to be flexible regarding processes, timing
10. Ability to ask a special favor
11. A supplier who understands the buyer's objectives
12. A supplier who understands the buyer's language, processes, terminology
13. Someone who will be honest and direct with you about problems
14. Greater ability to design-in features for the buyer's product line
15. Access to greater knowledge in components' areas
16. Knowledge of other uses or applications
17. Lower legal expenses
18. Less risk of legal exposure
19. Faster, shorter contracts
20. Managerial solutions to what were previously legal problems
21. Speed in resolving minor disputes, for example, payables terms
22. Ability to bring expertise to bear on the customer's customers

Some of these benefits—payables terms, lower costs of purchasing—show up directly in the buyer's income statement as lowered transaction costs. Others, like shorter time to market, show up several times removed in revenue and margins.

Loyalty based on points and miles and best-promotion-of-the-day can be worth a lot. But loyalty based on trust is worth much more, including profitability. When customers have your interests at heart, and you theirs, things are fundamentally different.

You can retain customers based on low price, or on preference for a style, or a level of service. But those factors don't motivate customers in ways that help you cross-sell, exchange valuable information, exchange ideas of mutual benefit to each partner, offer advice that is quickly taken, or take advice yourself. Only trust does that.

Proving the Link

Despite the benefits just described of a trust-based relationship, the broad business community has come to believe that success depends on being "tough." Variations on the theme include "nice guys finish last," and "you've got to play hardball." When someone in business talks about trusted relationships, or about doing well by doing good, many in the business community are inclined to believe he or she is soft-headed.

In the businesses I have seen in my 30 years of consulting and teaching, the economic value of a strong trust-based customer relationship exceeds that of being a "tough competitor." I know it—but I'd be hard pressed to prove it.

I'm not aware of a comprehensive statistical study proving that trusted relationships lead to greater profitability for seller or buyer. There have been studies showing powerful links between loyalty and profitability, but they define loyalty primarily as repeat buying behavior. Studies identifying microbehavioral responses to very specific aspects or definitions of trust exist, but they're academic and not comprehensive. One study of several thousand medium-complexity buying events suggests that buyers respond to a seller's understanding of their deepest wants.[1]

Philip Evans and Bob Wolf of the Boston Consulting Group identify greater trust as the antidote to rising transaction costs. By their estimate, ". . . in the year 2000, cash transaction costs alone accounted for over half the nongovernmental U.S. GDP! We spend more money negotiating and enforcing transactions than we do fulfilling them."[2] It's a powerful argument, but is it proof?

To define something as complex as trust—much less devise a large-scale study to isolate its effects from all other factors—would be difficult. Nevertheless, that doesn't mean trust doesn't exist or isn't powerful.

There's a passion in business today for empirical, fact-based, analytical justification for all decisions. As the saying goes, "if you can't measure it, you can't manage it."

But the saying is nonsense. People manage all the time without measurements. Facts are independent of our knowledge of them. The absence of proof doesn't imply disproof. The following box tells what Frank Johnson, Director, Enterprise Business Development at Intel, learned from Andrew Grove, one of its founders.

Back in 1991, we made what was—for Intel—a major shift, away from pure product sales. Andy Grove told us that in the new world, thinking of ourselves as pure purveyors of product just wasn't enough. Our sphere of influence had to go well beyond that. We needed to interact with many people besides the direct economic buyer—software, service, various engineering groups, and our customers' marketing people.

We were all very nervous about this new indirect sales role. Up until then what we knew was, "Tell me what products I have to move, the price structure, and my incentives and I'll do it." This was new. We said, "Tell us what it is you want us to do."

And Andy replied, "Hey, what was the ROI when Columbus went to the Queen of Spain and asked for money to discover the new world? I don't know, we'll figure out the right thing to do and do it." Sometimes you just have to make a leap of faith because you know in your gut it's the right thing.

And it absolutely was. Our products are now integral parts of complex engineered people and service systems. Everything is linked. Our job is to make sure it all works together—whatever that takes. That's what sales is for us. And it rests on trust.

The world Intel faced in 1991 was different from the old world. There was no longer one buyer; you couldn't get direct feedback about every meeting; you couldn't prove which actions led to what outcomes. Most frustrating, Intel couldn't control everything about the buying process for its products.

Andy Grove provided sage advice. You know what's right. Take a leap of faith. Trust your gut.

If you feel somewhat the same, you're reading the right book. You can't control everything about the markets and the buying process for complex products and intangible services. There are too many interdependencies. Sometimes you even have to cooperate with your competitors.

Trust-based Selling is made for a world that is daily becoming more interconnected in which the ability to work together with customers, or joint venture with competitors, is growing in importance. Trusted salespeople have always been valuable, and will become more valuable in the future.

If you want to know the best business case for trust, follow Andy Grove's advice—look to your own experience, and trust your gut. All I can do in the chapters that follow is point out a few things to watch out for along the way, a few perspectives to help you bring your own experience to bear on the question.

Low Business Trust

Often, very often, buyers are suspicious of sellers. They use request for proposal (RFP) or request for quote (RFQ) processes specifically to reduce the chance for personal interaction in the selling process. RFPs tend to force decision making based solely on features and price.

The suspicion of sellers, although perfectly understandable, is a real shame. Possible benefits to the buyer and seller alike are lost in order to protect against the risk of an untrustworthy seller. And the practice is more common than ever.

In our society, lack of trust in business—think Enron, insurance scams, mutual fund scandals, CEO behavior—has led us to rely too much on structural solutions. In particular, we focus on conflicts of interest. Are accountants being less vigilant on audits to get consulting? Then separate the businesses—get rid of the conflict of interest. Are Wall Street analysts shading their opinions to get investment banking business? Then separate the functions—get rid of the conflict of interest.

The violations of trust are real. But overreliance on the "break 'em up" solution is in part cutting off the nose to spite the face.[3] Every business transaction between a buyer and a seller is on some level a conflict of interest—because each party's interests are in some measure different. If we try to make all transactions at arm's length, impersonal, and driven only by price and features, we succeed in minimizing conflicts of interest—but we destroy relationships.

On a macro level, a business world full of RFPs and devoid of conflict of interest is a world full of transactions, but no relationships. Without relationships, there is no trust. Absent trust, every transaction becomes an opportunity for negotiation, posturing, contract writing, bargaining, tracking, auditing, record keeping, legal maneuverings, lawsuits, cross-checking, and verification.

That is a high-cost, low-creativity world. By focusing on structural solutions to the lack of trust, we drive up the number of transactions, which increases cost. At the same time, we reduce the opportunity to create the kind of value that only comes from collaboration. And it is a misguided effort to begin with, because trust is not structural—it is personal. Trust is about much more than the absence of conflict of interest.

Why Trust Is Rare

Most corporate buying decisions today don't involve high levels of trust. At the end of the day, there are three reasons why trust is rare.

The first reason is the dominant business ideology of today, which emphasizes competition, even between buyers and sellers.

The second reason is that most approaches to selling are based on seller-centric and rational models.

And the third reason is the natural fear that comes with all trust—putting oneself at risk with another.

Good salespeople can overcome all three obstacles and reap the benefits for their customers—and themselves.

Notes

1   Bill Brooks and Tom Travesano, *You're Working Too Hard to Make the Sale*, Irwin Professional Publishing, 1995.
2   "Collaboration Rules," Philip Evans and Bob Wolf, *Harvard Business Review*, July-August 2005.
3   There are other solutions. They include increased enforcement, more severe civil and criminal penalties, and greater publicity. But the biggest solution is simply increasing the number of object examples of the power of trust.

CHAPTER 4

A PRIMER ON TRUST

This Chapter at a Glance

Trust-based relationships are rare, partly because they require risk. This chapter covers the relationship between trust and sales; the four principles of trust; the process by which trust is created; and the components of trust.

Trust-based Selling is based on four principles: true customer focus, collaboration, a medium- to long-term perspective, and transparency.

The components of trustworthiness are credibility, reliability, intimacy, and low self-orientation. They are related to each other in the trust equation.

The process of trust creation happens largely in personal interactions and follows the five-step process: Engage, Listen, Frame, Envision, and Commit.

Trust and Sales

Buyers don't come to trust sellers easily. Part of the reluctance has to do with our cultural views of selling. And part of it has to do with how anyone comes to trust another.

Look up the word *sell* in the dictionary, and you'll find a range of definitions. Some sound neutral, but others are negative. And negative dictionary definitions don't come out of thin air. There is some justification for them.

The biggest reason sellers are not seen as trustworthy is very simple: they're not. They do not have the buyer's best interests at heart. They believe that their objective is to get the sale—as opposed to helping the buyer.

Put yourself in a buyer's shoes. Imagine you're with a salesman whose offering seems in some ways a little better than his competition's, and in others a little worse. Every time you inquire about the two offerings, you get answers that seem to shade things in favor of the seller.

What you're hearing is not overt. The salesperson uses language to make his pitch sound objective, unbiased, and transparent. But he always ends up emphasizing his company's benefits, interpreting your comments in ways favorable to him, phrasing questions that are just a bit loaded, changing the conversation in ways to favor his sale, insinuating delicately that the competitor isn't quite as good, and pushing you ever-so-slightly toward closure. You just *feel* like you're being pushed in the direction of a particular conclusion.

Do you trust the person? Of course not. He may do everything right by all the books. He may have used all the proper questioning techniques, the right body language, memorized your kids' names—and yet it still doesn't feel right. He's faking it. It oozes and bleeds out of him almost against his will. You know it in your bones, even if you can't point to just what the person is doing wrong—you can't really trust him.

Corporate buyers of complex products and services are smart and cynical, and have good instincts. Once in a while you may run across someone with whom you can fake trust, but you're not likely to get more than one chance with that person. When word of your deception gets out, you're stuck with a career based on nothing but new clients who've never heard of you. That's a high-cost and low-satisfaction career.

If your customers trust you, you will make a lot of sales and a great deal of money. But if you try to use trust just as a *tactic*—as a *tool* to make sales and money—then your customers will rather quickly see through you to your real objectives and reject you.

If people think you are acting from your own self-interest, they become suspicious. We don't trust people who put their own interests first—then why should we expect our customers to behave any differently?

If so few salespeople are really trustworthy, it's by no means all their fault. Nearly all the reigning belief systems in modern business today— as articulated by the Harvard Business School, the *Wall Street Journal* and *Fortune* magazine, and the bestselling business authors— enforce the idea that the purpose of business is to achieve sustainable competitive advantage for the corporation.

The leading business thinkers of the day equate business with competition. When they talk about "customer focus," the goal of that focus is to understand the customer better *in order that* the selling company can be more successful competitively. Buyers, not being stupid, sense that they are being treated only as objects and react with lowered trust.

In the face of such entrenched beliefs, a solitary salesperson has an uphill battle to even *think* differently. The idea that the purpose of business is to serve customers has been nearly overlooked.

To sell from trust is no easy matter. And it's a matter of beliefs and principles, not of techniques and processes.

The Trust Principles

Trust-based Selling cannot be reduced to pure behaviors. You can't bottle it in a competency model. Our actions are driven by our beliefs, and our beliefs are driven by our values—the principles we adhere to. Trustworthy behavior is way too complex to fake. If your beliefs, values, and principles don't drive you to behave in a trustworthy manner all the time, you'll be found out quickly.

Hence, the principles you adhere to are the most important component of Trust-based Selling. The way to become trusted is to act consistently from those principles—and not just any made-up set of principles will do. The four specific principles that drive Trust-based Selling are:

1. A focus on the customer for the customer's sake, not just the seller's sake
2. A style of selling that is consistently collaborative
3. A perspective centered on the medium to long term
4. A habit of being transparent in all your dealings with the customer.

Principle 1: True Customer Focus

Customer focus amounts to caring about the customer. The phrase "customer focus" in seller-oriented selling means learning about the customer *so that* the seller can make more sales. By that definition, a vulture epitomizes customer focus. It pays a great deal of attention to its prey—but only for its own good.

In Trust-based Selling, "customer focus" means treating customers as ends, not means. It means continually noticing and paying attention. The following box lists nine reasons why client focus is critical to complex businesses.

WHY CLIENT FOCUS IS CRITICAL

1. Client focus improves problem definition for customers who deal in complex problems.
2. Client focus allows constant learning on the part of the seller who can't know all the answers.
3. Customers won't let you *earn the right* to offer solutions until they feel you've understood their situation—and that comes about from truly paying attention.
4. True client focus works *competitively*—because few people really practice it.
5. Customer focus encourages the customer to *share more*, open up, and allow more access.
6. Client focus leads to *collaboration* by the client.
7. Customer focus fosters *acceptance* of recommendations.
8. An outsider's perspective often brings new insights that help all involved.
9. Focusing on another enriches our own lives.

Being customer-focused requires a state of mindfulness, of paying attention and being open to a client's issues and situation as well as to a client's concerns, desires, and fears.

It is only human to be distracted by our own thoughts when someone else is talking. The more stressful the situation, the more we are distracted by our thoughts. The more things we try to do at once, the more distracted we are. And when there is money at stake, the distractions are more difficult yet to ignore.

Selling triggers all those forces. It is very difficult to pay attention to what a buyer is talking about—much less feeling and not saying—

when we are focused on what the outcome means for us. Yet if we give in to the distractions, everything starts to fall apart. We are no longer paying attention to the client, but to ourselves.

Beliefs or actions that detract from this state of mindfulness are therefore destructive to client focus. Consider the list in the following box of unconscious, "harmless" actions or beliefs that serve to destroy client focus.

UNCONSCIOUS DESTROYERS OF CUSTOMER FOCUS

1. Seeking to control the agenda or outcome of a meeting or phone call
2. Focusing on one's own "share of client wallet"
3. Waiting too long to talk about money issues
4. An inability to confront customers on difficult issues
5. A belief that problems will get better if they are just left alone
6. Focusing on beating the competition
7. Cross-selling for its own sake, not the sake of the client
8. Pushing for a job when another firm is more qualified
9. Focusing on credentials, rather than customer issues, in the selling process
10. Seeing selling as unrelated to adding value
11. Being motivated by fears of how a client will perceive us as individuals
12. A preference for working "back at the office" rather than on the client site
13. Attachment to "winning" an argument
14. The belief that there are trade-offs between customers' interests and our own

---

Principle 2: A Collaborative Style

Having a collaborative approach to things means being willing to involve the buyer in all our activities. This goes way beyond customer satisfaction surveys or client dinners.

It means a willingness to involve the buyer in the sales process itself, even in areas where sellers typically keep buyers at bay. Instead of having internal meetings to guess what clients might want, it means picking up the phone to <u>ask</u> them. It means openly sharing assumptions. It means proactively suggesting joint working teams. It means daily habits of interaction, like routinely checking agendas in advance of meetings, or spending more time with the customer and less in the car or office. It means constantly defining each others' interests, and working to align them. If your interests are those of your client, then many opportunities to collaborate will reveal themselves.

BENEFITS OF COLLABORATION

1. Shared perspectives
2. Enhanced creativity
3. Efficiency through division of labor
4. Efficiency through enhanced communication
5. Efficiency through shortcutting where mutually agreeable
6. More buy-in on the part of the customer
7. Fewer misunderstandings
8. Less elapsed time
9. Greater honesty
10. Better working relationships
11. Improved understanding of each others' business
12. Greater understanding of motives behind words and actions
13. Staff development on the part of buyer and seller

Given all the benefits listed in the box, are there ever any reasons not to collaborate? Yes, a few. A loss of perspective must be guarded against, to be sure. You can't afford to confuse collaboration with codependency. And in certain situations, where even the appearance of conflict of interest must be avoided, you have no choice.

But for the most part, this is not why we actually *do* refuse to collaborate. The real reasons most salespeople have trouble with collaboration are far more self-oriented and fear-based. They come not from any objective conditions, but from our own minds, as listed in the next box.

REASONS WE RESIST COLLABORATION WITH CUSTOMERS

1. A belief that we compete with our customers
2. Ego—wanting to be seen as able to do everything
3. An inability to confront difficult issues constructively —especially emotional ones
4. Fear of sharing corporate secrets
5. Fear of being found out to have stretched the truth in the past
6. Lack of common goals
7. Fear of being seen as not knowing enough
8. Fear of sharing our economic model
9. Discomfort with speaking openly with customers
10. Fear they'll use knowledge learned to bring in a competitor
11. Fear they'll use knowledge learned to push for lower prices

Principle 3: A Medium- to Long-term Perspective

Having a medium to long-term perspective means focusing on multiple transactions and interactions over time, as opposed to the particular sale at hand.

The longer term is the right perspective from which to view issues of investment and return. If you believe you will *in the long term* do well by serving your client, then you will be willing to make certain investments, perhaps even recommending someone better qualified for a particular job.

The simple and sound economic reason for focusing on the medium to long term is that the most powerful selling-related economics take place across transactions, not within them. The cost of selling a dollar of business to a new customer is multiples higher than the cost of selling a dollar of business to an existing customer. That is true in nearly every business; heavily true in some, massively true in others. And by focusing on the short term, the transaction term, those economics are lost.

Don't let medium- to long-term focus excuse low margins and "investment pricing." The long-term view means that the provider firm must *also* prosper in the long run. A customer doesn't benefit from a few cut-rate golden eggs if providing them means killing the supplier-goose. You need the ability to have honest discussions with your client about the mutual levels of benefit accruing from a long-term view. In the long-term context, short-term problems often fade.

Refer to the box that follows to learn why a medium- to long-term perspective is so critical to Trust-based Selling.

WHY A MEDIUM- TO LONG-TERM PERSPECTIVE IS CRITICAL

1. It gives you room to invest in the relationship.
2. It provides better return-on-investment data.
3. Both sellers and buyers can make a few bad short-term decisions.
4. The consequences of trust-creating behaviors—and trust-destroying behaviors—become clear.
5. It often takes a while to develop a relationship.
6. Beyond the transaction, the economics of scale and of relationships take hold.
7. Over time, buyers and sellers learn about each other's businesses.
8. In the short term, relationships can look like win-lose or lose-win; in the medium to longer term, they all become clearly win-win or lose-lose.
9. Time allows multiple relationships to develop across buyer and seller organizations.
10. The value of trust relationships isn't just additive; it fosters more trust relationships. Time helps trust become scalable.

Despite the clear benefits of focusing on the medium to long term, a host of pressures keeps us as sellers from looking at relationships that way. At the heart of these pressures lies one overriding factor—fear. Fear that we cannot control the buyer, fear that we will be taken advantage of, fear that if we take a risk we might not get the return, fear that if we don't get some collateral in the matter of risk-taking we might get taken advantage of in turn.

Fear drives control-oriented behavior; fear drives us to the short-term perspective; fear drives us to do unto others before they do unto us. Fear shouts out one solution—let me get mine, here, now. A bird in the hand is worth two in the bush. Don't accept any return if the payback horizon is too long. What have you done for me lately? Refer to the following box for a list of those pressures that keep us from adopting the right perspective.

PRESSURES AGAINST ADOPTING A MEDIUM- TO LONG-TERM PERSPECTIVE

1. Quarterly earnings targets (for public companies)
2. Quarterly (or monthly) sales targets (if allowed to contradict longer-term good)
3. The desire to look good among one's peers—"the President's Inner Circle"
4. The lure of sales contests—"the trip to Hawaii"
5. Promotional pricing or other short-term incentives
6. The competitive sense between salespeople
7. The desire to help the team—"win one for the Gipper"
8. A fear of being taken advantage of by the buyer
9. A fear of establishing a precedent
10. A desire to get the maximum now, in case it doesn't come up again

---

Principle 4: A Habit of Transparency

Secrets break down trust. A habit of transparency is the best guarantor that motives will be understood. Being transparent means being willing to let the client into your business, and into your thinking, by sharing information you might normally think of as being proprietary.

In complex product and intangibles businesses, being transparent means being willing to think out loud (see Chapter 13). It means speaking difficult truths (see Chapter 12). For professional services businesses, it means being willing to be open about such key processes as staffing and professional advancement. For product-based companies, it means being open about such things as product life cycles and pricing structures. The next box lists some of the benefits of transparency.

BENEFITS OF OPERATING TRANSPARENTLY

1. Your customers have no doubt about your motives.
2. Your clients have the data to know you're telling the truth.
3. Little time is wasted in arguing about what the truth is.
4. You get a reputation for truth-telling.
5. Since your flaws as well as your strengths are evident, people can make sensible judgments about you.
6. For the same reason, people don't think you exaggerate.
7. Customers feel fairly treated by you.
8. Buyers are not suspicious of you.
9. Clients reciprocate by being open and aboveboard with you.
10. Buyers can see what is a fair profit for both of you.
11. You gain credibility—people believe what you say.

With all benefits listed in the box, it might seem surprising that everyone doesn't practice transparency. But of course, we don't.

Of all the values, being transparent is perhaps the most frightening. It gets to the very heart of the difference between seller-centric and customer-centric selling. In seller-centric selling, there is a brick wall between buyer and seller built from the difference in perceived interests. The purpose of seller-centric selling is to get the buyer to give you money—*and the seller is not supposed to admit that to the customer.*

That difference in objectives translates into the perception that the game is a zero-sum one, that interests are ultimately at odds with each other, and that the game of buying and selling is a competitive one. In such a game the last thing you want to do is let the competitor "see your cards." It goes against a lot of business thinking and tradition to let the buyer into your thoughts, your intentions, and your mind.

That generalized fear translates into more specific reasons we don't practice transparency. Refer to the next box for a list of these reasons.

REASONS PEOPLE DON'T PRACTICE TRANSPARENCY

1. A belief that, "They'll find me out and reject me—I'm not good enough"
2. Fear that we'll lose control of the sale
3. Fear that we'll have no value to add after all the information is out
4. Fear that we will be manipulated
5. Fear that the buyer will "cherry-pick" us for free ideas and then buy from a competitor
6. Fear that the buyer will use information to his or her advantage against us
7. Embarrassment or shame over our policies, products, organization, or ourselves
8. Belief that to be transparent is to give up advantage, therefore profits
9. Belief that transparency will help our competitors more than our customers

Trust is intuited, not deduced, and felt, not proved. Children instinctively know the difference between an adult who talks down to them and one who takes them seriously. Dogs seem to sense whether a stranger is friendly or afraid (or a cause for fear). Corporate buyers have the same kind of relationship with trust and know intuitively whether or not they can trust you.

Tiger Woods took decades to perfect a great golf swing and he says he's not done yet. A golf swing involves just one set of muscle movements, a few movements repeated ad infinitum. How much more difficult would it be to perfect trust in selling if we had to do it only through behaviors—tips, tricks, magic phrases, selling processes, and body language.

Principles are key. After all, you would not trust someone who:

- Always starts by focusing on himself
- Insists on working alone and only sharing end results with you
- Doesn't look past the transaction at hand
- Never lets you in on his situation and thinking

You would not trust such a person and neither would your customers.

The Trust Equation

(The next two sections of this chapter borrow directly from *The Trusted Advisor*[1]; if you have read that book, you may want to just skim them).

Often we intend more than one thing when we use the word *trust*. We use it to describe what we think of what people say. We also use it to describe behaviors. We use it to describe whether or not we feel comfortable sharing certain information with someone else. And we use the same word to indicate whether or not we feel other people have our interests at heart versus their own interests. Those four variables of credibility, reliability, intimacy, and self-orientation can be combined into the "trust equation," as shown in Figure 4.1.

Credibility has to do with the words we speak. In a sentence, we might say, "I can trust what she says about intellectual property; she is very credible on the subject."

By contrast, *reliability* has to do with actions. We might say, for example, "If he says he'll deliver the product tomorrow, I trust him, because he's dependable."

Intimacy refers to the safety or security that we feel when entrusting someone with something. We might say, "I can trust her with that information; she's never violated my confidentiality before, and she would never embarrass me."

Self-orientation refers to the focus of the person in question and, in particular, whether the person's focus is primarily on himself or on the other person. We might say, "I can't trust him on this deal. I don't think he cares enough about me. He's focused on what he gets out of the deal." Or—more commonly—"I don't trust him. I think he was too concerned about how he was appearing, so he wasn't really paying attention to me or to us."

Increasing the value of the factors in the numerator increases the level of trustworthiness. Increasing the value of the denominator—that is, self-orientation—decreases the level of trustworthiness.

Figure 4.1   The Trust Equation

$$T = \frac{C + R + I}{S}$$

Where: T = trust
C = credibility
R = reliability
I = intimacy
S = self-orientation

Since there is only one variable in the denominator and three in the numerator, the most important factor is self-orientation. A seller with low self-orientation is free to really, truly, honestly focus on the customer. Not for his own sake, but for the sake of the customer. Such a focus is rare among salespeople (or people in general, for that matter).

Looking at trust this way covers most of the common meanings of trust that we encounter in everyday business interactions. Note that the meanings are almost entirely personal, not institutional.

People don't primarily trust institutional entities. They trust other people. The components of credibility and reliability are sometimes used to describe companies or Web sites, but more often to describe people. The other components—intimacy and self-orientation—are almost entirely about people.

Trust in selling requires good "scores" on all four variables in the equation. But the most important, by far, is low levels of self-orientation. Living from the four trust principles is the best way to increase trustworthiness on each of these variables.

The Trust Creation Process

Has the following scenario ever happened to you? You have a customer who has a certain need; you can see that need very clearly, but the customer *cannot* see it and is resistant. The more you try to explain why your solution is the best, the more the customer resists, even though you are sincerely trying to do the best thing for the customer!

People come to trust others through interactions—conversations. And in selling, trust comes about not in the impersonal parts of the process, but in the interactions between people. This trust creation process consists of five sequential steps: Engage, Listen, Frame, Envision, and Commit (ELFEC for short), as shown in Figure 4.2.

Here's a description of each step in the trust creation process.

1. *Engage*—understand what your customer values and be well-prepared to discuss one of those issues.
2. *Listen*—to the themes and issues that are important and real *to the customer.*
3. *Frame*—the true root issue, problem statement or opportunity statement in terms that both of you agree to.

Figure 4.2   The Trust Creation Process

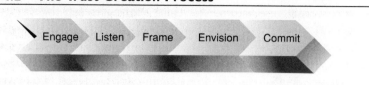

4. *Envision*—jointly, an alternate end-state—how things will look if the issue was resolved.
5. *Action*—offer specific actionable steps that are agreed upon by both parties.

The *order* in which these sentences occur in a conversation has as much impact as the sentences themselves. You could do a wonderful job on framing the issue or on the commitment to action—but if you do them *before* you do the listening, then the trust process breaks down or freezes. When we translate the trust creation process into a sales context, as follows, this becomes clear:

Engage: I hear X may be an issue for you—is that right?
Listen: Gee, that's interesting; tell me more; what's behind that?
Frame: It sounds like what you may have here is a case of Q.
Envision: How will things look three years from now if we fix this?
Commit: What if we were to do Z?

Let's briefly examine each step in turn.

Engage

The first step in a trust-creating conversation is "engaging." To engage a customer means to begin talking about something that is interesting and useful—*to him or her*. It may or may not be as interesting to you.

Getting engagement right is like a good tee shot to the fairway in golf—it makes all things possible. But a hook off the tee into the woods makes it very difficult to achieve to par.

Effective engagement has four results:

1. It identifies a subject of common interest to you and the buyer.
2. It shows the buyer you have done some homework.

3. It shows the buyer you are not afraid to offer a point of view.
4. It demonstrates customer focus, as opposed to self-focus.

You should not begin conversations with general, vague comments like, "How can I be of help to you today," or, "Let me tell you about us." Instead, good engagement statements might sound like, "I'm assuming that time to market is a problem for you—is that right?" or "A lot of our customers are concerned about growth these days—am I correct that growth is an issue for you too?"

Having a "point of view" is key to engaging and requires homework and research about the customer's business and company. Engaging is not about getting credit for looking energetic and smart; it is about you generating a point of view on how *his business* can be helped—probably, though not necessarily, by your company.

You, not the customer, must take the first step. You can't ask the customer to begin a trust-creating process. You must offer something of value to get engagement started, and that begins with having an educated opinion based on research or a point of view on an issue that is important to the *customer.*

Listen

One step is more critical than all the others. It is this one—listening.

> Michael L. worked as a trainer on the Manhattan Suicide Prevention Hot Line. His job was to train volunteers to handle incoming calls correctly.
>
> Michael says, "The average suicide call lasts 20 minutes. You absolutely must spend the first 10 minutes simply listening to the caller. If you try to engage them in problem-solving conversation or offer solutions to them without having listened—well, your calls end much sooner. It is a matter of life and death."
>
> A suicide hotline is an extreme case—but an accurate example of how people behave. People do not want to hear your ideas until they feel *you* have heard *their* concerns. As the saying goes, "They don't care what you know until they know that you care."

It's tempting to think that listening is about collecting information. With data, we can then identify the problem, craft solutions, overcome objections, and close the sale. But good listening is, perhaps, only 10 percent about getting the data. Good listening is about much more.

Good listening is about understanding the people in front of you, and I don't just mean what school they went to. It's about what drives them, what motivates them, what excites and frightens them. Sure, it's about what buying criteria they have in mind, but it's also about what issues are important to them in life and what they think is funny or profound.

Perhaps most important of all, good listening is about establishing relationships and making connections. You do that by actively listening—paraphrasing rational information and empathizing with nonrational information. By doing so, the buyer *knows* you've been listening—and gives you the emotional right to proceed further.

Listening earns you the right to be right. Being right by itself isn't worth much. You can have the best advice and the best service offering, but if the buyer doesn't think you understand his or her situation, doesn't think you "get" who he or she is, she or he is not going to accept your advice. That's just how we human beings work.

Frame

Framing is the third step. A framing statement is sometimes also called a *problem statement.* It is an attempt by you to summarize and state the root issue that you and the client are talking about. The purpose of a framing statement is to gain agreement between you and the client about the issue at hand.

Examples of good framing statements include:

- "It sounds like this is an engineering, not a marketing issue—is that how you see it too?"
- "It sounds like low bandwidth is the primary issue for you, not processing speed; is that right?"
- "It sounds like the frequent spot checks are what's driving the store manager turnover; does that sound right?"
- "It sounds to me like we have been operating under different approaches to communication, which has caused us problems."
- "The core problem here seems to be one of resources, not of tactics; what do you think?"

If customers nod their heads at your framing statement, they are in effect telling you, "Yes, that *is* the issue as I see it. Now that *you* see it that way *too*, I am giving you the green light to proceed further in the discussion." You have earned the right to proceed.

In a new customer sales call, the framing statement may be almost entirely about the customer. In later sales discussions—involving trade-offs, negotiation, or differing perspectives—it needs to address both seller and buyer.

Envision

An envisioning statement talks about a "to-be situation." It describes how things would look different if the issue at hand were solved.

Envisioning keeps us from jumping straight from diagnosis to conclusions. Sellers are always eager to provide solutions, but clients need to *own* the solutions, and the best way to get there is to help them envision moving from an as-is state to a to-be future reality.

Envisioning anchors the buyers in the real-life implications of the decision to be made. It makes benefits tangible. Envisioning is where the value becomes clear, as opposed to the price. Finally, envisioning makes clear the action implications of the buying decision. Time spent on envisioning is invaluable for making clear implementation plans and accountabilities for them.

Sample envisioning statements include:

- "We would have 35 percent less breakdowns if this works out."
- "If this goes ahead, we would need two more parking lots."
- "Your yield rates would go up by two percentage points."
- "These customer groups would end up collaborating rather than competing."

Envisioning is often left out of sales conversations. As a result, conversations can end badly because people move to action or closing before the value, implications, and next steps are thought through.

Envisioning means staying away from statements like, "Why don't we do X" or, "What if we did Y" or, "What we need to do first is Z." Instead, spend time first describing the *result* of whatever actions get taken.

Positive results of good envisioning include solid statements of value, understanding of implications, understanding of complexities and impacts on organizations and processes. Good envisioning also increases the customer's ownership of the outcome.

Commit to Action

The last step in the trust creation sequence is action—in particular, a commitment to move forward. This is the *only step* in the trust creation conversation that deals with specific actions.

Good commitment to action steps creates emotional commitment too, by forcing both parties to recognize what must be done to gain the value in the sale. Good commitment to action steps cements the relationship between buyer and seller, because both have obligations. Mapping them out creates bonds. And of course, commitment to action amounts to an implementation plan.

Sample action statements include:

- "So, it sounds like we're in agreement here; shall we move ahead, or are there other areas we haven't covered yet?"
- "Why don't I take care of the logistics, and you draw up the contract?"
- "What if we were to try it on Tuesdays?"
- "Have you thought of shipping by land?"

A Cautionary Note

It's particularly important to beware of the two most common mistakes in the process of trust creation:

1. Inadequate listening
2. Jumping too quickly to the commitment to action phase

The first mistake leads to conversations that continue on the surface but have stopped being connected beneath the surface—they are just polite, paying lip service, marking time. The second tends to shut down the conversation prematurely, often even without the politeness.

Notes

1 Maister, Green, Galford, *The Trusted Advisor*, Free Press, 2000.

PART II

HOW IT'S DONE:
TRUST-BASED
SELLING
IN ACTION

TRUST IS NOT A BUSINESS PROCESS

This Chapter at a Glance

Trust-based Selling isn't tied to a particular process; instead, it depends on attitudes and values based on principles. Each step in a sales process model can be infused with trust values. The trust creation process can also be applied to all the interpersonal steps in a traditional sales process model.

In 2002, Priscilla Myers took over sales and marketing for Prudential's life insurance third-party channel, that is, non-Prudential agents who sell Prudential policies. An experienced executive who had managed the initiative to take Prudential public, she nonetheless had never been responsible for selling or running a sales unit until she was handed the job by Prudential's chairman. "It's about people," he told her, "you'll figure it out."

Within six months, Priscilla violated four common sales practices. First, she announced to her top customers in a price-competitive business that Prudential would not compete solely or even primarily on price. Then, she deemphasized quotas to her sales force. On several occasions, she agreed with customers who said Prudential's value proposition to them was inferior to a competitor's. Finally, she developed nonlegally binding sales agreements with her key customers.

All these sound like suicidal policies in today's cutthroat business world. Yet Priscilla's unit achieved growth of more than 40 percent in the first full year, well ahead of plan. Second-year results were even better. Just what was it that Priscilla did?

She is the first to admit, "I didn't figure it out all at once. But after a while I realized that to be successful, I had to build the relationship. To do that, I had to really see things from the customer's perspective; I had to be honest and transparent. I had to work *with* them; and I had to focus on the big picture and the long run. I always asked, 'What would it take for us to have a long-term relationship with you?' And it was an honest question—I wanted to know the answer.

"Those who wanted price only, even if they were willing to buy from us—I wasn't looking for. I wanted to focus our efforts, and all of our attention, on those who wanted a mutually beneficial long-term relationship. It amounts to trust. The agreements we made, while not legally binding, were in many ways even stronger. They were mutual commitments we made to each other, and we stuck to them. In cases of real shifts in the business, we took that into account, rather than sticking to the letter of a legal agreement. I had to trust them; but, more importantly, they had to come to trust me. Those policies are just a few that flowed naturally from those principles. Trust works."

Priscilla didn't use a set of clever sales tactics or a magical sales process. Nor did she focus on competitive strategy. Her actions emerged from a deep belief that, if she focused on helping her customers, her needs would be met as well.

Instead of, "How can we sell better?" she asked, "What can we do that will make us more attractive?" Instead of bargaining with her customers, she directly asked them what they wanted. Instead of "motivating" her sales team, she asked them to hone in on what customers complained about. If the answers went beyond sales, then she followed the implications; if she heard a customer issue that required reengineering another function, then she got Prudential to reorganize to address that issue. And if she couldn't meet a competitor's offering, she would say so, to the customer.

Priscilla was customer-focused for the sake of the customer, not just for the sake of getting the customer's money. She was willing to be transparent about her pricing and her internal operations. She adopted a long-term perspective and a collaborative approach to working with her customers. That is Trust-based Selling, and it works.

There is no chapter in this book on "the trust-based sales process," because Trust-based Selling is about human processes, not business processes. It is business process neutral. Almost all failures of trust creation are human interaction problems, not business process failure problems.

Since this is unusual—most sales books are built around a sales process model—it is worthwhile explaining how Trust-based Selling coexists with process models.

A Word about Sales Process Models

Most sales process models boil down to a few commonsense steps, such as those shown in Figure 5.1:

1. Target
2. Contact
3. Meet
4. Present/Propose
5. Close
6. Maintain

Of the six steps in that model, five have some element of interpersonal contact. And all six are potentially affected by rigorously applying the four trust principles and the interpersonal process of trust creation to each step.

In Trust-based Selling, it is not the sales process that is critical; buyers will not trust you based on your ability to execute a business process. They will, however, trust you—or not—because of the way you conduct yourself throughout all business processes, and outside them.

Figure 5.1   Trust-based Selling Principles Applied to the Sales Process

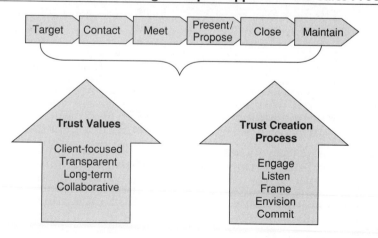

Trust should permeate the sales process. Table 5.1 shows the application of the four trust values across all steps of a conventional sales process model. It describes what each step in the process looks like from a seller-centric approach and what it looks like if the trust values are applied.

For example, in the first meeting, conventional selling focuses on demonstrating the seller's credentials and capabilities. Trust-based Selling makes sure the buyer also gets a clear idea of the boundaries of the seller's knowledge.

In the closing step, conventional selling aims to answer objections; Trust-based Selling aims to understand them as well as the buyer does. In the same step, conventional selling builds up to mentioning price after value has been established. In Trust-based Selling, price gets mentioned much earlier.

Table 5.1 Applying Trust Values to the Sales Process

Step	Not Living the Values	Living the Trust Values
Target	• Screen by fit with seller's offering • Quantitative criteria • Analyze data to define issues	• Screen by buyer's level of pain • Relationship criteria • Pick issues by reading/asking buyers
Contact	• Leading with seller offer • Time spent rehearsing pitch • Time spent writing, scripting	• Lead with buyer need • Time spent rehearsing listening • Time spent role-playing
Meet	• Present an agenda • Show how much you know • Show answers, early	• Present an agenda for discussion • Be candid about what you don't know • Focus on problem definition
Propose	• Write proposal at the office • Focus—qualifications, approach • Meet to present proposal • Write a winning proposal	• Write proposal at client site—with client • Focus—hypotheses, benefits, outcomes • Meet to review prediscussed document • Build a winning relationship
Close	• Seek a specific outcome • Answer objections • Build up to, make case for price • Make the best case for seller	• Seek a buyer-preferred outcome • Understand objections • Raise price issues earlier in process • Make the best case for the buyer
Maintain	• Suggest follow-on solutions • Pass leads to internal subject matter experts • Stay in your competence zone	• Ask about issues • Explore related issues yourself • Acknowledge your limits, then explore

The trust creation process, just like the trust principles, can be applied to any existing sales process model. The three sale process steps of contact, meet, and propose all require personal interaction, which means all three can be approached in terms of the five-step trust creation process. Table 5.2 shows what the trust creation process looks like in those three sales steps.

For example, framing during the contact step in the sales process might sound like, "Well, it sounds to me like we're both saying it'd be useful to discuss this particular issue further—is that how you see it?" Applying listening to the meeting step suggests the importance of open-ended questions, paraphrasing, and empathy.

Table 5.2   Trust Creation in the Sales Process

Trust Stage	Contact: Step 2	Meet: Step 3	Propose: Step 4
Engage	• We've noticed that [point of view] seems to be the case for your firm; might we talk about that?	• Reiterate earlier call • Share agenda • Is what we talked about still of interest?	• Here's an issue • Here's a perspective • Is this worth discussing?
Listen	• Is that a big issue? • If not, what is? • Paraphrase	• In our experience with others . . . where are you? • Open-ended; personal • Paraphrase, empathy	• Restate findings • Ask for concerns, incorporate • Identify individuals' stakes

Frame	• Sounds like it might be useful for us to discuss:
	    -our idea?
	    -your idea?
		• What are key issues you see arising here?
		• I think what I see is . . .
		• Sounds to me like . . .
			• Propose problem statement
			• Check for buy-in
			• Check for concerns
			• Restate problem statement

Envision	• Check agenda • Would you prefer just me at meeting? Purpose?	• I would imagine that . . . • What's at stake here? • Does that mean if . . .	• Restate benefits • Restate changes implied • Measures of success?
Commit	• I'll bring X content • Agree time contract	• Is this powerful enough to move on?	• POV on staying coordinated • Roles, responsibilities, critical success factors

CHAPTER 6

LIVE THE PRINCIPLES

This Chapter at a Glance

Why it's hard to live by the trust principles; how to know when you're not; and tips for living them right:

- *Start from the customer's perspective*
- *Behave in a collaborative manner*
- *Adopt a medium- to long-term perspective*
- *Be transparent*

Trust-based Selling puts more emphasis on the motives, objectives, and mindsets of the salesperson than on a particular set of techniques or behaviors. So it's important to explore how one lives out the four trust principles:

1. Start from the customer's perspective
2. Collaborate
3. Adopt a medium- to long-term perspective
4. Be transparent

True Customer Focus:
Start from the Customer's Perspective

Craig (not his real name) is a former sales and marketing exec, currently an organizational development consultant. He was dreading an impending meeting with a senior exec who had a reputation for being somewhat difficult. A good friend of Craig's, in fact, had had such a negative experience with this exec that it precipitated his leaving the company. The meeting was causing Craig some concern.

A week before the meeting, Craig attended a seminar that required that he simulate that meeting in a role-play exercise with Craig himself playing the role of the difficult executive.

"A minute into the exercise," he said, "the strangest thing happened. I was saying the very words I could imagine him saying to me, in his voice, with his tone. And rather than fear, I felt nothing but compassion for him. He was dealing with a messy situation and the answers were not altogether obvious. It was as if I could see where he was coming from. He wasn't angry at me, simply frustrated, upset and even afraid of the situation he was in. And I could see perfectly well why he would be afraid, given what he was up against.

"It became clear to me in that minute why I needed to put aside my fear and just be with him. I could go in and meet with him and help him to the best of my ability. All this simply because I was able to focus on him—and not on me."

Being customer-focused requires a state of mindfulness, of paying attention and being open to a client's issues and situation—as well as to a client's concerns, desires, and fears.

Is it easy? No. If it were, we'd all be doing it, and trust and customer focus wouldn't be such rare commodities. Refer to the box below for specific ways to get and stay client-focused.

23 Ways to Get and Stay Client-Focused

1. Before you meet with a client, do whatever it is that you know helps calm you down. If you don't know how to calm down, go ask someone. If you don't know whom to ask, then try deep breathing, or sitting still with your eyes closed for 60 seconds.

2. Go into customer meetings well prepared. Then be prepared to drop all your plans. The point is to be ready to meet reality, not to try to control it.

3. Go into customer meetings with an objective. If the objective turns out to be wrong, then ditch it.

4. When the client is describing something, first let him describe it in his words. If the description is about something that happened, let him describe it chronologically. Just ask, "Then what happened?"

5. Start all customer interactions with agenda checking; "I want to make sure we get done what you want today. I thought we might start with X and Y; does that meet your goals?"

6. Don't try to take notes while you're listening. Either get another person to take notes, or write them as soon as you leave the meeting. Or stop occasionally and say, "Oh I'm sorry, just give me a second. I want to make sure I get this, let me just make a note." Then do so. Then put the pencil (or the keyboard) down.

7. Let the conversation go where the client drives it.

8. If the client is drawing diagrams, ask her to draw it in your notes, rather attempting to copy her drawings.

9. If you think you're in a negotiating situation with the customer, define before the meeting just what you think it is the customer wants. And why. And what's behind that. Then check the "why" and the "what's behind that" with the customer.

10. Be curious. About everything. All the time.

11. Open-ended questions are almost always better. You knew that, of course. But here are four of the best open-ended questions:
    What's behind that?
    Help me understand [why] [how] . . .
    Please tell me more . . .
    That must have [been] [felt] . . .

12. Instead of thinking "What an idiot" (or worse yet saying it), say, "Help me understand how it is you see it that way? It's not clear to me."

13. Make a list of the four top issues that keep your customer awake nights. (Even if you're meeting that customer for the first time). Then ask him to review and correct your list for accuracy.

14. Restudy listening 101. Sign up for listening 201. Demand listening 301. And read Chapter 8 in this book.

15. Don't multitask. When you're with the customer, turn off your phones and mobile devices of all types, and look away from your e-mail. Sit with your back to the glass hallway door or to the window with the great view. The customer is view enough.

16. When you feel angry at your client, stop and ask why she is doing what she is doing. From her perspective, not yours.

17. Make a list of five things you wish you knew about your customer (see Chapter 9 for some ideas). Find them out. Every time you find out one thing, add one more question to the rolling list of five.

18. Pregnant pauses are your friend, not your enemy. Hold them just a bit longer. If the client isn't filling two-thirds of the pregnant pauses, you're talking too much.

19. What percent of the time should the customer be talking versus the salesperson? You'd probably say 70/30. But have you ever timed it? Try it sometime.

20. If you don't understand something—ask about it.

21. What was your client's last job? What's her next one likely to be?

22. If the buyer doesn't buy from you, what's likely going to be the reason?

23. Try role-playing your customer with someone.

Customer focus doesn't mean "the customer is always right." The customer is often wrong, as you well know. But if you don't begin with trying to understand the customer's perspective, from his or her point of view, and helping the person to know along the way that this is what you are doing, it will not feel like customer focus to the customer. Trust requires first that you walk a mile in your customer's shoes.

Behave in a Collaborative Manner

If your interests are those of your client, then there are many reasons to collaborate. Benefits include sharing of perspectives, enhanced creativity, greater efficiency, more buy-in, greater honesty, fewer misunderstandings, greater trust, and division of labor, to name but a few.

Brian (not his real name) works for a large systems and outsourcing firm. In the course of a long relationship, a client decided to form a subsidiary to take back some of the responsibilities that had previously been outsourced. This was done, but the subsidiary found itself lacking in some of the capabilities that, over the years, had been taken on by the outsourcing firm.

A series of negotiations followed, each slightly more testy than the last. The outsourcing firm felt it was constantly being told to renegotiate, and to cut costs. The client subsidiary felt constantly humiliated at having to go to the outsourcing firm to gain access to technical talent. "Basically" said Brian, "the relationship just began to go sour for all concerned."

"When yet another round of negotiation began, we decided we had to break the vicious cycle. We decided it was just not right—ridiculous, actually—for us to have this arms-length combative relationship with a client. So we decided to do something about it. We decided to put everything on the table, and see if we could turn this around.

"We started by asking them to describe everything that was bad for them, and how things could look better. And we resolved to just listen, and listen some more. To our delight, they welcomed our invitation to open up, and took a good long time to go through all their critiques and desires. Then they invited us to do the same, and we were equally candid.

"In this one session alone, we succeeded in setting a stage of trust and collaboration that led to a successful agreement. Our daily interactions now are in marked contrast—everyone likes working together. It's night and day, and all because we simply determined to work with them, not against them."

Like client focus, collaboration has to be lived "hard" to get it right. Refer to the following box, "How to Know When You're Being Truly Collaborative," for some stretch indicators.

HOW TO KNOW WHEN
YOU'RE BEING TRULY COLLABORATIVE

1. You write the proposal *with* the client.
2. You are willing to think out loud.
3. You run a sales meeting like an early phase project meeting.
4. You openly discuss prices, fees, rates, and discounts with the client.
5. You're perfectly willing to discuss personalities with the customer.
6. You aren't afraid to say, "I don't know" when you don't—which is often.
7. Both you and your client have strong points of view and express them freely.
8. You're willing to say what concerns you about this potential sale.
9. You're willing to work with the customer's staff instead of your own.
10. You can name three times when the client changed your mind on a point.
11. When you have a client relationship problem, the first call you make is to the client.

By contrast, you might think you're being collaborative in the following situations—but you're not:

1. You hold back some information from the client until a "better" time.
2. You answer the question you would have asked, not the one the customer asked.
3. In a presentation, you say, "I'm getting to that point a little later in the presentation, if you can hold on."
4. You give the customer a "special deal" that isn't really special.
5. You discuss with your team what the client really wants, rather than asking the client directly.

6. You assess customer satisfaction only through multiple-choice questionnaires.

Adopt a Medium- to Long-term Perspective

You may think, "We can't afford to always be giving things away; we've got to get something in return or have some clear hope of doing so." Ask yourself what you would have done in the situation described in the box below.

> Michael Fabiano worked for Accenture Consulting. "We had a transportation company client. They were undergoing a strike in the late 90s. The edict came out from the client that they had to cut back on everything, and of course that included consulting."
>
> Another firm, who was also doing some work for the same client, was miffed that it was getting cut back, and insisted, "We have a contract with you, you owe us, you can't cancel our contract without paying us, we'll hold you to the terms we agreed."
>
> The Accenture (then Andersen Consulting) partner in charge, when told of the cutbacks, behaved differently. In effect he said, "Look, we've made a big start on this; you'll come out of this fine, and so will we. We're not going to back out on you now. If we need to take price cuts we will. The important thing is to keep progress on this, and we'll figure some way to sort out the economics. We'll ride this out with you, we're in it together."
>
> The client was so impressed with Accenture's behavior that he told the partner of his irritation with the other firm's behavior, and voluntarily offered to continue doing the Accenture project at full rates.

Living in the medium to long term is not easy in sales. It takes a certain amount of personal strength to remember that long-term relationships are better for everyone involved than a series of short-term interactions. For some things you can do and cannot do, refer to the box "Ten Ways to Adopt a Medium- to Long-Term Perspective" that follows.

TEN WAYS TO ADOPT A
MEDIUM- TO LONG-TERM PERSPECTIVE

1. Remember that sales and earnings targets may be monthly or quarterly; but your career is long term. Sprinters don't win marathons—in fact, they lose them.

2. For any given issue—price, terms, timing—imagine doing the same deal 100 times. Ask yourself whether you would take that deal 100 times. Ask yourself whether the client would take that deal 100 times. If you both would, congratulations. If only one of you would, then talk about when and how the imbalance will be redressed.

3. If you think the prospect is taking advantage of you, be clear about your time horizon. Say, "This has to work for both of us in the long run; this price [or these terms] aren't sustainable for us. If we do this, it's a one-off."

4. Don't be greedy. Be willing to offer phased, partial, or incremental sales, rather than insisting on "the big contract" where it isn't necessary.

5. Accept that you have total control over your sales effectiveness— and very little control over its timing. Sales closed on trust are sales closed on the customer's calendar, not yours.

6. Be willing to push back on internal short-term pressures like sales goals and contests. I'm not recommending career suicide; but most sales managers will recognize the wisdom of choosing steadily growing sales over a few years versus pushing for the maximum every quarter until the balloon deflates, if you explain it well.

7. Learn to like deferred gratification. The benefits of trust usually outweigh the benefits of competition—you just have to increase slightly the measurement period to prove it.

8. Don't hesitate to say how this sale will lay the groundwork for X, Y, and Z initiatives that have to happen down the road, and how you might help. Say you'll bring it up again in three months. Then don't mention it again until the three months are up. In other words, be forthright about your intent to think long term; then don't sneak it into every conversation.

> **9.** In your benefits discussions, don't settle for short-term defini-
> tions of value, like payback time. Make sure you talk about
> longer terms as well; *annual* savings, *compound* growth rates,
> *cumulative* reductions and increases.
> **10.** Be willing to cut price, but be completely open about why and
> when you do it, and how you expect to recoup the investment
> over what time frame. (And don't cut price very often.)

Be Transparent

The U.S. auto industry still have a hard time sharing advance order information with suppliers, fearful that proprietary information could be used against them. By contrast, Japanese auto producers routinely share order information because without it their suppliers can't economically perform. The trick isn't to give just enough information to allow things like just-in-time; it is to be willing to provide information that will help the customer (or the supplier).

The auto industry is hardly alone. Most companies, and people, are fearful of sharing information. The rationale the companies give is fear of competitors getting an edge via inside information. But any edge achieved by a competitor from shared information is generally far outweighed by the advantages of a strengthened customer relationship.

The frequency and value of a "competitive edge" is also overrated. Many companies are so deeply in thrall with the "not invented here" syndrome that they discount, or look down on, or otherwise wouldn't know what to do with a competitor's strategic plan if they received a copy in the mail.

Individuals hold back on transparency for the personal version of the same fear—fear that the buyer will gain "an edge" on them. But hiding information just creates suspicion, which leads to more distance, which leads to more fear—and less trust.

The next box offers suggestions on ways in which you can be more transparent in your dealings with your customers.

13 THINGS YOU CAN DO TO BE MORE TRANSPARENT

1. Talk about price early on. If clients ask about it, tell them. If they don't ask about it, tell them anyway: "So that neither of us runs the risk of embarrassing ourselves, perhaps we should initially touch on price. This feels to me like a medium six-digit kind of price range we're talking about; is that the kind of range that you were expecting?"

2. Answer direct questions directly, with no spin control. All of them.

3. Be prepared to candidly discuss the relative merits of your company's offering with those of your competitors. Honestly.

4. Introduce all the customer-facing people on your team to the customer. Make people's e-mails and phone numbers available. Their pictures too, in the case of call centers or support staff.

5. If you're worried about your competitors getting the information you share with your client, say, "This is the kind of information we of course want to keep confidential with you, our customer." Look the customer in the eye when you say it, and say it seriously. But *don't* then follow it up with a legal confidentiality or nondisclosure agreement.

6. If you *must* use legal agreements, get them vetted by a literate nonlawyer. In such cases, say, "This is one of those things we need to have written agreements on, I hope you'll understand."

7. Don't think about "opening bid" positions with customers; be straight about what you need.

8. Within legal boundaries, answer questions about pricing to other customers.

9. Invite the client to your offices—on your nickel.

10. Invite the customer to speak at an offsite sales meeting.

11. Let your customers know your profit model; their profitability to you; and where they stand vis-à-vis your other customers' profitability to you.

12. When you don't know, say so.

13. Don't ever lie. Ever. Nope. Not once. Ever.

SELL BY DOING, NOT BY TELLING

> ## This Chapter at a Glance
>
> *This chapter discusses why selling by doing is the best selling and applying the principles of simple selling to complex goods and intangible services. Why do sellers nonetheless still practice selling by telling instead of selling by doing? We also discuss separating the value creation part of the selling process—the selling by doing—from asking for the money.*

The chief counsel of a Fortune 50 company tells this story.

"We needed to hire outside counsel; we looked at a dozen firms, narrowed it to three, and invited them in for 90-minute presentations.

"The first two were very good; they had solid expertise, industry knowledge, and had done their homework.

"Then came firm three. They said, 'We have 90 minutes with you. We can either do a standard capabilities presentation—which we're happy to do—or we can try something different. We suggest that we get started on the job, right now—as if you had already given us the contract—and begin the job, right here right now. After 85 minutes, we'll stop, and you'll have firsthand experience of exactly how it feels to work with us.'

"Well, we did their little exercise. It was quickly clear they were competent. But as we worked with them, we also got to know them better; instead of giving answers to questions, we had a dialogue. And for our part, instead of giving stock responses, we began to open up too. We felt what it was like to work with them. They came to listen and to work, and to show their smarts in real time, on our issues, not to report on theirs. You just felt you could trust them."

What this firm did was simple and sensible. But just what was it they did? Was it listening? Client focus? A sense of theater and willingness to take risks? A shrewd and clever way to differentiate itself?

It was all these, but first and foremost it was *selling by doing*, not selling by telling. Most sellers think there is a big difference between doing and selling. But the good news is that *the best selling actually looks an awful lot like doing*. The only difference is that with selling you haven't been paid yet.

This is good news in particular for all those businesses that depend for their selling on people with deep technical and delivery expertise. Most such professionals already have confidence in their ability to deliver. It's selling that's often scary.

Why Is Doing the Best Selling?

Remember: buyers of complex goods and services buy in a two-step process—first screening, then selection.

A great deal of the screening process is done at a distance—through promotional materials available in print or on Websites, through industry sources, through third-party references, and through initial rather scripted inquiry phone calls. The best screening materials consist of concise statements of focus and objective referent points of competence.

A common mistake made by salespeople is to continue behaving as if they are in the screening process when it comes time to work the selection process. They keep *marketing the firm* when they should be *selling the salesperson*.

Once you're in front of the client—in the selection process—it's time to stop reciting the company's expertise and to begin applying it to the client's own issues. This is what selling by doing does. Don't talk about your capabilities and what you've done with other firms. Instead, talk about the client seated in front of you and about her specific issues. People are far more impressed with your capabilities if they can see them applied to their situation than if they can only hear about them secondhand from someone else's situation.

Selling by doing means giving samples—doing real client work, in real time. It makes all that abstract expertise directly relevant. Selling by doing shows an other-orientation, demonstrates a willingness to take risk, and exemplifies collaboration. It adds value rather than talking about adding value. It shows a commitment to the client, feels genuine, is client-focused and collaborative, and makes the abstract feel tangible. No wonder it beats selling by telling.

In the last few years, I had occasion to interview a new personal financial planner and a new personal accountant. When I went to the financial planner, he described to me his approach to portfolio management, using a well-designed graphic slide set. He showed me track records of other clients, sample reports that he generated, and some testimonials from satisfied clients. His degrees were framed on the wall.

When I scheduled an interview with the accountant, he asked me to bring a recent tax return. When we met, he immediately started flipping through the tax form. "What are you doing about health insurance?" he asked me; "I think we can save you some money on that." He flipped through some more pages; "I think you may be leaving some money on the table on your treatment of home office deductibility; has someone explained the options to you?" More flips. "We need to look into getting you a SEP-IRA." And so on.

Which of the two impresses you more? If you're like most, the accountant's approach feels better. He focused on me directly. I didn't have to infer results from what he'd done with others; he gave it to me straight. He didn't tell me he gave good advice. Instead, he just gave me good advice. He practiced selling by doing, whereas the planner did selling by telling.

Buyers have a choice—they can try to evaluate the expert's level of expertise, or they can assess how much they trust the expert. To properly evaluate expertise, the buyer would have to possess the very expertise he is trying to acquire. Not surprisingly, buyers prefer to screen on acceptable levels of expertise, then base final decisions on trust. They prefer to assess trust not by qualifications, but by sampling: selling by doing.

Why Sellers Still Sell by Telling, Not by Doing

Two factors lock sellers into selling by telling, not selling by doing. First is that selling by telling is the norm in other businesses, and, therefore, the norm for most sales books, sales training, and salespeople.

But other businesses are different from the complex goods and intangibles kinds of business we're talking about here. Quality in physical-product businesses means zero defects; but in private banking or consulting, there is an unlimited upside. In product businesses, sales contracts typically imply a change in legal title, with financial implications like insurance and liability. Not so with professional services, where contracts often can be broken at any point. Finally, in some simpler businesses, sellers speak plain language, rather than the language of engineers or professionals.

Sellers often overrate the importance of expertise. They do so because of the huge investment they have made in mastering their area of expertise and because all of their career, including rewards and reinforcements, has been focused on increasing technical mastery. Buyers contribute to this as well; for their own complex set of reasons, buyers also act *on the surface* as if the evaluation of technical expertise is what is important to their buying decision. They frequently ask technical questions, even if they're not sure how to evaluate the answers because they feel it is a required part of their role as buyer.

So most sellers sell by telling. They stress credentials, qualifications, years of experience, office locations, functional depth of capabilities, industry credentials, and other features.

Think back to the most recent client sales opportunity you faced. Ask yourself what proportion of your prep time was spent on how to communicate credentials and qualifications versus how to ask great questions and engage the client in meaningful dialogue about the real issues at hand.

Then think about your concerns just before the meeting. Were you worried about how to control the meeting to get your points across? Or about how to move collaboratively toward a joint understanding of the issue at hand? Finally, in the meeting itself, how much time was spent by your firm talking about your capabilities versus how much time was spent by the client giving you answers to rich, open-ended questions?

Ron works for Towers Perrin, an international human resources consulting firm. "One day," said Ron, "I was working on a small project we were doing at the headquarters location of a client."

"The controller of the company knew I was there and called me into his office to ask me a question. Apparently there was some disagreement between the client's accounting firm and their actuarial firm about the implications of a certain HR policy issue.

"It was an issue I knew something about. I figured we'd spend 30 minutes together sorting it out, and then I'd go back to my work and that would be that.

"So we worked together—I was right, it took only about 30 minutes—and I was able to resolve the issue and to explain it to him so that he could understand it.

"At the end of our conversation, he said, 'You know, I think we'll just hire you instead of both the other firms.' I was floored. I had no idea he was thinking of changes in hiring. I hadn't the slightest intention of trying to sell anything. And I think, looking back on it, that's precisely why it resulted in the sale. Because all I was thinking of was doing a good job helping out the client. And in the end, that's exactly what sold him."

Ron sold without even knowing he was a salesperson. It is the purest form of selling by doing.

Selling by doing doesn't mean forgetting about economics. It just means separating the two discussions. Focus almost all the time on doing the right thing for your existing and future clients. Periodically, have another discussion—the discussion about how you get paid.

Approach that conversation with an attitude of, "OK, we've been doing some exciting work together on this. Unfortunately we can't keep doing this for free. Let's talk about what it takes for us to be able to continue doing this interesting, valuable work together with you."

AVOID MISTAKES IN THE TRUST CREATION PROCESS

This Chapter at a Glance

Any of the five steps in the trust creation process can go wrong. This chapter identifies how they go wrong, what to do about it, and how to avoid those mistakes.

Doing the Sales Trust Creation Process Right

Trust gets created between people. But how does it work? What do you actually say? And where does it go wrong?

The trust creation process was described in Chapter 4. It can be used successfully, or incorrectly. This chapter describes how to use it correctly, and what can go wrong with it.

There are five steps in the sales trust creation process: Engage, Listen, Frame, Envision, Commit. You can derail the process at each step—and so can the customer. That makes ten possibilities of error in total. Two of those ten errors stand out as the most common and serious: errors in the listening and commit phases.

On top of that, the steps can be done out of sequence in a far greater number of ways. By far the most common of these is doing the last step—commitment—too early in the process. Exploring how all these steps go wrong can be more instructive than simply saying how to do them right—so each mistake is highlighted throughout this chapter.

Figure 8.1

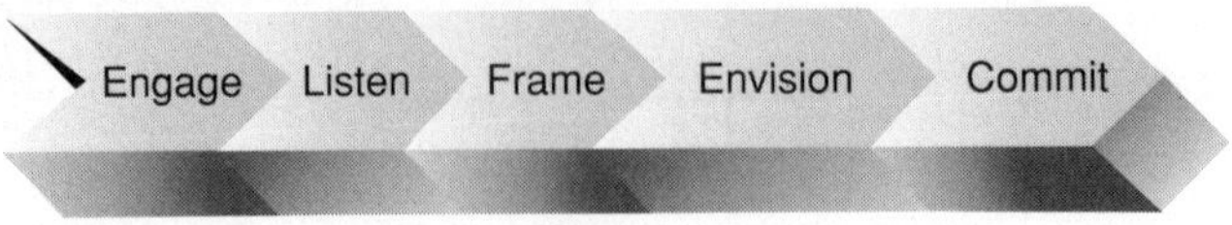

Doing Engagement Right

Good engagement does two things:

- It identifies an issue of interest to the buyer.
- It brings something to the game from the seller

What's of interest to the buyer? Do your homework. It doesn't even have to be a lot.

> Karl Almstead, a vice president at Turner Construction Company, describes the power of "other-focus" in engagement.
>
> "We were in competition for a major project management assignment and struggling to find a theme and focus for the sales presentation. We felt we were the best qualified firm to provide the service the owner needed. The problem was the best way to convey that to the owner.
>
> "We had many false starts attempting to align the unique needs of the project with our staff, experience, and procedures. One of the team suggested that there might be some background material we could use in an article about the project that appeared in the Sunday paper. The article was short and simply described the owner's goals for the project, not in cost and schedule, but the project's importance to the facility and impact in the community.
>
> "We made a decision to structure the presentation around the newspaper article. We stopped thinking about our staff, our experience, and our procedures; instead we focused on what we could do to help the owner realize their stated goals. Although it may have been a subtle shift it was important.

> "We were awarded that project. I was told several weeks later 'you were the only one of the competitors that understood our needs, concerns, and issues, and based upon that we had to award you the project.'
>
> "I was a little surprised," says Karl. "In retrospect all we did in the presentation was restate the owner's goals from the newspaper article and tell them how we thought we could help them achieve the goals. Sometimes it doesn't take much to be client focused—but it makes a big difference."

Bring something to the game. Have a point of view. Walk in with something to say. It doesn't have to be great; it doesn't have to be wildly insightful.

But it *does* have to be intelligent and thoughtful and offer some evidence that you've taken at least some time to think about this buyer's situation. Buyers don't expect you to be experts during the engagement phase. But they do hope you'll at least appear to care.

Here are some examples of good engagement statements:

- "Your industry's growth slowed for the last two years, making it imperative to get more productivity out of your existing accounts. How have you responded to that challenge?"
- "I would imagine that, with so many small competitors, quality is an important issue for you. Is that true, and what problems do you encounter trying to achieve it?"
- "We believe customers in your sector have gotten far more sophisticated; hence, they're probably demanding more flexibility in your offerings. Is that true, and if so, could we talk about ways to offer it?"

Engagement Errors

The biggest engagement error salespeople make is to assume that the customer wants to hear about them and their company. Customers—like everyone else—want to talk about themselves. If you don't have something to say of interest *to them*, don't make the appointment.

Customers don't expect you to walk in with all their problems solved. They don't even expect you to understand them! All you have to do in the Engage phase is to identify a particular issue and confirm that it is of interest to the customer.

Once you've identified the issue, move on to listening. If you continue to try to show expertise and knowledge about the issue without having heard the customer's take on it, you are violating the trust process. You have not yet earned the right to offer an opinion; to do that, you must now listen.

Customers can drive engagement errors too. A customer might begin a conversation with, "OK, tell us all about you and why we should use you." Don't fall into this trap. The trap consists of talking too soon about specific solutions, which is the commit step.

Customers enter sales discussions with as much fear and trepidation as do salespeople. They are afraid of being taken advantage of, looking ignorant, and being put in difficult positions of guilt and obligation. They often automatically resort to a defensive tactic—asking the salesperson to talk about herself and her company, rather than the issue at hand.

A customer who asks you to talk about your company and your capabilities may even seem genuinely interested; but in fact, it's usually an avoidance tactic. They are hoping that they will hear something that will allow them either to decide they trust you or to rule you out on general principles. That way they have no emotional exposure.

When a customer asks you to talk about yourself, it seems like you have little choice. But you do. You can just say, "Well, many people use us because of X or Y. But people use us for different reasons, depending on their unique situations. Could we talk more about your specific situation? Then I could talk about our abilities as they apply directly to you, or not."

Listening to Earn the Right

The single most important step in the trust creation process is listening.

"People often ask me how I, an American Jew, have been able operate in the Arab/Muslim world for 20 years, and my answer to them is always the same. The secret is to be a good listener. It has never failed me. You can get away with really disagreeing with people as long as you show them the respect of really listening to what they have to say and taking it into account when and if it makes sense. Indeed, the most important part of listening is that it is a sign of respect. It's not just what you hear by listening that is important. It is what you say by listening that is important. It's amazing how you can diffuse a whole roomful of angry people by just starting your answer to a question with the phrase, 'You're making a legitimate point' or 'I hear what you say' and really meaning it. Never underestimate how much people just want to feel that they have been heard, and once you have given them that chance they will hear you."

(Thomas Friedman, *New York Times* columnist, in a commencement address at Williams College in 2005, as reported on Williams College's Web site http://www.williams.edu/home/commencement/friedman.php)

Listening to earn the right means earning the right to give advice, or ideas, or suggestions. Listening is how you earn the right to be right. Without it, your ideas will fall on deaf ears, even if your ideas are absolutely what the customer needs.

Good listening does three things: gets the data, gets the context, and acknowledges the message. And it does all three both for rational and for nonrational issues, as shown in Figure 8.2.

In the example in Figure 8.2, an interviewer asks a client about the number of transactions that must be gone through a given process in a month. The answer "3,000" is an example of rationally getting the data. A follow-up question ("So, how big is 3,000?") elicits a rational contexting answer, "The most ever." The third row, acknowledgment, is called *paraphrasing* when applied to rational issues. In this case, something as simple as, "OK, you're currently at 3,000 per month, which is the highest you've ever been—did I get that right?"

In the nonrational column, the interviewer asks something personal: "So, what was your role during this tumultuous month?" The answer in the example is, "I was in charge of the operation." A nonrational contexting question might be, "That's interesting, what was it like to be running this operation at that time?" And the answer comes back, "They doubted me."

Figure 8.2   Listening to Earn the Right

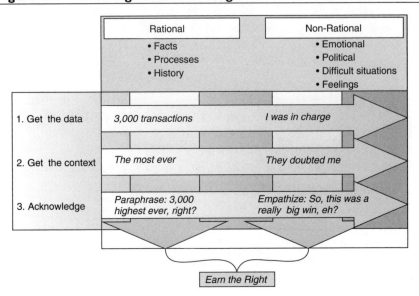

You now have a choice. Don't treat emotional data like rational data—"OK, they doubted you . . ." In this example, some kind of emotional acknowledgment is called for. "Gee, that's really great, that's quite an accomplishment. Good for you, I guess you showed them," and so on.

Listening Errors

The biggest errors in listening come from shortening or skipping the third row in the listening model—acknowledgment—and in particular, the nonrational form of acknowledgment, empathy.

If you don't acknowledge rational data by paraphrasing, then the clients aren't really sure that you have heard and understood what they have to say. The reaction is to continue the conversation, but only at a surface level. If you don't validate, the client emotionally checks out. You haven't earned the right to anything beyond politeness from the client. In particular, you haven't *earned the right to be right.*

That's bad enough. But if you don't acknowledge nonrational data—that is, if you don't empathize when it's called for—then you not only don't earn the right, you may shut the conversation down and move the relationship backward. When people share something emotional about themselves, they take a risk. If you don't acknowledge it, they feel naked, exploited, embarrassed—and they shut down.

You don't have to be a therapist to empathize; the right language depends on the client. "Darn, that really stinks" (or something more explicit, depending on the two parties) could be a perfect empathy statement.

Of course, customers can cause listening to shut down too. All of us know customers who insist that are very busy, they just want the facts, they don't have time for idle chatter, and so on.

More often than not, these comments mask fear or discomfort. The customer is afraid of revealing rational contexts as well as emotional facts. It is our job as salespeople to be gently insistent.

We do this in two ways. One is by taking on 98 percent of the responsibility for understanding. Use questions like, "Please help me understand . . ." or "What's behind that?"

The other is by pointing out the importance of understanding contexts and emotional facts. That means you have to know the importance yourself. If you don't know why your customer's context affects the solution you offer, you won't be able to explain it to him.

If you ask a question about the company's past and the client seems unwilling to give more than a perfunctory answer, be ready to state why the question is important. "The reason I ask that is that I find people have long memories; if that policy is less than ten years old, then I am guessing a lot of people still remember the old days and won't react as well as newer people. Is that right, or am I missing something?"

In the late 1990s, a Midwestern U.S. office of the accounting firm then named Deloitte & Touche was informed by its largest client that the firm would be putting the audit work out to bid.

"This came as a real shock to us," said one of the partners. "We hadn't seen it coming, and they were very clear that this was final. They told us that we could bid, but that frankly it was a nicety—a way for us to save face. The fact is, they were going to change auditors.

"We decided that, if there were ever a time where not to take a risk was to take a risk, this was it. We might as well do something dramatic. And we did."

What the firm did felt risky. The client review team consisted of four executives from the finance organization. Instead of using their 90 minutes of presentation time to do a conventional presentation, the four partners decided to act out a play. And the play they acted out was a representation of the four client executives having a meeting, deciding to fire Deloitte & Touche. In other words, the four partners role-played the very clients sitting in front of them deciding their fate.

They said things like, "Well, those Deloitte folks just haven't showed us what it takes." "That's right, they've haven't been proactive enough." And so on, echoing the very criticisms that they imagined the client had in their minds.

"We were prepared to get yanked out of there in two minutes," said one partner. "And in fact, after five minutes, we stopped and asked them if they wanted us to stop. But they were fascinated; they asked us to keep going. And we did, for nearly an hour. We just kept talking—as if we were the client—about the things that we, Deloitte & Touche, had done wrong and should have done better. And they listened, fascinated.

"At the end, they gave us the job back. And it was clear why. They told us that we, and maybe only we, had been able to show them convincingly that we understood just what their concerns were. We showed, in the most dramatic way possible, that we had finally been listening to them. And so they gave us the right to try again."

I don't recommend you try the Deloitte partners' approach; they only did it after having been through an actors' workshop, and in a unique situation—having just been fired from a relationship lasting decades. But their story emphasizes the importance of earning the right.

Framing

If you've done a thorough job of listening, then it is much easier to state the root issue at hand. However, sometimes even after good listening, salespeople can frame a problem the wrong way.

The most common mistake in framing a problem is to make it all about you. A good framing statement will be about both you and the customer, and it will have not a hint of blame in it. Table 8.1 lists some examples.

Table 8.1   Framing—Poor and Good Examples

Situation	Poor Framing	Good Framing
Presentation	What you need is deep expertise in this area—which we have	One possible need is greater expertise; we can help explore that one. Another possible need is . . .
Contract negotiations	The problem is, we need your people to fill this out first	Our people and yours are having process problems on paperwork
Price negotiation	I can't go any lower on price	We may be getting stuck in a blind alley on price
Execution or delivery	That wasn't in the specs; I assumed you knew that	It sounds like we've had a miscommunication on the specs
Execution or delivery	Your people are just not being responsive	What we have here is a failure to communicate

It isn't just salespeople who are tempted to frame issues too soon or in a one-sided way. Customers do so too. When they do, it sounds like this: "Let me tell you our issue, what the problem is, and what we need from you."

It's important to remember why customers do this. They do it partly from the natural human desire to do a good job, but mainly for purposes of control. Customers want to make sure they exert considerable control over sellers—until and unless they trust them.

Unfortunately, when customers frame the issue, they implicitly preclude the seller from adding value by involving both parties in a mutual process of problem definition. Work the trust process—go back to listening. Don't fight framing with framing—don't argue the case. If you simply engage in dueling framing statements, you will only frustrate the customer and create an argument that you will lose.

Envisioning

Envisioning is potentially the most comfortable step in the trust-based sales process, because you and your customer can jointly spend time on positive, forward-looking thoughts. Two things derail this positive experience, however.

One is an inclination to be vague. Good envisioning will have a lot of far-reaching, big-picture ideas, but it will also have a lot of very specific, tangible examples. Without the tangible examples, both customer and salesperson can end up nodding their heads in feel-good agreement about something that doesn't really exist.

If you stay longer in precisely describing a future "to-be" state of affairs, you will gain insight, gain commitment from the buyer, and develop and internalize relevant performance metrics to help describe the sale and to evaluate postsale.

The risk of being vague is sometimes even bigger on the customer side. Customers may say things to you like, "We want this new system to have a really significant impact on the way we hire people around here."

That is an exciting statement to hear from a customer, because it implies a willingness to be bold. But it also is very low in specificity. Be careful in agreeing to such statements. You may agree to something that neither of you understands or, worse yet, that each of you understands differently.

In the above case, you might say, "Well, that's an exciting prospect and one we ought to explore a lot more. Tell me how that significant impact would show up against some specific recruiting statistics, like cost-per-hire, acceptance rate, and rate of tenure six months after hire? And how much of a change can you envision in those measurements?"

The second way envisioning gets derailed is by confusing it with action steps. Envisioning describes future-state "to-be situations"; action steps tell you what to do to get there.

Don't confuse "what will it look like when we get there" with "what if we try this to get there."

Commitment

The other most common error in trust conversations along with poor listening is jumping too quickly to answers or actions, the commitment step. For a hundred reasons, salespeople are tempted to jump to "the answer" as soon as possible; they are even more tempted when the answer is clearly a product from their company.

Salespeople think that customers want a fast answer and practical, implementable actions. After all, that is what the customers say!

But it isn't what they want.

Customers don't measure speed-to-answer. If anything, the right answer too fast makes them suspicious! Think how you feel when you worked hard to get an answer or insight and someone else tosses it off like it was the most obvious and simple point in the world.

Litigants don't want the answer until they feel their lawyer has heard all the grievances. Patients don't want the diagnosis until their physician has understood all their pains. Building owners don't want the design until the architect has listened to their interior space ideas. Software users don't want systems forced down their throats until they've had their say about design requirements.

People don't like being told what to do until they have been understood (listening), until they have agreed on the problem definition (framing), and until they have understood and taken ownership of the value of a solution (envisioning). Then and only then are they ready to listen to action steps.

Working the trust process in sequence is about earning the right to be right. Violate the sequence, and the buyer won't buy in.

Customers can also drive a conversation to action steps prematurely. When a customer says, "You're the expert. What should we do?" it sounds like she is asking you to provide actionable advice. But that's not what's really going on.

What's really going on is that the customer is anxious or fearful about engaging in a dialogue and wants you, the seller, to take the risk in the conversation. That way, if something goes wrong, she can blame you.

So what do you do? You can't hem and haw and hedge; you'll look evasive and incompetent. And you can't beg off and say you don't have enough data. She'll accuse you of false advertising, calling yourself an expert, and then refusing to deliver.

When a customer asks a direct question like that, you must respond. How do you get out of the dilemma?

You anwer directly and completely. First directly; then completely. "Based on what I know now, I would recommend you go with an order of 1000 XP-27s. That is based on my assumptions about speed to market requirements and memory access speed. There's a 30 percent chance that two other solutions might be better. So, can we talk about speed to market and memory access speed?"

What you've done is to take the trust process back to Engage and Listen. The direct answer is the Engage statement; and the invitation to discuss assumptions is the beginning of the Listen phase.

CHAPTER 9

CHECK YOUR EGO
AT THE DOOR

This Chapter at a Glance

There are many tempting opportunities to focus on oneself in the sales process; but doing so reduces the connection with the customer and decreases the odds of getting the job. Final presentations are often loaded with high self-orientation. Harboring resentments toward customers—past, present, or future—raises self-orientation. The concept of "the elevator speech" is inherently self-oriented. Most high self-orientation is rooted in fear.

Solutions to high self-orientation lie more in mindset than skillset. Focus on the relationship, not the sale. Requests to "tell us about yourself" are only surface deep. Dare to be authentic. Do the right thing and detach from the outcome. Cultivate an attitude of curiosity.

Salespeople are subjected to an enormous amount of hype, particularly about winning and losing. We are urged to "get psyched" before going into "battle," coached on how to "win," taught to "go for the kill" on the close, and, finally, encouraged to celebrate "victory" mightily. Most of us do enjoy the adrenaline flow from the hunt, the thrill of victory, the congratulations, and the rewards.

But let's face it—all of that is pretty much about us, isn't it? It certainly isn't very much about the customer.

Let's examine the penultimate moment—the pitch, the final presentation, the dog-and-pony show, the beauty contest—when it is just you and the client. The job is on the line, when all your hard-earned work is going to either pay off or not. What do you do?

Here's what most of us usually do. Rehearse like crazy, if only in our own minds. Add yet a few more slides to the PowerPoint deck at the last minute. Have in mind every objection that could possibly be raised at any page, with the perfectly scripted response ready-to-mind as required. Power suit, best tie. Deep breaths. Fist-bumps with the team going into the room. And then go into the conference room *pumped!*

Now let's shift perspective. Put yourself in the position of the people sitting in that conference room 60 seconds before you make your grand entrance. They've just finished interviewing someone else, gotten a fresh cup of coffee, and checked their voicemail. They're thinking about how long this interview will last. Mainly they're thinking about how good, or bad, the last people were and how difficult this business problem is. The more people they interview, the more complex the issue looks, and the less qualified all the salespeople seem to be.

Then the door opens and in you walk. Your audience may get up with smiles to shake your hand, but what they're really thinking is, "Oh groan, another set of power ties and closing suits. They look like they just did some fraternity fist-bump exercise before walking in, trying to be all high-energy pumped up. Why can't we get someone who's interested enough just to listen?"

Sometimes you're lucky, and they continue to act polite, saying, "Why don't you tell us about yourselves?" Other times, they've gotten irritated already, and they say more aggressively, "OK, tell us why we should hire your firm for this job?"

Your answers to those two questions may not make it for you, but they can break it. Here's what *not* to say.

Case 1—Polite Client

CLIENT: Why don't you tell us about yourselves?

YOU: Glad to. First, thanks for having us here. We're really pumped to be able to talk to you today. We bring some incredible talents to this assignment / We think we can really make a difference for you / The XYZ way is really the most outstanding value proposition in the market today / blah blah.

Case 2—Irritated Client

> CLIENT: OK, tell us why we should hire your firm for this job.
>
> YOU: Glad you asked. We're the best for this job because we're the biggest player in this market / We're the specialists who focus on your niche / We can save you the most / earn you the most / deliver you the most. Plus, we're really hungry for this job.

Either one of these answers will lose you the job in 20 seconds, unless you're only up against other firms with the same lame answers. Let's explore what's wrong.

- The core of Trust-based Selling (and frankly, on this one point, any good approach to selling) is that it's not about you. Drop the "we" in almost every case.
- Telling buyers that you are "really pumped" or "really hungry for this job" is even worse. It is presumptuous. It makes buyers feel manipulated, like you're trying to make them feel guilty if they don't pick you. Being pumped is about you. It doesn't add anything objectively to how good a job you'll do. It is not their fault that you feel pumped or hungry, and it's not their fault if you leave disappointed. To suggest that somehow these are affirmative reasons for their buying from you leaves them feeling vaguely resentful. Guilt-tripping is not good Trust-based Selling.
- Both answers are arrogant. The only conditions under which you should begin a first sales presentation with "We're the best for the job" are if you've already been speaking with them for a week, you've already done five jobs for this client before, or you personally spent five years working for them in the past. Short of that, you have no basis for knowing when you just walk in why you are the best for the job. So be honest about that—say so.

I am on a school board. While interviewing for a new principal recently, one of our committee members asked a candidate, "What makes you think you're the best candidate for this job?"

He said, quite rightly, "I have no idea if I am the best for this job or not. You'll have to make that choice. The best thing I can do for you is help you to envision what the school would look like if you were to choose me. And the best way to do that is for us to talk about the issues together."

So let's rewrite those answers the way they should sound.

Case 1—Polite Client

CLIENT: Why don't you tell us about yourselves?

YOU: I'd be happy to. If it's all right by you, I'd also like to make sure we learn about you and your issues. May I give you the three-minute version of XYZ, and then move on to your issues?

CLIENT: Well, we want to make sure we learn about you.

YOU: I'll give you as many three-minute bits about us as you feel you need; but I also want to make sure we don't spend more time on us than is necessary. You may learn the most about us by hearing us react to your specific situation.

Case 2—Irritated Client

CLIENT: OK, tell us why we should hire your firm for this job.

YOU: I don't know if you should or not. We want to help you make the right choice, whether that's us or someone else. The last thing we want is to get a job it turns out we're not right for. So let me tell you why some delighted customers chose us for the job and why some other customers chose someone else. Then we can discuss what's important to *you*. Out of that discussion we can come to see whether you should hire us or not. By the way, if I believe you *should* hire us, I won't hesitate to say so. But we don't know that yet. So let's talk.

In other words, try something completely different. Check your ego at the door. Most likely this job is already won or lost. Not because it's wired or the clients have made up their minds, but because the kind of job you will do and the kind of people you are will appear so different from your competitors that the tuning of details around the edges makes virtually no difference. The deal is already won or lost—you just don't know which it is!

Drop your self-orientation to a level of zero, and just be prepared to do what is best for the client in the interaction. Don't be fixated on controlling the time; don't think you've got to get to your clincher slide; don't push back on questions to prove your point. Simply be there to offer the excellent wisdom that you have to give, and be present to help the client move the ball forward in whatever way presents itself.

If you can do that, certain things happen:

- You increase the client's ability to see the real you.
- You let the client co-manage the sales presentation, which shows collaboration.
- You increase your ability to hear a question from the client's perspective.
- You appear client-responsive—because you are, in fact, truly, really *being* client-responsive.
- You reduce your likelihood of a stroke from being overly pumped up.

What gets in the way in these and other situations are some basic beliefs. To be trusted, you have to stop thinking it's all about winning. You have to lower self-orientation. You have to see yourself as a channel for client success, and you need to cultivate an attitude of curiosity.

It's about the Customer

In John Feinstein's book *The Open*, about the history of the U.S. Open, he describes how ABC sports for many years had the contract with the USGA to broadcast the Open. But the USGA decided ABC had gotten too lax, and it decided to open the bidding—much to the chagrin of ABC, who felt betrayed.

When the bids were opened, NBC's bid was far more attractive than ABC's. Over the weeks remaining in ABC's contract, relations between the USGA and ABC became strained. A USGA official was quietly told it would be better if he not visit the ABC tent at the Open. Things culminated in an on-air incident in which the USGA felt the ABC commentator could have prevented a rules error, but instead said nothing as the error unfolded on TV.

At that point, a USGA official said, "Put it this way. If NBC had come to us after the '94 Open and said, 'We've changed our mind, we just can't do this,' I'd have given the rights to the Home Shopping Network before I would have gone back to ABC."

This is a telling example of how the instinct for client service can become perverted. Over the years, ABC had come to view its relationship with the Open as an entitlement. Things started out, most likely, as an excellent client relationship. But the relationship apparently stagnated, as ABC came to take it for granted. How else can a sense of resentment on the part of a seller over a buyer's decision to consider alternative proposals be explained?

"Justified" resentment, "righteous" indignation—if indeed there are any such things—are inappropriate attitudes for a seller to hold toward a buyer if the seller hopes to sell on trust. Trust is earned every day; it cannot be taken for granted. If trust is lost, the seller has first to look inward, rather than to blame the customer.

Kill the Elevator Speech

You know the popular sales training exercise, "the elevator speech." It's the answer to the question, "If you had 60 seconds in the elevator with the prospect's CEO, what would you tell him about your firm?" Note that the elevator situation is a special case of the first step in the five-step trust creation process—engagement.

Some firms use the elevator speech as a concrete way to exhort the troops to clarify their mission statements, to be explicit about their value propositions, to get client-focused, to be dynamic about the value the firm can add, to be succinct and hard-hitting in differentiating the firm from others. These all sound like worthy goals; after all, it's useful to everyone to know what a firm can do for a customer.

But it's the wrong idea. Don't use it. Kill it.

Instead of the elevator speech, think about *the elevator question*. If you had 60 seconds in the elevator with a prospect's CEO, what question would you ask that person?

Why a question instead of a speech? Because *it's about the customer*. If all you do is tell the CEO something, you learn nothing, and you demonstrate high self-orientation in the process. You learn nothing about the CEO, the organization, what's on his or her mind, how you might add value. Leading with the elevator speech squanders an opportunity to establish a relationship.

By contrast, the elevator question gives you a huge insight—the issue that is top of mind for the CEO. With that piece of insight, you can return to the office and put together any number of approaches that have a good chance of being listened to, because they're based on a real-world felt need. The obvious one is a letter to the CEO saying, "I couldn't stop thinking about what you told me in the elevator . . ."

What would a truly client-focused elevator question look like? It's not easy to come up with one. Ideally, a perfect elevator question would raise a big issue—big, that is, for the customer. Ideally, it would add to the formulation of the problem statement beyond what the client had been able to achieve to date. A perfect elevator question would add value. If you do all that—even if you come close—the client will form a positive impression of you and want to know more; you will accomplish more than with the elevator speech.

Finally, the ideal elevator question would take only the first 10 or so seconds of the 60. After all, the best Trust-based Selling comes more from the client talking than from the seller talking.

What are some examples of successful elevator questions? First, what's your reaction to these questions?

- What issue keeps you awake at night?
- What legacy do you wish to leave?
- What's the scariest outcome of the current situation?
- Where do you see this company in five years?
- What achievement are you most proud of?

These questions are good enough in some other situations; they are more or less open questions and somewhat client-focused. But they're *not* good enough to be elevator questions. They don't add value in the question itself.

A great elevator question has to be more than just an open-ended, client-based question. Those are too mechanical for a great CEO elevator question; they don't give the buyer any reason to believe you care or are interested.

Here are a few better elevator questions:

- "Lou Gerstner, at the beginning of his tenure with IBM, said, 'The last thing IBM needs right now is a new vision.' For this company now, is that true too? Or is a new vision just what the company does need?"
- "You've said in the past that changing culture will be important for XYZ; do you envision doing that through new people or new systems or new values—or perhaps all three?"
- "XYZ's flagship product is facing new competition—can you share with me, obviously in broad terms, what's key to meeting that competitive threat? Is it engineering? Marketing? Market research?"

- "You've got a degree in engineering, but you also spent 10 years in marketing; which talent bucket do you expect to draw upon most in this new situation facing XYZ?"
- "You've announced a program to get more customer-focused. In meeting that goal, will the leading role be played by training, new hiring, customer research, or some other approach?"

In each case, you are demonstrating that you're aware of a specific issue known to be important to the client. You're offering some specific ways of thinking about the issue, which are known to the clients, but which might not have been expressed to them in quite that way. *And you're keeping it short—because it's not about you!*

Most of the time, a great elevator question will result in interest. In *all* cases, you should have a point of view ready to explain in case the CEO were to ask you what *your* recommended answer would be. If so, give your point of view and wait for a reaction. If not, don't push it on the client.

Do I really mean "kill the elevator speech"? Four out of five times, yes, I really do. There are some cases in which the customer *is* sincerely interested in seizing this random event to hear all about you; but those instances are rare, and you'll know when they arise. If you lead with a great question, no one will begrudge your handing over a business card when you get to the 34th floor. Depending on the customer's response, you could even ask for a follow-up phone call. A great question is more likely than a great speech to earn you the right to make that call.

Just Do the Next Right Thing

Judy Lutzy is a successful financial planner in West Orange, New Jersey. After raising three daughters, Judy began her planning career at age 40. She is extremely successful. Here's how.

"People tell me," she says, "that if you have a really successful client relationship, you should ask that person for five referrals. But if I did that, I'd be turning away even more people than I am already!"

Judy gets referrals constantly, without asking. As she puts it, "You simply have to care more about meeting your client's needs than you do about what you get out of it.

"One couple," she says, "had a $1.5M retirement nest egg, and they were confused by their retirement options. I could have switched them into alternative funds that would have generated either fees or commissions for me. But their funds were very well-managed, and they valued stability. So I helped to educate them about their options. They were so happy with my help that the husband will roll over his retirement accounts to me when he retires next fall.

"I personally meet with and input the raw worksheet information from all prospective clients," says Judy. "I could have someone else do it more cheaply; but I think if you're going to talk to people seriously about their financial lives, you need to really feel their lives. Sometimes when I ask them questions, it raises real life issues for them. I'll get health insurance coverage for my clients; they ask me for advice about doctors, lawyers, accountants, mortgages, second homes, even divorce mediators. I make it my business to have good advice and referrals to give—no charge, it's just part of my job. If I don't know the answer to a financial question, I seek out the correct answer from an expert. I like my clients a lot, and I want to help them to achieve their financial goals."

One of today's business trends is linking all your actions and interactions as tightly as possible with improved efficiency, lead generation, time management, profitability, and so on. It all sounds good in theory. But always thinking like that will seep into your intentions and make clients feel like objects. As you can see from the above box, Judy Lutzy never does that. If she decides to take on a client, the profitability decision is made. The only thing left is service—great service, all the time, for the client's interests.

You might be skeptical that Judy can be profitable "giving away" all that service without charging for it. But she gets a larger return for it; her costs for marketing and prospecting are zero. Her satisfied clients don't just serve as references; without being asked, they often perform lead generation and lead qualification functions for her. She just has to meet with the prospects, complete the sale, and convert them into trusting clients.

Judy does not subject every transaction or every service decision to a profitability analysis—she simply does the next right thing for that client. This works because the critical profit decision for Judy is whether or not to take on a particular client. Once that decision is made, the profitability die is cast. Her per-client profitability may be high or low, but that is not a critical issue to her, because doing the next right thing for all clients ensures that the systemic profitability is high. The economic payoff is in reduced sales and marketing costs.

Judy doesn't pay attention to client needs *in order to be successful*. She is client-focused for the clients' own sake. She actually, really, truly, honestly cares. The success of her business is proof of the paradox that if you don't focus too much on making money from your clients, many things happen—including being very profitable.

It's Not All about You—Even When They Say It Is

There are plenty of reasons a customer in a sales situation might want to hear about your qualifications and experience. Only one of those reasons is to learn more about your qualifications and experience, and it's not the most important one.

My first job out of college was with a new town development company. I was given mostly gofer jobs, not being qualified for much else. But one day I was asked to investigate contractors for the building of half a dozen swimming pools.

I identified two contractors readily enough; but then came the hard part—how to choose between them? One dealt mainly with gunite (cement) pools; the other, pools from a form of vinyl lining. I immediately became nervous. One was more expensive, but supposedly lasted longer. One seller was more personable, but had less experience.

The more I looked into it, the more nervous I got. How could I judge what was important? How could I keep from looking ignorant, being taken advantage of, or—worse yet—having to say no to someone without a strong reason?

I delved deeper into each vendor's literature and asked each of them questions, hoping to find salvation in the specs. Steel walls, polymer walls, cement walls? Liner versus pressurized concrete? Maintenance costs per square foot per year? Statistics on previously satisfied customers?

> Somehow the specs never did save me. Nor could they. I was looking for someone to help me make a decision—and all I found was people trying to sell me.

Most buyers have a lot more experience than I did, as described in the box. But their reasons for asking questions are not fundamentally different from mine. They want to know some basics, yes. But they are also trying, as best they can, to see if you are someone who might actually be able to help them make a decision. Someone they can trust.

Look to the next box for 11 reasons—other than to find the answer—why customers ask us as sellers questions about our qualifications and expertise.

REASONS CUSTOMER ASKS ABOUT QUALIFICATIONS AND EXPERIENCE

1. Fear of dealing with other more psychological and scary issues
2. Desire to find some chink in your armor
3. Desire to become expert quickly in your area so he can defend himself
4. Desire to buy time while she figures out what to say
5. Desire to see if you can connect with him
6. Trying to see if you understand her business
7. Desire to check off the box on what he is supposed to do
8. Collect information on what you've said so she can relate it to others
9. Desire to see if there is a basis for connection, common geographic or educational experience or leisure interests
10. Protecting himself by covering all the bases
11. Comparing her own understanding of issues with yours

To sell from trust, the seller must continually remember to focus on the buyer. That doesn't mean you're not important; you have to have two to tango, and sellers have to be profitable to do good work.

Be Yourself—Everyone Else Is Taken[1]

There is a solid business case to be made for authenticity; it goes like this:

- If you behave authentically—being who you claim to be at all times to all people—you will be seen to have integrity.
- Having integrity allows people to evaluate your trustworthiness confidently.
- Trust is a powerful driver of sales.

Customers are much more interested in who you really are than in who you are trying to pretend to be. If you have the courage to be open about who you are—what you know and don't know, how you are feeling, how you think—then you allow customers to know the real you.

Doesn't it seem odd, then, that we spend so much energy rehearsing and trying to be other than what we really are?

This book isn't meant to provide a course in human psychology. But then again, buying is first and foremost a psychological event, not just a rational event, so we can't avoid talking about it. So let's touch on the reasons why we as sellers (really, we as people) have so much trouble being authentic; then examine why it's so important that we conquer those fears. Look to the following box for a list of the common fears that keep us from being authentic.

FEARS THAT KEEP SALESPEOPLE FROM BEING AUTHENTIC

1. Fear that we haven't got what the buyer is looking for
2. Fear of being found out for not having done our homework
3. Fear that defects in our product or service will be found out
4. Fear that we have to exaggerate to get the job and will be found out
5. Fear that we'll disappoint customers
6. Fear that we'll have to cut price to get the business
7. Fear that our personality won't fit
8. Fear that we're not as good as we think we have to be

The fears listed in the box are deeper than just fear of rejection. This list boils down to, "The weak, bad person I am is not the strong, competent person they want, and so I have to pretend to be something other than what I am. Otherwise they'll reject *me*—for *who I am*. And I can't stand that."

Such fears can come from good motives. For example, a desire to please is not a bad thing in and of itself. In fact, it is the root of a lot of good work.

But there are what we call *people-pleasers*: those whose desire to help is out of control, rooted in a need for others to think well of them. Those needs often lead to gross overcommitments. Then, when things don't work out, they have a hard time understanding why the client doesn't appreciate all the well-intended effort they put into the job. And guess what? A lot of salespeople are people-pleasers.

But clients don't want good intentions. They certainly don't want sellers whose psychic identity is all tied up in getting the buyer's approval. *Because you can't trust such people in a fundamental way.*

Let's say your eighth-grade son gets a D on his report card and tries to keep you from seeing it. Worse yet, suppose he tells you he got a B. But you find out anyway and demand an explanation.

He says to you, "I know I should have told you, but I know how much you want me to get good grades, and I didn't want to disappoint you—and I know I can get my average up to a B by the end of the semester, so I didn't want to hurt your feelings."

You feel upset. The least of it is that you're angry that he got a D. You're much more upset that he lied to you, saying he got a B. But you're probably the most upset at the reason he gave for lying to you.

It's bad enough that your son lied; it means you can't trust what he says. But his reason for lying makes it worse: it means you can't trust his *motives*. He may love you and mean the best for you, but you can't trust even those good feelings and motives because he has stolen from you the right to decide for yourself.

Other relationship examples are even clearer. When couples begin hiding things from each other "because it would just upset him" or "because she really wouldn't want to know," they are on a slippery slope. By arbitrarily making a decision for people, we are stealing from them the freedom to make up their own mind. We are substituting our judgment for theirs, and doing so without even telling them.

This is the problem with being inauthentic. And it's relevant in spades for those of us in sales.

You may have the best of intentions. You may have transcended greed and self-interest. You may have genuine client focus in mind and in deed. But if you refuse to let customers make up their own minds about who you are, then everything you say and do gets called into question because you have usurped *their* right to make up *their* own minds.

The solution is simple. Be yourself. Everyone else is taken anyway. It takes a certain amount of personal courage to acknowledge who we are, warts and all, to admit our shortcomings, and to not cringe and hide from what we see as our shortcomings.

But it also works amazingly. If you are willing to let a customer see the real you, notice what happens. The customer thinks, "Well, she certainly isn't pulling any punches with me. What I see is what I get. I don't sense any hiding, any insincerity, any faking. The person I'm seeing here is a real human being. Flawed and imperfect to be sure, but genuine, real, and authentic. I trust this person to do the best she can, given who she is, and I'll work around the deficiencies.

After all, who would you rather buy from? Someone who once got a D from another customer and tells you the truth about it? Or someone who tells you she gets As and Bs from all her customers so that you won't be disappointed?

Be a Channel

Try the following exercise just before your next sales call. Maybe do it before leaving the hotel room, in the car in the parking lot before going in, or sitting in the waiting room at the client's office.

Here's what it is.

Close your eyes and say, "Let me be a channel in this meeting, to share the great things that I know, in order to make things better for my customer. Let me check my ego at the door, and don't worry about the outcome—just be a channel."

Now, if you consider yourself a religious person, then you might think of this as a prayer. If you consider yourself a spiritual person, then you might think of this as a mantra. If you consider yourself a cold, scientific atheist, then you might think of this as a preflight checklist.

It really doesn't matter what your belief system is. The point is the same. View yourself as a channel, a vehicle, for the powerful things that you know which can make a significant difference in the business and life of your customer.

If you can see yourself as full of potential to help your customers, several things happen. First, you become less attached to your part of the outcome. Second, you become customer-focused. Third, you leave your ego behind—you are not here to win, to impress, to settle scores, or to rack up points. You are here to do what you do best, which is to improve your customers' business. And divorce yourself for the moment from the outcome. You are not here to close a deal; you are here to help a customer.

The idea of being a channel is a curious mixture of attitude and fact. The fact is you almost certainly do know things—often a great many, and very significant things—that your customer doesn't know. And your customer could benefit from learning those things from you. But your customer is prevented from learning those things to a great extent by her lack of trust. Can she trust your motives? What agenda are you really working? Do you really care, or are you trying to shade things just a bit to ensure you get the sale?

If you maintain a be-a-channel attitude, your motives become an open book. You are there to improve things for the customer. Maintaining that attitude lets customers see for themselves that you have no hidden objectives or agendas; that allows them to relax and to take your advice, perspective, and wisdom and use it as it was meant—in ways to help their business.

By going into a sales meeting and thinking, "Let me be a channel," you clean up your motives. The customer can see that and can better hear what you have to offer.

And the paradox is: if you can do that, benefits come back to you in increased sales. But only if you keep your motives clean. That's why it's a paradox.

Cultivate an Attitude of Curiosity

Remember that in the trust equation, the single most powerful variable affecting trustworthiness is the perceived level of self-orientation of the seller. If your focus is on yourself—whether driven by fear and greed, a need to be right, or even a sincere desire to help the client by getting him to see your point of view, the result is the same—the perception that your own self-interests are the dominating motives.

Short of going in for years of serious psychotherapy, is there anything practical that a salesperson can do to lower his or her levels of self-orientation?

Yes; you can cultivate an attitude of curiosity. An attitude of curiosity means you make it a habit to wonder about various aspects of your client and his or her business, and you translate your wondering into questions.

Look at the box that follows for a very small sample of "curious" questions you might want to know about your client and your client's business (not every question on this list fits every industry; see how many fit yours):

A Beginning List of Curiosity Questions

1. How many organizational levels are there between your client and the CEO?
2. How is your customer's business organized differently from its chief competitors?
3. Where did your client go to high school?
4. What percent of total cost does your product represent for your customer?
5. What percent of cost does your product represent for your customer's customer?
6. How many members of your customer's sales force do you know?
7. Does your client's organization do 360 feedback? Why or why not?
8. About whom does your client use the term "vendor?"
9. Which of your client's competitors has the highest return on equity?
10. Which purchase—from you or others—did your customer feel best about last year?
11. Who is your client's boss's trusted advisor?
12. When it comes to your customer's competitors, how much of what you do is outsourced versus done internally?
13. What do your client's customers like best about your client?
14. What's the biggest threat to your client's business as they know it?
15. What does your customer annually spend on advertising?

16. Is your client's company the highest or lowest priced in its industry?
17. When was the last time your customer significantly altered his or her main product?
18. What's your client's go-to-market time for new offerings?
19. How do your client's salespeople approach selling?
20. How else might your client consider organizing the sales function?
21. What functions might your customer conceivably consider out-sourcing?
22. Why is your client's company headquartered where it is?
23. Who are your customer's biggest customers?
24. How long has the company's CEO been in the job? Where was that person before?
25. What are your client's kids' names?
26. Why isn't your customer's office in [name that city] or in [name another city]?
27. When was the last time your client got promoted?
28. What's the level of staff turnover in your client's business?

You could, of course, add hundreds of questions to the list in the box.

Now, ask yourself: when I think about my client, what percentage of the time do I think, "How can I get them to . . ." kinds of questions, and what percentage of the time do I think "curious" questions like those in the box?

Suppose the ratio is two to one: twice as much thinking about, "How am I going to get them to accept this proposal?" or "What will they buy in terms of services on this next deal?" versus the curious questions.

What would be the effect of flipping that ratio around so that twice as many of your thoughts are curiosity thoughts?

The result would probably be profoundly different:

- Just thinking up curious questions will lead you to think differently about your client, which adds new perspectives and insights.
- By asking questions, you will learn some new information.
- By asking questions, you will meet new people and generate new questions.

- By asking questions, you will stimulate thinking within the client organization.

But more important is the fact of curiosity itself. Being curious *lowers your level of self-orientation*. You stop worrying, and you focus your energy on potentially client-value-adding topics. Your client sees that you care, appreciates your showing interest, and becomes more involved in working collaboratively with you.

Notes

1. Thanks to James McSherry, of CIBC, from whom I first heard this phrasing.

THE RELATIONSHIP IS NOT THE SUM OF THE TRANSACTIONS

This Chapter at a Glance

Your approach to the transaction clearly signals your attitude about the relationship. In particular, it signals whether you really have a commitment to helping the customer, whether you value the relationship over the transaction at hand, and whether you have a short-term versus a long-term perspective.

Operating from a relationship perspective means adding value where possible, often beyond the boundaries of the good or service you sell. It implies a different economic model; the economics of trust are systemic, not transactional; costs are often investments, not expenses, and require discipline to manage.

It's tempting to think that relationships imply measuring profitability at the customer level; but if the measures are too microtuned, they actually destroy trust and hence the relationship.

Suppose one of your customers stops buying from you, and it's unclear whether and when the customer will buy again. Do you stop calling on the customer, or not? And if you keep calling on the customer, what do you say on the sales call?

The answers to those questions tell a lot about whether you're practicing Trust-based Selling or some version of seller-centric selling. In Trust-based Selling, the relationship is not the sum of the transactions.

If you stop calling on customers after they suspend sales, then the message you send to the customers is that they only mattered to you when they were buying from you. Most likely, that means:

- Your objective was clearly to get the sale, since you stopped visiting once the transactions stopped.
- You focused on the transactions, not the relationship, since when the transactions ended, you ended the relationship.
- You are not willing to look at the relationship as long term.

So much for shutting down contact after a customer drops you.

Now suppose that you *do* continue to make sales calls on the customer for a while. Maybe your conversations go something like this:

SALESPERSON: Hi, James, good to see you.

CLIENT: Uh, you too, Bill.

SALESPERSON: I was nearby, thought I'd swing by the old neighborhood and say hello.

CLIENT: Well, that's nice of you.

SALESPERSON: How about those Bears (Yankees, Clippers, etc.)! Say, I have some tickets for the game in two weeks, if you're interested.

CLIENT: Uh, thanks, I'll have to let you know.

SALESPERSON: Say, there's a new model of the XP-27, your old preferred item, coming on stream in a month or so, and my guess is we'll make it available at attractive prices. Think you'd be interested in my ordering some for you?

CLIENT: No, Bill, we haven't changed our mind yet about that.

SALESPERSON: Sure, OK, well no harm in asking, right?

CLIENT: Uh, sure, Bill.

The discomfort in that conversation comes not from any lack of technique in the salesman's pitch or process—it's that Bill is still trying to sell transactions, when the customer has closed the transaction window, and Bill has no idea what else to do.

The result of that conversation is the same as if you just stopped calling.

- Bill's objective was still clearly to get the sale, since he couldn't talk about much else of substance.
- He focused on the transactions; the only meaning of "relationship" in that example is joint attendance at sporting events.
- He's probably not in it for the long term, since such surface-facile conversations will quickly get uncomfortable for both parties.

If you're serious about having a trust-based relationship with your customer, you must distinguish the relationship from the sum of the transactions. That means a number of things:

- Providing value *beyond that* provided by your goods or service
- A different economic model
- A change in your thinking about customer profitability

Providing Value Beyond Your Goods or Service

Trust-based relationships require that you invest some energy, time, and attention in issues important to the customer, issues that are sometimes only loosely linked to what you are selling.

For example: suppose an insurance company chooses to write all kinds of insurance for its clients in Florida—except for hurricane insurance. If the agent never discusses hurricane insurance needs with his client, then he will be of limited value to his clients. They will buy less of the other kinds of insurance he is offering; perhaps even less than if he had given them advice about where else to buy hurricane insurance.

If you're just doing transactions, you'll talk about what you sell. But if you're developing trust-based relationships, you'll talk about what the customers buy, *even if it's not what you are selling*.

Higher-level forms of seller-focused sales will define customer needs and link them to the good or service that the seller is selling.

In Trust-based Selling, that's not enough.

Not only do you have to know about what the customer is interested in, including topics beyond your offering, but you have to have a *point of view* about it.

A firm that doesn't offer hurricane insurance nonetheless would make prospective client calls prepared not only to answer questions about hurricane insurance but to proactively offer up a point of view about various issues surrounding hurricane insurance as part of a sales call.

For example, "At these prices, our underwriters think the insurer can't make much, which is why we don't write those policies right now. But that's good for you—if someone offers you that rate, I'd buy it if I were you." Or, "I think you might want to look at more coverage in this one area—I can suggest a few firms that would help you out."

The first step in the trust creation process model (Engage) says, "offer something of value to the customer." That is, something of value in the eyes of the customer. Almost by definition, the customer's perspective on what is interesting will be different from your perspective as a seller. If you limit yourself to what you sell, not only do you miss a chance to be interesting to the customer but you tag yourself as being highly self-oriented as well.

On sales calls, make it a point to have a point of view going in about an issue of interest to the customer, even if you're not selling the solution to that particular issue.

Different Economic Model

People prefer to buy what they have to buy anyway from those they trust. That means if you can manage to be first in the hearts and minds of your potential customers through trust, you greatly increase the likelihood of their buying from you when they *do* choose to buy what you are selling. And therein lies a very different economic model.

Think of traditional selling as being largely a direct and variable cost. That is, you can sensibly allocate most of your sales investment directly to particular accounts. Because of this, you focus on lead qualification: you don't want to spend much time on accounts that aren't going to buy what you have to sell. There is a fairly direct connection between your time invested and the sales you get as a result.

Trust-based Selling costs are much more indirect and fixed. You can't match them up so much to specific transactions or even to specific customers. You have to invest time in developing information of interest that you will use across your clients. You spend time with clients who might not pass a transaction-based qualification. You stay in touch with former clients who are not current buyers of your goods or services.

And, since your goal is to improve your client's situation, you may incur unusual selling costs unrelated to the transaction even when the client is doing transactions with you.

These are the indirect fixed costs of Trust-based Selling, and they are higher than those under seller-focused selling. But they are more than offset by the lower direct costs of clients who choose to do transactions with you. Because, if you have developed a trust-based relationship, people are far more inclined to buy what you have to sell when they have to buy it anyway. And to buy it with less hassle, to buy more of it at better prices, and so on. Because of the prior relationship investment, the per-transaction costs are dramatically lowered.

Trust-based Selling requires slightly more sophistication to manage. You can't rely on a simple qualifying technique, as you can with transactional sales, because your investments are based more on potential than on orders in-hand. Assessing profit by transaction or by customers buying who are the easy way out. Selling by trust requires discipline and tough thinking about where you choose to make investments and where not. It is easy to let optimism cloud your judgment.

Customer Profitability

These days, with customer relationship management (CRM) systems, online sales management systems, and greater availability of analytics for the sales function, customer profitability assessments have become much more common.

This focus on customer profitability is enhanced by emphasis on competition, as well as by relentless focus on short-term performance. Even "customer-friendly" programs built around concepts like customer loyalty describe the difference between lifetime customer profitability and short-term customer profitability.

The message is the same: Figure out how much money you get from each customer, then decide which ones to fire and which ones to focus on as candidates for yet more profits. Customers may be forgiven for not finding this kind of "customer-friendliness" particularly customer-friendly!

Measuring customer profitability in trust-based sales relationships is a little bit like the principle in physics called the *Heisenberg principle of uncertainty*, in which the act of measurement changes the thing being measured.

Micromeasuring short-term customer profitability in trust-based customer relationships is a sure way to kill trust. Once you start seriously asking things like, "What if we tweaked our mix of product sales to customer X?" or "Can we get some savings through fewer sales calls to customer Y?" you are well down a slippery slope.

If you're a customer, you don't like being reduced to a series of minutely examined transactions that treat you like an object.

At the heart of trust economics is a paradox. If you're willing to put client service and the relationship at the front of your goals, one of the consequences is that you'll get very high profitability. But if you move profitability to the head of the goals list, you turn the customer into an object, simply a source of funds. And that destroys trust.

I am *not* saying you can't or shouldn't measure. You can, and you have to. But it matters what you measure. Micromeasurements have a way of turning customers and people into objects. There's nothing wrong with measuring customer profitability any more than there is with measuring the health of a marital relationship. It goes wrong when the measures become short term and ubiquitous, when every action is analyzed for its effect, and when the relationship itself takes a back seat.

That's the economic paradox. In order to be high profit, you have to give up seeking it all the time as a primary goal. It only comes if you're not obsessively looking for it.

If that sounds to western business ears like some bizarre Zen version of capitalism, think of it this way. In all other human relationships, what you get out is pretty much a function of how much you selflessly put in. Why should business be any different?

THE NEW ABCs: *DON'T* ALWAYS BE CLOSING

This Chapter at a Glance

Most approaches to selling say, "ABC—Always Be Closing." In Trust-based Selling, closing is simply another of many steps in the development of a relationship. It is not the point or the purpose or the aim of selling.

The common approach to closing is to focus on objection handling. But this approach views objections as rooted in concerns about the solution. In complex intangible services businesses, the objections are based on psychological unreadiness, not on a concern about the solutions. The solution to objections lies in going back to the listening stage in the trust process. The penultimate question in closing is not, "Are you now ready to sign?" but rather, "What do you want to do now?" Closing becomes a point in a process, not a goal.

One of the "obvious" truths about selling, as it is usually presented, is the belief that closing is the end-point objective of all selling. This belief has been enshrined as the ABC rule, or Always Be Closing. Much has been written—entire books, in fact—about techniques and approaches to closing. But in Trust-based Selling, closing isn't the end point. Closing is just another step along the way in the development of a strong trust-based commercial relationship.

Ask yourself: when was the last time you got "closed" as a buyer—and liked it? In my unscientific sample of seminar attendees, 80 percent of buyers' experiences with being closed were negative—and 80 percent also failed. If being closed isn't a positive experience for the buyer, then just why would we be doing it? In all other relationships, closing isn't some big event; it's a natural and mutual decision. And it's generally positive. It should be that way in selling too.

Closing: Theory and Reality

Closing is often presented as a process in which objections are voiced by the customer, then handled by the seller, until all objections are overcome and the sale is closed.

Here's how the model dialogue is supposed to go:

SELLER: OK, we've pretty much covered all the details; are you ready to sign?

BUYER: Well, I'm still not entirely sure.

SELLER: What is it you don't feel sure about?

BUYER: Delivery timing; and, I guess, just overall value.

SELLER: What if we speeded up the timing to two weeks? No extra cost.

BUYER: Good; then that's a deal on timing. But I'm still not entirely sure about the value.

SELLER: Well, let's go over the value. We talked about cost savings and quality enhancements. Which is it you're not sure about?

BUYER: Cost savings.

SELLER: OK; we talked about savings from transportation and savings from assembly. Which are you not sure about?

BUYER: Oh, yes, I forgot about the transportation savings. All right then [happily], I'm ready to sign!

Now, be honest—how often have your closing discussions gone this way? Have you more often had conversations like this?

SELLER: OK, we've pretty much covered all the details; are you ready to sign?

BUYER: Well, I'm still not entirely sure.

SELLER: What is it you don't feel sure about?

BUYER: Delivery timing; and, I guess, just overall value.

SELLER: What if we speeded up the timing to two weeks? No extra cost.

BUYER: Well, that might help. But I'm still not entirely sure.

SELLER: Well, let's go over the value. We talked about cost savings and quality enhancements. Which is it you're not sure about?

BUYER: I'm not even sure it's the value thing, to be honest. I'm just not sure it's the right move for us right now.

SELLER: Is it a timing issue? If it's not the cost savings side of value, is it the revenue gains? I want to be helpful to you here.

BUYER: You've been very helpful, I'm just not sure yet. I think I just need some time to think about it.

SELLER: Time often doesn't help; let me help you nail down just what it is you're not sure about.

BUYER: Let me think about it some more and get back to you.

SELLER: I'm sure I can help you.

BUYER: Not *now*, okay? I *said* I'll get back to you.

Now, which scenario is more realistic? How often have you had the second type of conversation and felt bad about it; wondering what it was that you did wrong, since the conversation didn't go the way it was supposed to in the model?

What if the problem was not with you, but with the model itself? In fact, the problem lies with the concept of closing as it is usually approached.

Ending Sales Conversations: What's Wrong with Closing

Recall from Chapter 4 that the second most common problem in trust conversations is moving to action steps too soon. Closing is a major case of exactly that problem.

In classic closing, the seller typically attempts to finalize the deal: "Are we ready to sign?" The buyer either agrees to finalize or raises an objection. If he has an objection, then the seller is supposed to move into "objection-handling mode," meaning she tries to answer the objections, usually by referring to prior benefits discussions.

The problem lies in the whole approach. The presence of an objection means that the buyer has an objection *to something*. The "something" is assumed to be the proposed solution. But that assumption is based on a misreading of a basic fact of human psychology.

What buyers are often resisting is not the proposed solution but the fact that they are being offered a solution—any solution at all—before the seller has earned the right to do so.

Except for simple sales that operate entirely in the rational realm, this means that *objection handling is doomed from the start.* It assumes that the problem is the fine-tuning of a specific solution to the customer's pre-cise needs. The *real* problem is the seller's premature proposal of *any* solution—before the buyer is ready to *accept* any solution.

The problem is not the objection, it is the timing. The answer is not to change the solution but to reengage at an earlier step in the trust pro-cess. The answer is not to keep saying better things—it is to *stop* talking and listen.

This is a profound case of the problems that arise from treating selling as a subcategory of rational decision making. The common approach to closing and objection handling ignores the nonrational component of the buying process. It offers more answers from the seller when what is required is more listening to the buyer.

The Alternative to Closing: Envisioning and Actions

You may now be wondering, "Well, how am I supposed to close a deal at all then? Aren't I supposed to ask for the business?"

Yes, you are supposed to ask for the business; but only at the right time. And the right time is determined by a simple but powerful fact of human psychology:

People are far more likely to accept an idea they perceive as their own than they are to accept an idea they perceive as someone else's.

The answer to the closing problem lies in the fourth and fifth steps of the trust creation process, which is where people come to accept ideas as their own.

Human beings take ownership of new ideas most powerfully by envisioning their impact—both broadly and selectively, in great detail. It is important that we help our customers envision the impact of having a solution in place. We do them a service by helping them feel sure about their decision. And that in turn also helps us in making a sale.

Involve the Customer in Envisioning

Suppose you go to a travel agent about a vacation in Europe; probably Paris. You have been to Europe, but never Paris.

A poor travel agent will say, "Okay, we have many packages to Paris; what kind of hotel, location, and what price range?" You are being asked to make rational decisions with very little sense of confidence about what you are getting into.

A better travel agent knows that:

1. First you envision a general change.
2. Then you envision a specific change.

Envisioning a general change might sound like, "So, you've been to Europe before; what do you like about it? Why are you going this time?"

Envisioning a specific change might sound like, "What do you imagine you will most like about Paris? What do you like about the idea of Paris as compared to, say, Vienna?"

Asking the customer to proactively envision does many things:

- It lets the buyer talk about wants as well as needs.
- It reminds the buyer of his or her motivations, as well as the benefits of the prospective purchase.
- It reminds both parties that there may in principle be more than one solution.
- It shows that you, the seller, are willing to engage on the customer's best interests, across all solutions.
- It makes the buyer more comfortable with making a decision.

Envision through the Eyes, the Heart, and the Brain

Suppose the customer says, "I've always heard about the Eiffel Tower and want to see it." And suppose the travel agent has been to Paris. Which comment is more effective?

Yes, the Eiffel Tower is one of the landmarks of the world; built in 1889, they thought it was ugly at the time. It weighs 7,000 tons, and was built for an exhibition. It's an easy walk from many hotels. You can do it in several hours, though lines are biggest in late afternoon.

Or

When I stood in front of the Eiffel Tower, my neck was exhausted from bending so far back—it is so high! It's all open, and there are elevators—you can see across all of Paris, in every direction. I can't believe they thought it was ugly at the time it was built. And the light is gorgeous in the late afternoon!

Three things to remember about good envisioning:

1. *Stories are better than lectures.* Stories let people draw their own conclusions, rather than someone else's.
2. *Sensory descriptions help:* sight, smell, sound, touch, even taste.
3. *Your own experiences* are very valid—*as long as* you keep them descriptions, not recommendations.

Introducing Envisioning

There is a temptation to jump from framing statements right to action statements. Here is some language to help you make sure you spend enough time envisioning before moving to action and commitment steps or to closing.

First, envisioning the change in general:

- "I want to make sure we have a common understanding of what is at stake in this decision."
- "Help me understand what will change around here once we solve this problem."

- "If we look back at today from the vantage point of exactly four years in the future, tell me what problems we will have solved."
- "Whatever solution we end up with here—tell me, in some detail, how things will look or feel different."

Second, envisioning the change in particular:

- "If we go with the XP-27, how many cars do you see in the parking lot at the plant in two years? And what kinds of cars?"
- "If we go with the XP-27, which processes will be changed, and just how?"
- "If we go with the XP-27 and we get the performance improvement you hope for, tell me what that does for sales and returns."
- "If we go with the XP-27, where do you see this product in terms of its life cycle in three years?"

Staying in Envisioning Long Enough

Customers are just as likely as we are to jump too soon to action steps. How many times have you heard a customer say something like, "Well, you guys are the big experts here—what do you suggest we do?" Or "Come on, let's get to the point here, I want to know pricing on the XP-27."

Unfortunately, even if the customers are the ones demanding you jump to the action stage, they are still just as likely to push back in the face of solutions if they haven't gone through the trust process. How do you spend enough time in engaging if the customer pushes you to action?

The first answer is, have a good reason. All the trust techniques in the world can't cover up weak technical skills. If the only solution honestly is your company's XP-27 at price-point Q, then say so, and be prepared to explain why.

But if there is an honest possibility of more than one solution, then use this answer: "Right now, I think the right answer is the XP-27, but there's a chance it could be the XP-25, and even an outside possibility of the QR-10. Until I understand Z, I can't recommend one answer over the other. That's why I want to talk about Z. Would that be OK?"

Difference between Envisioning and Action

You may think that envisioning includes questions like, "Why don't we go with the XP-27?" But, in general, they are not the same thing:

- Envisioning describes future conditions.
- Action steps describe consequences of and commitments to specific actions.

Look at Table 11.1 for some examples of the differences with respect to the decision to buy a particular chipset for a cell-phone product.

Good Action Steps

Good action steps accomplish two goals:

1. They describe what must be done not just to complete the transaction but to make it successful.
2. They list mutual responsibilities for taking action.

Table 11.1   Envisioning versus Action: Examples

Envisioning examples	Action steps examples
Look back two years from now, and tell me how error rates will be affected by this decision; and how important is that?	Going with the XP-27 means we don't need the subassembly from the mainland; who will manage that termination?
In 2 years, which do you think will be the hottest features this chipset decision enables?	We will need a further discussion about manufacturing commitment; that must be done by 3 weeks from now.
Where does the XP-27 rank for you in terms of importance among the other decisions you'll make this year?	The XP-27 will require minor assembly setup changes. Whose job is that, and when must it be done?
The XP-27 is rated faster than the other choice; tell me again how much that increase in speed is worth to you in sales?	There are minimum quantities with an XP-27 order, but I don't think they're an issue at the level of systems orders you're talking about.
How much do you think this decision will help you in competing with XYZ phoneset company?	Your lawyers will need to go over this; our lawyers have a standard agreement; I'll e-mail it to you.

Good action steps, therefore, go beyond a joint, legally binding agreement; they get into implementation issues. Good action steps frequently go well beyond the bare minimum of describing the transaction. They describe what it takes to make the transaction valuable to the customer.

Thinking of action steps this way makes them simply a continuation of the whole trust creation process. The purpose of the whole process is to deepen the relationship and to add value to the customer. When we think of it this way, closing isn't the end of a something—it is just another point along the way to a deepening relationship.

What Is Left of Closing?

In Trust-based Selling, we might even say there's really no such thing as closing.

Closing suggests an end, a closing off of something. But in Trust-based Selling, the goal is the relationship, not the transaction, and the relationship continues beyond the transaction.

Closing is often not a point-in-time event, but a decision that emerges slowly and organically, and it is sometimes clear only after the fact. Often the customer will do the closing, saying something like, "All right, let's do this thing. What do we have to do to complete it?"

When the customer doesn't close it, the right question is not "Now are you ready to sign," but "What do you, the customer, want to do? Does this idea work, or do we need another one? Do we have more work to do on this one, or shall we try something else? What do you want to do now?"

It should always be—no surprise here—about the customer.

BUILD TRUST INTO YOUR NEGOTIATIONS

This Chapter at a Glance

Much negotiation is competitive, power-based, and focused on the transaction at hand. Approaching negotiation from a trust perspective changes things.

It's sometimes said that in a successful negotiation, both partners walk away unhappy. In a marriage relationship, that approach to negotiation results in divorce. Successful relationships require trust-like principles: focusing on the relationship, not the transaction; being transparent, not secretive, about goals and feelings; and actually being committed to the long-term good of both parties. These same approaches work in business negotiations.

All salespeople want to be trusted, but they also want to negotiate good customer deals. In their hearts, they feel those goals are in conflict. So they try not to think about it—and end up negotiating poor deals and destroying trust in the process. Some bargain!

You may have heard the old line, "If both parties walk away unhappy, it was a successful negotiation." What a recipe for underachievement and bad relationships!

It doesn't have to be that way. Customer negotiation based on trust not only creates superior results, but increases trust in the process as well.

The Problem with Negotiations: Competitive, Power-based, Transactional

Do these comments sound familiar? "We've got to get tougher. Being trusted is one thing, but you've got to make money. We're leaving too much on the table. They're forcing us to deal with tough negotiators. We don't realize our power, and we don't use it. Our people need to be more hard-nosed. This is business."

In beefing up their negotiation skills, many firms end up using approaches that are competitive, power-based, and transactional. It doesn't add to trust, and it isn't even very effective as a negotiating approach in the long run.

Some approaches to negotiation give lip service to "win-win" and "growing the pie." People know they are not supposed to focus solely on the zero-sum component of any negotiation. Yet it's apparent in many firms' approaches that this is just lip service. Consider some recommendations that are commonly offered in negotiations programs:

- Always open high.
- Keep your cards close; don't reveal your true position.
- Make small concessions, not big ones—and don't be first.
- If you're weak, negate the other's power; if strong, use it.
- Have a figure in mind below which you'll walk.
- Don't jump at the first offer.

Of course, every negotiation has some inherently zero-sum, competitive, me-versus-you component. But focusing on that aspect of the negotiating relationship makes it feel like basic, permanent competition. The object is to win, the game is about gaining and deploying power, and the final transaction is the end—literally—of the negotiation. It drives out the critical part of the negotiating relationship: the part which focuses on the longer-term common good.

Consider other relationships. Negotiation happens all the time in marriage. Couples are constantly negotiating about key issues like money, time, division of labor, deferred gratification, and the goals of marriage itself.

Imagine a couple negotiating who will do the dishes. If they use the competitive model, each would think, "Hmmm, I've got to win this one.

I'll start with high demands and not reveal my true position. I can bluff, and I can hold out. I'll make him(her) give up the first concession. And if I don't get X, I'll walk."

In such a case, if "both parties walk away unhappy" often enough, it's not a successful negotiation—it's a divorce!

How do partners in a healthy relationship negotiate? By doing three things consistently:

1. Focusing on the marriage, not the dishes
2. Being transparent with each other about their feelings
3. Focusing on the long-term good of both partners

Such a couple will recognize that the outcome of the dishes conversation is itself trivial; that it is one of many transactions which will happen in the life of the relationship; and that, in the long run, this and other transactional conversations must contribute to the health of the individuals to sustain the relationship itself.

Does this simple model have relevance for sellers and buyers? Absolutely. In fact it's a must, if the seller is to operate from trust.

Reframing Negotiation: Working from Trust

Do the trust principles seem abstract or idealistic? There are circumstances under which the competitive approach to negotiation arguably works better. They include:

- If you expect never to do business with your customer again
- If you have good reason to believe your customer will never talk to future potential customers
- If you have massive market power, expect to maintain it for a long time, and don't mind using it

You have to decide if that's your business—or if your business is one for which ongoing relationships, even once- or twice-removed, are relevant.

Trust-based negotiation works with the same generalized three principles as a successful marriage. This isn't surprising if one considers buyer-seller negotiations as really being about relationships. Those principles are:

- It's about the relationship, not the transaction.
- Seek all information and lead by sharing all your own.
- Generalize this transaction multiple times into the future.

Negotiating by these principles fundamentally changes the rules. If you focus on the relationship instead of the transaction, you have a very large set of options to achieve fairness. You find it easier to agree to fairness over time than fairness in one instance. If you know that people will only tell you the truth and are willing to be examined about any aspect of it, then suddenly you have reason to trust them. If you trust them, then you can tell them the truth as well. If you project the transaction multiple times into the future, then you have a more practical measure of fairness by which to operate.

Here are a few implications of these principles for buyer-seller negotiations:

1. *Agree that if there is a fair solution, it'll be clear to each party.* Lack of perceived fairness by either party is a fact in itself. It says one of the two of you doesn't feel good about this. Perceived unfairness is prima facie evidence that the negotiation hasn't succeeded. Aim higher.
2. *Be willing to share 100 percent of your economic model—and all information.* How can the other party know what you want if you don't honestly tell him or her? Not sharing information decreases trust. Further, if previously withheld information ever comes out, you will appear to have lied. By contrast, if you behave transparently, your customer has the information on which to make sure that you feel fairly treated and knows you haven't behaved in an untrustworthy manner.
3. *Have a principle-based rationale for when you do or don't give discounts.* Many buyer-seller negotiations are over money. Arguments can be prevented by having a very logical and transparent pricing policy that you adhere to. This goes to the sense of perceived "fairness." Many clients aren't so much upset by a price as they are by the possibility that someone else might be getting a better deal.

4. *Project this transaction times 100 and assess the impact on each party.* Trust-based negotiation is about the relationship. So presume the relationship and envision each particular settlement multiplied a hundred times. Is it fair? If not, what is required to offset it—if not in this negotiation, then in future dealings?

5. *Never lie, withhold the truth, or even knowingly mislead the other.* Even just leading the other party to believe something that isn't true destroys trust. It puts your motives into question; it destroys your credibility; and it makes you look like you'll sacrifice the long-term relationship for short-term gain.

6. *Assume agreement; then try to justify the agreement to each party.* The competitive approach to negotiation keeps focusing on you, your needs, what you will do. But if you can each approach negotiation from the other's perspective, you lower your self-orientation, help yourself see the other side, and generally improve the overall offering.

Joseph Duane, a lawyer, worked for ABC,[1] a large U.S. document management company, in the early 1990s. ABC had a large contract with XYZ, a major IT outsourcing firm, to manage its data centers and to implement EDI (electronic data interchange). At the same time, XYZ had an outsourcing contract in reverse with ABC to manage its internal document requirements. The two deals were roughly the same size. Joseph was the only ABC person who was directly involved in both deals.

After two years, ABC became unhappy with progress on the EDI initiative and asked XYZ to renegotiate. Joe says, "Now, I knew XYZ has a lot of experience renegotiating contracts like that. In fact, they're often happy to renegotiate, because they keep good track of all the out-of-scope requests a customer makes—they don't discourage requests for changes. Most of their renegotiations end up a better deal for XYZ as a result. And I knew that."

"XYZ was pretty decentralized, so it took time to get the key players to the table. Finally we threatened to invoke the arbitration clause in our contract. That got the president of XYZ to come visit us.

"At that meeting, I decided to share everything with him that I would use in an opening argument for arbitration. I showed him all the initial communications and proposals. I didn't hold anything back in reserve for the arbitration itself. And I said it all with a sense of what I thought was fair. I wasn't trying to win, and I wasn't just trying to just split the difference. I was trying for what I thought was fair.

"The president was impressed; 'There's some new news here,' he said. He asked for a half hour with this team, then came back with an offer to take off the table what could have been $400M of income to them.

"I'd been a litigator," Joseph says, "and I know being a gladiator doesn't work; I also don't believe in just splitting the difference. I was open, and honest, and shared all the facts. And XYZ's senior leadership could see that—they were getting the truth, the whole truth, from me—maybe even more truth than from their own people. And they met me in the same spirit."

Notes

1   Both ABC and XYZ are disguised names of real companies.

BE A RADICAL TRUTH-TELLER

This Chapter at a Glance

The distinction between not telling all the truth and telling a lie is a distinction lost on most customers; they feel lied to in both cases. Trust requires transparency about both parties' economics, feelings, strategies, and aspirations.

Name It and Claim It is a technique for radical truth-telling in a socially acceptable manner. It provides emotional risk insurance, while at the same time increasing truth-telling and intimacy. Courage and low self-orientation are necessary to do it, but the technique is highly rewarding.

The notion of "exceeding expectations" is a peculiar case of lying; done with good intentions, it nonetheless suggests saying one thing and doing another, thus reducing credibility and reliability. You're better off being known for truth-telling.

Here are two practical rules for conducting yourself successfully in sales—for that matter, in business in general:

1. Pretty much, mostly, just about, nearly, basically, largely all the time—tell the truth
2. Never—never, never—tell a lie.

There is just a bit of wiggle room between those two; and that wiggle room causes all the problems. "There's no point in bringing up that conflict with him right now, it'll just cause him pain; and me too." "It wouldn't be appropriate to discuss price just now, it's too early in the relationship." "No point in raising those issues, we'll just leave and let it be." Not exactly lies; just an unwillingness to speak the truth.

If you tell a lie, you're a liar. Liars cannot be trusted, because they are not credible even when telling the truth because you can't know for sure if they're telling the truth. Which means that their motives are suspect, and they are perceived as highly self-oriented. This makes a potential trustee unlikely to share confidences, which means the intimacy level is low. Telling a lie is one of the most—perhaps the most—corrosive things you can do to a relationship. If you're not willing to speak the truth, you are almost by definition not trustworthy.

Worse yet, it's a slippery slope from not mentioning something, to letting someone believe something that isn't true, to deliberately withholding some truth, to telling a "white lie," to flat-out lying.

And the truth is we lie all the time. I mean outright lies.

- "How are you?" "Fine, fine, never been better."
- "We want your best people on this job." "Absolutely, you bet; all our people are the best."
- "We want you to feel like you're our most important customer." "But we're not."

Not everything always has to be said. There is a reason for wiggle room. There are such things as secrets and discretion and quirks to be tolerated. And there are serious cultural issues; entire societies are more discreet about what they choose to talk about than are others.

Yet, of the two errors—being too candid and being too deceitful—being deceitful is by far the bigger problem.

Dare to Be Transparent

From a customer's perspective, there isn't much difference between being lied to and not being told the whole truth. Both destroy trust, and the antidote to both is the same—transparency.

One of our biggest fears as salespeople is being asked a question when we don't know the answer. A close second is knowing the answer—and not liking it. What do we do in such a case?

Most of us try to present the truth in the most flattering light. We emphasize what we do know and downplay what we don't. We emphasize the advantages of what we have to sell and downplay the disadvantages. We do this out of an attempt to appear competent and to offer the customer the best we can do.

The alternative is to be transparent, to tell the truth—the whole, complete truth. When you don't know, say so. When the customer asks you a question that feels disadvantageous to you, answer it directly. It may feel suicidal, but this approach generates higher levels of credibility then trying to emphasize what you do know or what is advantageous to you.

Being transparent raises another paradox. By giving up the attempt to control the client and simply speaking the truth as you see it and as it is presented, you make it clear that your motives are not selfish. Your level of self-orientation drops because you are not trying to manipulate the client's perception of you.

Things become easier when you resolve simply to speak the truth. You don't have to rehearse your story; all you have to do is remember reality. You don't have to remember who you told what version of the story; one version fits all. Suddenly you don't have to worry what will be in your best interest to reveal and what not; you can be guided by simple courtesy and a motivation to help the customer. Sir Walter Scott said it best: "Oh what a tangled web we weave, when first we practice to deceive."

Transparency enhances your trustworthiness. If people trust you to tell the truth—not to shade and spin things to enhance your own interests—remarkable things happen. They become much more open with you. They take your advice. They seek you out. They listen carefully to your words.

And why shouldn't they? People who don't tell the truth do so from a desire to control the other in order to further their own interests. So when people lie to us or conveniently leave out significant parts of the truth to accomplish the same thing, we automatically assume they are acting from a high level of self-orientation.

Low levels of truth-telling attack the very foundation of trust: the level of self-orientation versus orientation to another. It's deeper than just, "He lied to me about that; how can I believe him on anything else?" It goes to our very character—whether we treat others as a means to our own ends or as ends in themselves.

You may be thinking, "This all sounds a little too pie-in-the-sky. Besides, it feels very counterintuitive. My customers would think I'd gone softy on them." So let's look carefully at how you "do" transparency in the real world.

Read the (fictitious) example in the box that follows of a postsale situation (which could rapidly turn into a cancelled-sale situation if not handled well).

THE SELLER

William is XYZ's project manager on his firm's new assignment with ABC. His first significant client meeting without John, XYZ's officer in charge, is coming up. William and John had worked hard to get the right staff for the project. Mary had some prior experience with ABC and probably would have been the very best, but she was unavailable. However, Susan was available and in fact had more industry expertise than Mary. The upcoming meeting is with Laura, the head of HR for ABC; the stated agenda is scheduling, though William suspects staffing might come up.

THE CLIENT

Laura is the head of HR for ABC. She is going to a meeting with William, the project manager on the new XYZ job. She has worked with XYZ before, with good results, though with some effort. It makes a difference, she has decided, whom you get from XYZ to staff the assignment. She knows that Mary is probably the best at this issue and is inclined to insist that Mary be staffed on the job. Laura is willing to postpone the assignment by up to four weeks to get Mary. The meeting is about project scheduling, but Laura feels staffing must be made an issue early on.

Does the situation described in the box sound familiar? Here's how it usually plays out.

WILLIAM: Hi, Laura, nice to see you again. As I suggested, I'd like to go over scheduling with you today.

LAURA: Nice to see you too, William, I look forward to working together. And yes we have to talk scheduling, but I'd also like to cover another important issue, staffing.

WILLIAM: [looks just slightly pained] Well, that's fine, we can talk about that, we have—

LAURA: As you know, Mary worked with us on the last assignment, and we had a terrific experience with her. She is very strong, and worked very well with us. This is a particularly challenging assignment, and the ability to have someone on the team who really knows us is very important, so I'd like to make sure we're able to have Mary on the team. Would that be all right? [smiles sweetly but firmly]

WILLIAM: Well, yes, Mary really is great . . .

LAURA: Yes, she really is a credit to your firm.

WILLIAM: . . . but I would also like to tell you about Susan. Mary is not available right now, but in many ways, Susan is a superior choice. In particular, she has greater industry experience, and, as we have discussed, knowledge of your industry is something very important to you. We really think Susan would be a better choice for the assignment.

LAURA: Well, I don't know Susan and you're right that industry experience is useful, but I also know what works for us, and I'm inclined to be pretty risk-averse on this very important assignment. Mary would be critical to this assignment, I think. Have you discussed this with John?

And so on. This is a discussion heading south fast. The positions hardened so fast that William didn't even get to find out that Laura was willing to negotiate.

The conversation can be upgraded from an F to a C+ simply by following two rules:

- Don't lead with a solution until you've heard the client state the problem.
- Listen, listen, listen.

As soon as Laura said she wanted Mary, William should have said, "Sounds like there's definitely something about Mary. Please tell me more about why she was so effective for you, so I can fully understand your concern on this issue." Then he should have continued to use open-ended questions like, "Tell me more," "What's behind that?," and "Then what happened?" until he had a full understanding of the situation.

But that only gets us to a C+. What if he does a great job of listening, and then says, "Well, I really understand why you liked Mary so much; thanks for explaining that. Unfortunately, she's still busy, and I really can't do anything about it. So let me tell you more about Susan."

If that's what William says, Laura will feel even more used, since William gave her reason to believe that being heard would have an effect—and it didn't. This fear is precisely why most of us in William's position are fearful of listening too much to the client: the client might make a persuasive case, and we'd *still* have to say no, which we hate to do.

Now let's get beyond that C+ level. Let's see what happens when William is willing to be transparent.

LAURA: As you know, Mary worked with us on the last assignment, and we had a terrific experience with her. She is very strong and worked very well with us. This is a particularly challenging assignment, and the ability to have someone on the team who really knows us is very important, so I'd like to make sure we're able to have Mary on the team. Would that be all right? [smiles sweetly but firmly]

WILLIAM: Well, we have some staffing issues ourselves with Mary; but it sounds like I need to hear what you have to say. Can we start with that, and then I can share our situation with you? Then we'll figure out together what to do.

LAURA: Well, let me tell you more about why she's important. This is a high-visibility job; I am risk-averse, and we have to be. She's a proven commodity with us; no surprises. That counts for even more than expertise. And I'm even willing to delay the project start for some period of time if we need to. She's that important.

WILLIAM: Hmmm. OK, you're telling me there are some risk levels here—both business and personal—that we need to be cognizant of. And Mary is a vehicle for lowering risk, so that naturally attracts you. You personally, I mean, and the company as well.

Also, that's interesting; I didn't realize you would be willing to alter fundamentals like timing. Clearly that says she means a lot to you.

Am I getting all this right?

LAURA: Yes; I just want to make sure you understand also the upside here too, which I feel is kind of limited. The upside isn't going to come from industry experience; it's going to come from solid execution and timely delivery.

WILLIAM: OK, thanks for that addition. So, Mary has a proven capability to lower risk; risk is a personal and corporate issue for you; and you don't see much upside here from abilities like industry experience. Yes?

LAURA: Yes, that's right.

WILLIAM: All right, good. And interrupt me if some other thoughts come to mind. Now let me share some other pieces of the puzzle with you.

Mary is up for promotion in 10 months; she needs to get more varied experiences in order to be promoted; I share your high opinion of her, but she does need more breadth, and your assignment would be the fourth of this kind she'd work on. We worry about her getting stale and losing value to our clients.

This happens all the time, of course, in our business; we have to balance client-useful experience with development needs of our people. We also need to be fair to our clients; we think it's fair that everyone take on some share of developing new people, and in return we owe clients their fair share of experienced teams.

Mary is tentatively slotted to work on our upcoming ARD assignment; as you may know, ARD is our biggest client, so we obviously need to be sensitive to them as well.

So those are some of the issues on our side—her need to get promoted, our need to make sure she gets broadened, and our need to balance legitimate client needs. On your side, I'm hearing a high-risk project, for which you quite properly have a high degree of risk aversion. Further, you have had experience only with Mary in this area.

Each of us has a lot of legitimate issues at stake here. Could we reframe this as a joint problem? I fully expect we're going to do more work together in the future: My biggest concern is how we do an equitable job of meeting your needs in the long run, consistent with our needs to develop our people and to serve multiple clients. I am confident that the two of us can arrive at a solution to that problem.

And if you are willing to entertain things like project delays, then maybe I can put Mary back on the table for consideration on this assignment, if we can come up with a great solution to the bigger issues.

Can we talk about those bigger issues?

In the above case, William's willingness to be completely open offers a radically new perspective on Mary's situation. Laura, who probably has a good personal relationship with Mary, is likely to take seriously Mary's need for development, seriously enough that she's at least likely to meet Susan. And if the final decision is indeed to deploy Mary on ABC, you can be sure it will be along with a process which benefits Mary and XYZ in the long run as well.

This is more than just a "win-win approach" to negotiation. It starts with a willingness to be transparent about issues that are not usually put forth. When we perceive ourselves as negotiating, the instinct is to hold back on information, not to show our cards, to keep something in reserve.

The trust-based approach is again paradoxical. If you're willing to show customers the truth, you give them the ability to see your side of the story. It becomes apparent that you are not shading the story to fit your own needs. *Acting transparently with consistency becomes a personality characteristic, not a tactic.*

When people know you are being open, they believe what they see; and they are motivated by a strong human instinct to treat you fairly. They are also motivated by a much simpler business instinct—not to cross someone you're likely to do business with in the future.

It all depends on climbing out of the business mindset that says customers are the enemy and you must hide things from them. Customer are not the enemy, and hiding things from them just makes them suspicious. Have the courage to believe in the paradox—be transparent.

Name It and Claim It

What do you say when there's a difficult issue that is very hard to talk about? What is a socially acceptable way to speak about things that no one can speak about? How can you handle "elephant in the living room" issues—problems that everyone knows exist, but which everyone tacitly agrees not to talk about.

The most common tactic—leaving such issues alone—virtually never works; they only get worse.

In *The Trusted Advisor*, my coauthors and I talked about a technique for dealing with these situations. It's called *Name It and Claim It*, as in, "if you name it, you can claim it." Let me quickly recapitulate so we can apply it to selling.

The trick is to acknowledge publicly the issue that has not been publicly acknowledged. The truth, in this case, shall set you free. Consider it radical truth-telling in a socially acceptable manner. It is being able to speak the truth in a way that allows you to manage the emotional risk surrounding it.

The basic technique is a verbal one: Use as many caveats as are necessary to slightly overcompensate for what you are about to say—then say it.

Caveats include:

"I may have missed this, and . . ."
"I realize this is awkward timing, but . . ."
"I wish this could wait, but . . ."
"I appreciate that this must be difficult . . ."
"If this is not the right time, please say so, but . . ."
"I'm sure you've seen this many times, and . . ."

The caveats acknowledge all the negative consequences of what you are about to say. By speaking them out loud, you rob them of their power. Because you are the one taking responsibility, the other person feels relief.

Slightly overcompensating accomplishes two things. First, it deflects objections that you have forgotten something. Second, it does so through humor, which is always helpful in difficult situations. The following box gives an example of this tactic.

> Walter Dellinger was U.S. Solicitor General in the late 1990s. It is the Solicitor General's job to argue cases on behalf of the Executive Branch before the Supreme Court. Of the nine Justices at the time, two were women—Sandra Day O'Connor and Ruth Bader Ginsburg. They sat at opposite ends of the court, as perhaps befitted their differing perspectives on many issues.
>
> One day, Dellinger was presenting a case and was asked a question by Justice Ginsburg. He thought quickly, and began his response with— "Well, Justice O'Connor . . ."

He instantly knew his mistake. As did Justices Ginsburg and O'Connor and every other Justice and every other sentient being in the Court that day. It was bad enough that he had confused the names of two people he knew very well; this was worse. This wasn't like mixing up Ginsburg with Souter—it had the potential appearance of objectifying the two women as women—in short, sexism.

The natural, first-order, reptilian-brain temptation of any person when faced with having committed a faux pas like this is to hope no one noticed and to rush blindly along as if it hadn't happened. And, of course, that never works, as Dellinger well knew.

Instead: he stepped back from the podium, and out of the formal role of advocate, and said, while shaking his head with his hands at his temples, "I can't believe I said that, I can't believe I said that." He then turned to Ginsburg and said, "I would like to apologize to you, Justice Ginsburg," (and pivoting to face O'Connor) "and to you Justice O'Connor." Dellinger then squarely faced Chief Justice William Rehnquist and said—with a straight face but a twinkle in his eye—"and to you Chief Justice Souter!" The embarrassed silence quickly turned to a roar of laughter.

Was Dellinger's error forgotten? No. Forgiven? Probably, though not necessarily. What *did* happen was that, in a stroke, Dellinger spoke the truth, thereby avoiding the prison created by unspoken truths. If he had said nothing—or inadequately called it out—everyone would have focused on nothing else, and the incident would have festered and grown worse over time.

Dellinger named it and claimed it. His "I can't believe's" functioned as caveats. He further parodied himself with his humorous misidentification of the Chief Justice. The combination managed to overcompensate for what he had done.

Elephant-in-the-room issues are resolved by the kind of constructive confrontation—Name It and Claim It—that Dellinger used, so that the two parties can arrive at a shared view that increases trust.

A similar concept is the idea of errors of commission and errors of omission. An error of commission means doing something wrong; an error of omission means not doing something right.

When we don't do something about elephants in the room, we are allowing them to remain by an error of omission. The right thing to do is to acknowledge the situation for what it is—in short, tell the truth.

Applying Name It and Claim It to Sales Situations

You may be wondering what all this talk about wild animals and psychology has to do with selling at your firm.

Imagine a customer who aggressively focuses on the issue of defect rates and who is sarcastic, cynical, and doubtful. The elephant in the room is the customer's aggression. We are usually afraid to say anything about it.

We usually respond with one of two approaches. One approach is to ignore it. Simply behave politely, overlook the other's rudeness, and reveal only the smallest signs of annoyance, hoping he will come around. Which usually results in the client misbehaving further.

Or, we can respond with equal amounts of aggression. Sometimes this works—with the kinds of clients who are simply looking to find a "worthy competitor." But more often, it just breaks down in an argument.

There is another choice. State the truth, head on, in a direct and factual manner. You might say, "I could be wrong here, maybe I'm being a little overly sensitive, but I notice you're focusing a lot on concerns about defect rates. Have you had some negative experiences before in this area?"

Or, you might say, "I don't mean to be presumptuous, but you sound pretty worked up over the issue of defect rates; you seem to have a lot of energy about it. Am I hearing you right? Have you had some really bad experiences in the past?"

Most likely, you'll get a positive response. "Yes, I have had bad experiences," or, "Yes, now that you mention it I am worried." You can then explore those issues openly.

What is the worst result? Either, "No, I don't feel worried about defect rates," or "You're darn right I have, and I'm worried about yours too!" Either way, you are no worse off than before, and you have shown you are willing to talk. Further, you have acknowledged the customer's feelings, and by your taking the first step, you have lowered the risk of intimacy.

Almost any outcome will create more trust than continuing to let the elephant stay in the room.

The opportunity to use the name-it-and-claim-it tactic comes up in selling quite frequently, but particularly in:

- Mentioning price too late
- "Scope creep" after the sale; the postsale disagreement between buyer and seller about exactly what extras were or were not included in the original scope of the sale
- Personality conflicts on teams
- Finding yourself involved with the wrong sale—even the wrong client

The Trap of Exceeding Expectations

One of the more destructive pieces of unexamined business "wisdom" these days is the idea that you should always exceed expectations. Perhaps your own company's performance evaluation forms have a column labeled "exceeds expectations." You've probably been to sales training programs or read books that advocate you should "delight" the customer by exceeding his or her expectations.

Here's the problem. Imagine you run the office. Suppose you want to come up with a really great surprise for morale, and you settle on— the Christmas turkey. Everyone loves it. What a great company this is, they say. Never expected it at all. What a fine, fine place to work.

Next year, everyone expects it again. Now you have a choice. You can say flatly it was a one-time thing and decide not to do it in year two. But if you do, you are sure to disappoint at least a few people who had expectations of a repeat.

Of course, you could repeat the Christmas turkey; but if you do, it's no surprise. The great boost in morale you got last year is gone; it's an entitlement. The new people had been told to expect a Christmas turkey; it's a perk, along with getting their parking tickets stamped and coffee in the break room.

So, you work to manage expectations. Throughout the year, you drop little reminders that last year's Christmas turkey was a one-time thing, a special bonus, not to be repeated. And then you surprise them and give out a Christmas turkey again! And again you get that great buzz! "Boy they really surprised me this year; I thought it was never going to happen again, lightning never strikes twice, but this company really came through. What a great company!"

But now in year three you've got a real problem. Two points make a straight line, and now everyone expects the trend to continue. Worse yet, last year's gambit won't do; you can't claim it was a one-time thing, because you did that last year and, "You wild and crazy boss, you big galoot, you came through for us anyway, so wink wink nod nod, sure, we understand there's no turkey this year."

But woe is you if you don't come up with the turkey for year three! You'll have hell to pay. So you're stuck—you now have to have a Christmas turkey forever.

But wait, that's not the end of it. Remember, you started all this to get people excited, to surprise and delight them. You can't drop that ambition! So in year three, it won't do to just have the same old boring Christmas turkey that everyone expects; you've got to *exceed* expectations! Say hello to—the Christmas turkey and the cheese and fruit basket! Or some other equally inflationary item.

Bad enough? No. What is at stake here is not just the inflationary cost of keeping everyone in turkey-cost-plus; it is credibility and trust. Because if your aim is to exceed expectations constantly and you establish a pattern of doing so, that becomes the new pattern. The only way to play the game is to manage expectations, and then beat them.

The fact is, exceeding expectations is just another way of misleading the customer—a temporary version of lying. You'll either understate what you're really going to do, or you'll do something other than what you said you'd do. Either way, you misled the customer. It works for a while with kids and Santa Claus; but even kids get wise soon. Customers get wise a lot faster.

Customers learn quickly that "under-promise and over-deliver" means you're not being straight with them. They start setting their own expectations, making their own forecasts, having their own set of private offline books and conversations with themselves. And suddenly you haven't got a collaborative, open relationship; you've got a shell game going on.

This game gets played out on a grand scale with companies who try to manage Wall Street earnings expectations. They become known for a while for always "delighting" Wall Street by exceeding expectations;

but the excess quickly becomes factored into the next quarter's forecast. Those companies have traded a few short-term stock price surges for longer-term losses in credibility.

What's the alternative? Again, truth-telling. Share the truth with the client. Nothing says credibility like showing the client you've got nothing up the sleeve. The truth is your friend. Don't hesitate to name it and claim it.

MAKE LISTENING A GIFT, NOT A SKILL

This Chapter at a Glance

The single most critical step in the five-step trust creation process is listening. It is one of the two biggest sources of failure in trust-based sales conversations.

Being right is vastly overrated; people don't accept advice or suggestions or buy if they don't feel the seller understands them. Earning the right to be right is the more critical part of influencing or selling.

The best listening is not "active" listening or behaviorally based listening (i.e., mirroring, eye contact); it is the total concentration of the mind on the whole message the customer is delivering—that is, paying attention. Paying attention means not borrowing mental bandwidth to think about your response; it simply means paying attention.

Being willing to think out loud after listening frees the mind to pay attention; it also models collaborative behavior with the client.

Question: What are the lessons learned from the bust that will be applied to the recovery and any future boom?

Answer: The biggest lesson is that the customer is now in charge. . . . From now on, the technology companies that succeed will be those that have developed skills at listening and a sophisticated understanding of their customers' industries.

SAM PALMISANO, CEO OF IBM,
BUSINESSWEEK DOUBLE ISSUE
"THE FUTURE OF TECHNOLOGY," AUGUST 18–25, 2003.

Not all sales training books, programs, and approaches agree on everything. But if they agree on any one thing, it's probably the importance of listening. And they're right. Most people think that if you want to convince someone of your point of view or to follow your advice or to consider your service offering, you have to convince him or her of the rightness of your point of view. There are two problems with that.

The first one is that just being right is vastly overrated. You first have to earn the right to be right—and you do that by listening. The second problem is that what often passes for listening isn't listening at all. It's fake listening, and it makes things worse. True listening requires paying attention, and there are some specific things you can do to achieve it.

Jennifer Nelson is an acting branch chief in the Office of Procurement and Grants at the Centers for Disease Control in Atlanta. (The CDC's mission is to protect and support the health and safety of people, which includes disease prevention.) Her branch handles building and facilities contracts totaling over $1 billion per year. Jennifer also used to teach third grade.

"It never fails to surprise me," says Jennifer, "but I'd say a good half of the people who try to sell to me actually don't listen. That's 50 percent! And these are people who are educated, technically competent, in positions of responsibility. They are representing big companies, trying to get me to write six- and seven-digit purchase orders. Yet they somehow expect I won't notice that they're not paying attention to me, believing I'm unaware they have zoned out while pretending to listen to me. Well, let me tell you—I sure do notice.

"And it's not that I take it personally," Jennifer continues. "You get beyond that. It's that, if they can't listen, then they are preoccupied with themselves—and not with CDC. And at the CDC, we need to work with people who care about the work we do controlling diseases. If they can't focus on me, then they can't focus on that either. We want to work with suppliers who understand us and care enough to pay attention.

"One of the life skills you teach third graders," she laughs, "is how to listen, how to pay attention. I guess a lot of people out there—well, let's just say maybe they missed that day of school."

Earning the Right to Be Right

Suppose I go to a doctor, complaining of a pain in my right elbow. "It happens when I raise my arm above 90 degrees," I say, "and it seems worse after I've had fried chicken," proud of having catalogued clues that will be useful to the doctor's diagnosis. "Uh huh," says the doctor. "Take ibuprofen as directed, and I'll see you at your regular checkup next month."

I am not satisfied by the doctor's response. I feel unheard, unlistened to, unappreciated. I may not even feel like taking his advice—*even though it may be right.*

By contrast, suppose the doctor asks me, "Wait a minute—fried chicken only? What about fried fish or French fries? And what time of day does this happen? And only at home or at the office as well?" On hearing my answers, the doctor says, "There's been an interesting phenomenon lately, a combination of low pressure zones together with low temperature that have the effect of aggravating some soreness of joints for people over 40 who haven't been exercising; especially if they're eating fried fast foods, and especially on lower floors near the damp ground, not upstairs where your office is. It's nothing to worry about; just take ibuprofen according to normal instructions, and I'll see you at our next regular appointment. Though it would do you good to get back on the exercise regimen, OK?"

In this second case, the doctor provided exactly the same advice, but this time I am far more likely to take it. Why? Simply because we, as human beings, are far more likely to be influenced by and to take another's advice if we feel that the other has understood things from our perspective.

Being right by itself isn't worth all that much. In fact, it's overrated. Unless you have *earned* the right to be right, the customer isn't going to listen to you or take your advice. It may not seem fair—especially if you really *are* right—but fair hasn't got much to do with it. If you want to be listened to, appreciated and trusted or have your advice valued, you'd best earn the right to be right. And you do that by listening.

Listening versus Paying Attention

So, how do you listen to earn the right to be right?

First, let's deal with the obvious. If you're the one talking more than half the time in your customer interactions, you're not likely to be successful. You can't talk and listen; and your job is to listen, not talk. Your customer should probably be doing 70 to 80 percent of the talking.

But you knew that. Let's even assume that you are successful at not being the primary talker in your customer interactions. Now comes the bigger problem.

Much of what passes for listening is not really listening at all. It's fake listening. It consists of—let's be honest—waiting for the other person to stop talking so that we can once again start looking smart. And, while we are waiting, we are thinking of what it is we are going to say next, so that we do in fact look smart.

During this fake listening, we may practice several little behavioral tics—nodding, doing nonverbal verbals ("uh huh"), switching our gaze from the customer's right to left eye, and so forth—but what we are really doing is thinking up our next brilliant comment. This fake listening is aimed at getting the customer to think we are interested in him, when all we are after is information we have predecided we need.

Fake listening is not much better than talking. It can even be worse, since your attempts to be seen to be truly caring are likely to make you look selfish and insincere.

The human mind has limited bandwidth. Incredible though the brain is, it has only a finite ability to process information. Furthermore, most research suggests that, as we multitask, we get less efficient. Doing two things at once engages more than twice the brainpower, since some of it is used up in keeping the two things separate.

People can tell the difference. If you talk to a 10-year-old on the phone, you know when she is instant-messaging on the computer while talking with you. And it's not much more difficult to tell when an adult is doing the same thing to you. And if that's true, how difficult is it for your customers to tell when you're multitasking (the benign word for fake listening)? Not very.

Customers know when we're doing fake listening. The solution is *not*, however, to get better at faking it. You don't fix fake listening by taking courses in listening skills. You fix fake listening by—*not faking it!*

Fixing fake listening starts with understanding the purpose of listening. The purpose of listening is not just for you to get data from the customer; it is not just about you. The point of listening is also to connect with the customers, to truly understand what motivates them—who they are, what is important to them, and how things affect them.

You cannot find those things out if you believe the only point of listening is simply to acquire information. You can find those things out only if you are willing to *truly pay attention* to others—to let them take you *where they want* and to be willing to go along for the ride.

In working with the in-house legal team at a biotech firm, I was discussing some types of questions that worked better and worse for listening. One lawyer said, "But we're working with [he named a top consulting firm], and one of their people is using exactly those techniques. And it feels fake to me, manipulative; so I think those techniques are wrong."

I said, "The techniques aren't wrong—they're just no substitute for caring and paying attention. Here one of the best consulting firms in the business uses these tools, and even they can't blow it past you. The fault is in the consultant, not the tools; the intent is not clean, and you can sense it. Your gut feel is right. Technique cannot substitute for intent."

Have you ever had someone in business really, really pay attention to you and your ideas? I don't mean someone who's trying to flatter you or who depends on quoting your ideas back to you. I mean someone, like a boss or a customer, who doesn't really have to pay attention to you—but who does. It's a pretty good feeling, isn't it?

(In my experience, the people who are capable of truly paying attention—putting away other distractions for the sake of giving you their undivided attention—are more often than not senior people who are quite successful. There's a reason for that: they have the self-confidence to stop thinking about themselves for a few brief moments).

When we are listened to in this way, we feel heard, understood. Once we feel that another person has heard us out and can appreciate our perspective, we become much more willing to engage in a discussion, including being able to consider that person's points of view.

If you would like people to listen to you—people who don't have to—you are best advised to listen to them first. And you can do so by paying attention.

Make listening the gift of your attention. Be willing to let the customer lead; follow where he or she goes. Show your customers they are important to you by being willing to let go of control for a period of time and simply pay attention.

The Surprising Key to Listening: Thinking Out Loud

To pay attention, you have to clear your mind of distractions. The external distractions are easy: it's the internal distractions that are tough.

Start with the easy things. To do a good job of listening, turn away from your computer screen, even if you're on the phone. Turn off your cell phone or beeper. Have conversations in quiet places, without other distractions.

The big job is getting rid of those internal distractions—especially the distraction of thinking about what you're going to say when the other person finishes talking. Here's the key:

1. When you're supposed to be listening, pay attention.
2. When you're supposed to be thinking, do so out loud.

In other words, don't do two things at once: do them in sequence. And think out loud.

What do I mean by thinking out loud? I mean just that. Imagine you have just finished listening to a customer by paying full attention. You might lean back, stretch your arms a bit, and say, "OK, well, now, let me think out loud with you about what you've just told me. Um, you're saying you're nervous about being dependent on just one supplier; I'm not sure I heard that before. So, now, I'm just thinking out loud here, does that mean you'll consider multiple sourcing? I realize I don't know, do you do that already in your other lines of business? Or does that mean— no, wait, you only have one supplier in the office area, right? So, then, help me understand . . ." And so on.

In other words—you do your thinking verbally, in the presence of the customer. This has two enormous advantages. First, it frees you up to pay attention when you are supposed to be listening, which is how you earn the right to be right.

Second, the willingness to think out loud is a powerful way of collaborating with the customer. If you're willing to think out loud—to share the very formation of your thoughts—then it sends a signal that you have nothing to hide, that you are being completely transparent. You are behaving collaboratively. It increases intimacy, a key component in the trust equation; it allows the customer to add to or to freely correct your thoughts, and it invites the customer to participate.

The big objection to thinking out loud is, of course—it's scary. Something could go wrong—in particular, we might have a half-baked thought that shows we misunderstood something or is just a bad idea. In which case, the customer would see that we were imperfect, and we'd be embarrassed. And it's true—thinking out loud carries with it the risk of sharing our thought process and the possibility of being wrong.

But how big a risk is this? When you think out loud, the customer recognizes that you are taking some risks. This means you have managed the risk! Being willing to think out loud invites the customer to do the same, at a higher shared level of intimacy.

When you view it that way, it's not a risk. It's actually a technique of risk management! A small amount of emotional discomfort now buys you protection against much larger discomfort down the road.

CHAPTER 15

WORK THE SAME SIDE OF THE TABLE

This Chapter at a Glance

The value of collaboration comes from being willing to do together what is usually done apart from the client. This should be a general attitude, but it also includes specific circumstances, such as proposal writing and satisfaction assessment.

Write your proposals with the client—not alone. Make some significant portion of satisfaction assessment a joint process that goes well beyond ratings and scores.

Collaboration means being able to see the customer's emotions as just another set of data, not an emotional state that triggers a reactive emotional response from you. A customer who is angry at you is not someone who is personally attacking you; she is a partner who is feeling angry and who could probably use your help.

Our business culture and thought leaders tell us that business is about competition—even with our customers. Too often, the same message comes through in our approaches to selling and to negotiation. The truth is that everything works better if you're working on the same side of the table as the client.

Opportunities to work the same side of the table come up in all the interpersonal steps of the sales process; but interesting opportunities present themselves particularly at the proposal and the maintain steps.

Write Your Next Proposal *with* the Customer

Suppose you're in a services business where proposals are commonly written. Here's what that conversation usually sounds like.

> *"Okay, Joe, we'll get this proposal wrapped up and out to you by next Wednesday; you should have it by Thursday midday. It'll contain qualifications, methodology, approach, schedule, and pricing. I look forward to discussing it with you. Please don't hesitate to call us with any questions or comments whatsoever. We're very responsive. We want you to know we really want this job!"*

The proposal goes out on time. Of course, Joe never does call with any questions or comments. The only response is either a "thanks very much, not this time" call or an invitation to come in to work on the details. And it's usually the former.

How would this conversation look if you were working from the same side of the table? It might sound like this:

> *"Joe, thanks for taking the time to go through this. Now, you need this proposal by next Thursday, right? So let's do this:*
>
> *"Let's book Conference Room A for a half-day this Friday, and we'll write this proposal together—you and me. I'll have everything we need from our side. You need to come with the specs you need to have addressed—what you need to see in the proposal. You tell me what you need in terms of qualifications, and I'll have it in hard copy and digital.*
>
> *"We'll work out the trade-offs between speed and cost. I'll share with you our pricing worksheets and our discount policy sheets. We'll come to some agreement on what level of staffing to apply to it. And we'll walk out Friday afternoon with all the tough issues solved. I'll get it document-ready over the weekend, and you'll have a best-shot proposal ready for Monday morning.*
>
> *"We may or may not win it, and I know that. But you will know absolutely that you saw our best shot at it. No second-guesses. In writing it together, I'm sure some issues will arise that need to get addressed anyway by whomever you end up hiring, and that can only help you. And if we do get it, we'll be that much farther down the road.*
>
> *"I'll bring the donuts. OK, the bagels. See you at 8 a.m. Friday, all right?"*

Sound scary? Try it. First, look at the benefits. There are all the pluses stated in the conversation, plus the opportunity for selling by doing, not selling by telling.

Now look at the downside. The client says, "No, I don't think we're quite ready to do that. Just send us the regular proposal." In which case you say, "Fine, no problem, maybe you'll think about it for next time." And they most certainly will. Most likely, you'll get credit for being willing to be so open and transparent, even if they don't take you up on it.

It's the Journey, Not the Destination

Being trusted isn't something that stops after you close a sale. It has to be an underlying attitude before, during, and after—in other words, all the time.

Assessing How Things Are Going

Some years ago, Deloitte & Touche set about implementing a comprehensive approach to assessing client satisfaction in its audit and tax businesses. There were two camps. One said, "We need a set of metrics that is comparable both longitudinally, so we can assess progress, and horizontally, so that we can compare performance across clients. We need a survey."

The other camp said, "We're looking to talk to CEOs, CFOs, and chairpersons of the Audit Committee; they're not going to fill out surveys. We need white-space open-ended interviews to ask what's on their minds."

Like many large organizations, D&T forged a compromise. It would send out a 12-question survey in advance of a scheduled meeting and then use half the meeting to review the survey and the other half to discuss more open-ended topics.

When they pilot-tested the approach, they found a stable pattern. First of all, they got near 100 percent acceptance of their request to meet. In nearly all cases, the interviewee would say, "OK, here's your questionnaire, all filled out; good questions, I had fun. But now—

what I want to know is, how did you come up with that wonderful idea to use options pricing models to solve the problem?"

In other words: the survey questions qualified D&T to get the interview. Then, in the interview itself, the clients went all over the map. The data from the survey was good, but the results of the meetings were superb. D&T learned where it had problems, and what it needed to do to fix them. The clients appreciated the attention. And, even though it had not been their intention whatsoever, in many cases the interviews resulted in new business.

Finding out *how the work is going* is what most people have in mind when they begin to think about interviewing their clients. Firms are partly looking for a report card—ideally, a source of benchmarking. They are also looking for specific behavioral feedback to be used for performance feedback.

But *how the relationship is going* is something most firms would like to know even more—and don't know how to ask. The value of that discussion is huge: identifying new issues, surfacing unspoken concerns and even business development. And the value lies in the discussion, not the answer.

"How the work is going" can refer to the project or to the performance of the individuals on the project. Structured, regular project review meetings are invaluable for the former—but not for the latter.

Client surveys are ineffective at evaluating personal performance for a great number of reasons. Clients hate to give negative feedback about professionals, and as a result any feedback is suspect. By the time the survey is done, the opportunity to fix things is usually past. And professionals tend to take feedback very badly, challenging the validity of the data or blaming the sources.

For performance reviews, there is no substitute for ongoing, direct interaction with the client. Problems should be surfaced all the time and fixed on the spot. Performance evaluation is primarily the responsibility of the selling firm—not of your clients. Don't lay your problems off on them.

On the other hand, "How's the relationship going?" is a question that demands customer interaction, yet requires sensitivity. When it comes to the relationship question, it's the discussion that counts, not the answer.

That means you should not contract out the discussion to a third party. Objectivity here is not the point—in fact, subjectivity is. You can't send someone else to discuss your relationships.

How often do you fill out service assessment cards in your hotel rooms? Probably not very often. And that may be OK for the hotel business; it has large numbers to draw from, and it can describe its service attributes successfully in terms of a few multiple-choice questions. That is not, however, a good model to follow for complex goods and intangible services customers.

To engage clients in relationship discussions, you need personal one-on-one interviews among senior people, using open-ended questions. Conversations should go where the client dictates, not where a prepared interview guide has predetermined.

Because they are relationship discussions, they should not be done after each sale, project, or engagement. Some firms find them appropriate on an annual basis, but that can seem too mechanical and cyclical. Some combination of every 18 to 24 months and "as needed" may be a better rule.

The person in charge of the relationship should be at the heart of the discussion, not excluded from it. Remember that the point is not to get data but to reexamine relationships. It is very useful if he is joined by an equally senior or more senior person not involved in the relationship. That ensures two sets of ears to hear what is said, and it offers an opportunity for intrafirm mentoring and candid discussion, as well as another ear for the client. For smaller firms, this is a key CEO task.

Setting up customer relationship review meetings is easier than many people fear. Once it is understood that your focus is not a report card or a source for performance review feedback but rather an honest discussion about how to work together going forward, most customers are more than willing to devote time.

Emotions Are Just Facts

One reason it's difficult to stay on the same side of the table is that we tend to read emotional judgment into the behavior of our customers.

Remember the last time you stood in front of an angry customer? Perhaps that customer was yelling at you; or perhaps she was annoyed or disappointed or frustrated.

Whatever the reason for the anger, how did you feel? Maybe you were embarrassed, upset at the customer and at yourself, and generally uncomfortable at being in the situation. You probably wanted to fight back or apologize or simply get away—or do all three at once.

All three reactions are just reactions. You need to not take it personally, simply *notice* the anger the other person is feeling. If you can notice that she is angry, then perhaps you can begin to understand why. And if you can understand why, you can empathize with her and begin to earn the right to help.

The following box provides an example of this from Mike Heal, a sales VP at Hewlett Packard.

"HP has had a relationship with AT&T that began in the 1980s," explains Mike Heal, a sales VP at Hewlett Packard. "At the time, we were first to market with RISC architecture and were trying to sell to AT&T. But they had a lot of surrounding systems—networking interfaces, UNIX—that didn't fit our off-the-shelf products. So it became increasingly apparent that we had to do some serious product customizing.

"We put on a major full-court press to do it. We scrambled to find the right technical people internally. We had folks working 24/7; Chairman John Young came down at one point and gave people certificates. We really pulled out the stops.

"At a critical venture, we had to present to a senior Bell Labs product group we hadn't met before. I brought in Joe, one of our senior salespeople. He was a few slides into a presentation about our global support, capabilities, and so forth, all of which were important, but the head of this group—who was known for being a little feisty—jumped up and said, 'I only want to know one thing—can your products do the job? If you're not going to talk about that, I don't want to hear about the rest.'

"In that instant, I was pretty upset. Joe didn't deserve to be talked to that way. We had a lot of marbles on the line here, and of course I was the one who had set it all up.

"But before I could say anything, Joe responded. He said in a calm and sincere voice, 'I hear you loud and clear, and what I have to say isn't about product, so let's deal with this later, and move ahead to the issues that are critical to you.' And we did.

"Most people's natural inclination would have been to get all bent out of shape and respond either by confronting the customer or to complain about the customer later behind his back. But Joe didn't do that. He just heard the client's request at face value and responded to it.

"It was made clear to me later that if Joe had responded in any of those other manners, we would have lost the whole deal right there. Turns out it was something of a pivotal moment. And by the way, that gentleman on the client side remains one of our biggest friends and fans to this day."

Don't take it personally. It's personal, all right—but it's personal about them, not you.

When you have an angry customer, don't get angry in response. The fact that your customer is angry—even if he or she is angry at you personally—doesn't have to have anything to do with how you feel. Your feelings are under your control; you don't have to let others rent space in your head.

Seeing emotions as facts is a facet of emotional intelligence; it is the ability to recognize feelings in oneself and in others and to act upon them.

PICK THE RIGHT CUSTOMERS

This Chapter at a Glance

It's tempting to view customer selection, screening, and qualification as simply ways to make selling more efficient. But they are also great marketing opportunities. Add some value to your interactions with leads, even as you screen them out or disqualify them. Those leads can influence your market image, and even your lead stream.

Quantitative approaches to customer selection can play to a desire to overanalyze and reduce meaningful customer contact.

Still, some customers are more trusting than others. This is mainly a personal attribute, but varies also by industry and company. The frequency of trusting customers is also influenced by factors like decentralization, public versus private, market performance, and the customer's attitude toward its own customers.

A lot of sales books and training programs focus on the efficiency and effectiveness of selling. Part of that focus is on spending time with the highest-probability prospects. This is why we have systems of account planning, sales funnel systems for lead qualification, and complex exercises aimed at defining the ideal, targeted customers.

That's fine as far as it goes, but what of the leads you disqualify? What about the impression you leave behind with any contact or query that you decide is unlikely to be efficient or effective or profitable for you?

Any interaction you have with a potential customer has an impact. The process of selling is a marketing function as well as a selling function. In the rush to qualify leads and prospects, we can shut down the most powerful marketing tool there is—a firsthand knowledgeable referral.

Another risk in account planning is that, because the account planning process is largely analytical and can be made as complicated as one wants to make it, salespeople end up using those exercises as ways to avoid face-to-face selling.

Yet there are customers who are more receptive to trust-based relationships than others, and it is worth spending some time identifying them.

Replace Qualification with Marketing

What do you think of when you think of account qualification? You may think of "qualified leads" or some way of weeding through potential customers so that you don't spend time where you're not likely to get sales.

Most salespeople think the point of qualification is to spend their time wisely. Here's what one sales coach suggests:

> *It's really easy to waste our time in front of customers who aren't going to buy . . . remember, if it's not real, or we can't win it, or it's not worth it—you're wasting your time—find something else that is!*

The message this coach delivers is that time is money; your efficiency matters, and customers are infinite and undifferentiated, so that if one doesn't fit, drop him or her quickly and go find another more likely candidate. The implied message to the customer is: My time is important, and you are not. You are important to me only in terms of how fast I can sell you and how many dollars I can get in the sale, and I want to figure that out as quickly as possible so as to minimize my potentially unproductive time.

Think about this approach as applied to some other aspect of human relationships. Suppose a teacher looked at her students this way? What's the reputation of someone who approaches dating solely as a screening mechanism, rather than as an exploration and learning opportunity? What would you think of a father who screened his interactions with his kids to determine what was in it for him?

The approach is built around a transactional, seller-centric model. You judge that you won't run into this person or this company again, so that the only thing that needs to be done is to evaluate, as quickly as possible, whether or not there's anything in it for you.

It's the equivalent of a military scorched earth policy. If there's nothing good for me, leave it behind, pay them no mind, they're irrelevant. I'm busy and the monthly quota still needs filling.

Trust-based Selling has a different approach. Of course, if you're selling widgets, you don't want to spend time talking to buyers of window shades. But usually buyers and sellers get put together for some sensible reason. There may or may not be a sale coming out of it, but some common interest brought them together.

These situations are not potential wastes of your time—they are the best marketing opportunities you have. A lead that you disqualified isn't just an empty hole where you invested some time. A disqualified lead is a human being you talked to or met or who sought you out—someone who has now formed an impression of you.

A lead you disqualified is someone who knows enough about your business to have sought you out, who has enough of a relevant business issue to think you might be of help, who has a business close enough to your customer base to warrant conversation. Such a person is very likely to walk with or near the clientele that interests you. A positive impression can result in second- or third-level referrals. People put far more weight on personal testimonials than they do on unvalidated images.

Never get rid of someone the minute you find out she's not qualified. Never leave unsolicited e-mail inquiries unanswered. Instead, invest some small amount of time to give these people the benefit of your knowledge and wisdom. Help point them in the direction of solving whatever problem or issue it is they have. If your product or service isn't right for them, they don't expect you to continue to give charity. But they will be mightily impressed if you care enough to give a bit of your expertise to help them, *knowing* it isn't going to result in a sale.

Isn't such an encounter a free opportunity for personalized publicity? Isn't it a chance to send someone out into the market who understands your business and the kinds of clientele you seek, together with a testimonial that you behaved well toward the person—when you didn't have to?

Investing over time in those kinds of leads generates a reasonable rate of return. You can't tell which unqualified lead will result in a qualified lead, or when; but if you live your selling life according to the principle of doing good when the opportunity presents itself, those leads will pay back severalfold the minor investment you made.

All that is required is to stop seeing leads as opportunities to be *dis-*qualified; and to see them as opportunities to help clients, with a payback stream less distinctly linked to the client than in qualified lead cases. The only difference lies in how fast you get paid and from whom.

Thinking this way means you're operating less from tactics and more from principles. If you just "do business" this way, you become known for it—in a positive way.

Avoid the Colored Paper Trap

Large-scale account management programs in big companies depend a lot on processes. There are sales funnels for lead management; strategic analyses for account qualification; and sales reports to track customer information. Some of these programs use color-coded sheets to help keep track of which actions are required by whom and when.

It's easy to get lost in evaluating and scanning data regarding blue sheets and yellow sheets and green sheets; or A, B, and C in a funnel; or running analyses of net present value of various probabilities. But people don't get lost because it's complicated; they get lost because it helps them avoid personal contact that might be uncomfortable.

The colored paper trap is the trap of thinking you can analyze your way into selling from trust. You can't.

There are sales systems out there that track and analyze everything you can think of. You can track and analyze who the decision makers, influencers, gatekeepers, and coaches are. You can track and analyze your market share and that of your competitors. You can analyze industry trends and trends in your own sales. You can analyze trends by segment, sector, slice, section, and subdivision.

Having spent that analytical time, you'll have greater insights into who has how much power, who has what needs, and what to expect. But what you won't get is a sense of whether the customer will trust you because that depends on how trustworthy *you* are.

Analytical tools are seductive. You can apply endless levels of analysis to lead stream profiles and account selection criteria. It is tempting to believe that increased levels of rigor will result in increased sales effectiveness.

But getting a case of analysis paralysis doesn't build trust.

Evaluating Trust Partners

That said, there *are* some places to look that are more likely to be trust-ing than others. While trust is experienced individually, people capable of trusting are not equally distributed across business. If you're look-ing for apples, you're better off in an orchard than in an orange grove.

Do all customers respond equally well to Trust-based Selling? How can you qualify good prospects for Trust-based Selling? Who is an ideal customer?

One answer may surprise you. Suppose you would like to target Big-GoodCo, which is number two in the widget business. Suppose you are the number two supplier to the widget industry, and the widget indus-try is your number one sector. Suppose further that the widget industry is itself high growth and high profit; that your margins on widgets are high; and that your product quality is at least as high as that of your com-petitor, WidgetSupplyCo.

WidgetSupplyCo is the market leader in the widget supply business, and BigGoodCo is its biggest customer. BigGoodCo has had a strong trust-based relationship with WidgetSupplyCo for several years. You would love to get the BigGoodCo business, and you feel you can make a good business case to BigGood.

Here's the catch. If WidgetSupplyCo *really is* a trusted advisor-supplier to BigGoodCo, you can put your chances as somewhere between slim and none. A true trust relationship is the strongest driver of sales loyalty possible. It cannot be overcome by anything short of massive product, quality, or price dislocations. If all you have is a slight edge, you're very unlikely to get a customer to change.

The best thing to do is make a short, respectful call on the customer, saying, "If you really are as deeply trusting of WidgetSupplyCo as I have understood, then congratulations; that is a rare and very positive rela-tionship. I won't waste your time trying to persuade you otherwise. If you don't mind, I'll send you a note every six months or so to remind you of our existence, in the remote event something bad happens to that rela-tionship—though for your sake, I hope it doesn't. Have a nice day." Then go back to the office and take any numbers associated with BigGood off your next year's sales plan. In other words; write it off. You can't beat trust.

The good news is, those relationships are pretty rare. You know how hard it is for a competitor to knock you out of a trust-based relation-ship. So move along. Find your own trust-based customer relationship. It shouldn't be that hard—there aren't that many!

Wanted: Customers Willing to Trust

In all businesses, some clients are more profitable than others. The most practical application of business strategy is asking, "What customers should we do business with?"

But more importantly, if you do business based on trust, then you have to give up the fine-tuning control of profitability by client and process. You can't suck profit at every step out of customers because that objectifies them; which means the critical profitability decision is the acquisition of trust-capable relationships, not the management of these relationships after the fact.

The biggest single factor driving successful trust-based seller/buyer relationships is the trustworthiness of the seller. Yet trustworthiness alone is not enough. If the client or customer is unwilling or unable to trust, there can be no relationship. The dancing metaphor is apt—it takes two to tango.

While trustworthiness and the ability to trust are often indicators of each other, they are distinct.

The most important factor in the ability to trust is, of course, personal. But there are others. You can improve the odds by looking more in some places and less in others.

Three characteristics suggest a high propensity to trust in an organization—the structural characteristics of an industry, the business's organization and culture, and of course the personal characteristics of individuals in the business.

Some Industries Are More Trusting Than Others

Environments mold people's propensity to trust, and to be trusted. Some of those environmental factors act at the industry level, conditioning all people within the industry. Those include the level of value added in the industry, the regulatory history of the industry, and the pace of growth and change in the industry.

All else equal, low value-added industries are less likely to be candidates for trusting buyer relationships. Successful firms in these businesses tend to pursue low-cost strategies, which imply things like standardization and outsourcing, and they lean toward a transactional relationship with suppliers—including those of intangible services. This is the norm. Ironically, though, some of the better-performing low-cost strategy businesses are candidates because they know they can lower cost by being willing to trust.

However, a lot of companies get pegged as low value adding that really are not. A highly successful brick company is, surprisingly enough, in the fashion business. We may think of bricks as just mud plus marketing costs—the ultimate commodity—but a successful brick company sells a great many models of bricks, is constantly changing models, and appeals to architects and aesthetically inclined purchasers, neither of which is price-conscious. Managers who understand such subtleties often appreciate the value of trust.

Regulation is a double-edged sword. Industries which have been regulated, even 10 or 15 years ago, have senior management that grew up in a culture of clannishness, rewarding inward-looking abilities and politics (in the bad sense of the word). These norms are so deep-seated that they're invisible to those who hold them.

Managers in regulated industries are often well disposed to personal relationships of trust, and they are often in positions to buy significant amounts of complex goods and intangible services. So at first glance they look like very good candidates for sales approaches built on trust.

And some may be. But the downside is that they tend to see the relationship in very narrow terms—largely terms of self-interest. If one sees the world in clannish and political terms, then allies are very important; but they are seen in largely personal terms. There is not a deep sense of loyalty to the business or to the customer. If the seller's advice strays too far from a very narrowly perceived view of the client's self-interest, the relationship is at risk. Which means it wasn't a very strong relationship to begin with.

The challenge here is to the seller's honesty and integrity. The seller must constantly educate the client about the importance of her own company's customer and firm goals, and the seller must be constantly on the lookout for ways in which the client's individual demands might be at odds with those goals.

Up to a point, growth and change drive trusting relationships. They are the cause of a firm's need to evolve constantly, which benefits from advice, which in turn suggests an ability to trust. (By contrast, firms that are in stable, low-growth, low-changing industries succeed by becoming masters of rather glacial processes—capital investment, process management—rather than of change. All else being equal, they are less likely to be trusting, because they focus more on arcane details at which they are masters.)

At the extreme, however, the growth and change factors may produce fewer trusting customers. High-tech firms are notorious for leadership by forceful personalities—think Steve Jobs, Bill Gates, or Larry Ellison.

In such cases, the candidates for trust-based relationships are fewer—perhaps a handful in any company. And those potential candidates are often very skeptical. But for someone who can form a personal relationship with those clients, the power of that trusted relationship can be enormous.

What does this mean for you? Given your product or service offering, you probably don't have much say in whether or not you sell to a given industry. But there are other implications.

If you're selling to a low-trusting industry, be aware of several things:

- You'll find fewer trusting partners, but they may be very appreciative.
- Don't be discouraged—it also means you have less competition.
- You'll have to work harder to point out things that are mutually beneficial.
- At the same time, working hard probably means more acting and less talking, since the language of trust isn't widely spoken in such industries. Make sure to behave in trustworthy ways: focus on the reliability trust factor, and pursue intimacy by winks and nods, not by sincere eye contact.

Conversely, if you're working for a high-trusting industry:

- Be aware that your competitors are probably reading this book too.
- Make sure your company is aligned behind your customer trust message.
- Use more of the verbal techniques mentioned in this book—listening, name it and claim it.

Some Companies Are More Trusting Than Others

Industry structure is not the only environmental factor affecting people's propensity to trust and be trusted. Within industries, such factors as corporate organization, strategy, and culture greatly affect individuals' behavior. Some companies have higher propensities to trust. Factors affecting trustingness include:

- The company's experience with buying complex goods and intangible services

- Levels of decentralization and integration
- Private versus public ownership structure
- Industry leadership
- The trustworthiness of the client to its own customers and clients

Experience

In general, you'd rather sell to someone who has experience buying complex goods and intangible services than someone who hasn't. Successful experiences with trusting generate a propensity to trust further.

Decentralization

An organization which is highly decentralized and integrated will be more trusting than a firm that is centralized or nonintegrated. This is often true because there are more general managers in a decentralized firm and because an integrated business has managers with experience forming trusted relationships with each other.

The lowest levels of trust are found in pure functional organizations (only one general manager—the CEO), and in "siloed" organizations which compete rather than cooperate with sister business units).

Private versus Public

All else equal, privately held firms tend to be more personality-driven in their management, and that is a double-edged sword. Personality-driven organizations are likely to have fewer trusted relationship candidates simply because power tends to be more concentrated at the top. However, relationships at the top are if anything more likely to be candidates. And those that are high in trustingness tend to be very high. The freedom of a private company allows top managers to take longer perspectives, for one thing, which helps trust.

Market Performance

All else equal, firms in the top tier of an industry (say, the top 20 percent) tend to be better candidates for trusting relationships. Because they are more likely to be principle-based, they understand the importance of adhering to a long-term conception of the business, rather than being diverted into one short-term focus after another.

Customer's Customers

Finally, there is the issue of the customer's behavior toward its own customers—the best indicator of all. If a customer does not behave as a
trusted seller to its own customer base, it is not likely to be very trusting
either. The inability to be trustworthy strongly implies an underlying
inability to trust.

What are some indicators of the inability to trust? One is a vocabulary
of short-term focus. Excessive use of phrases like *bottom line* or sentences
like *We're all in this to make a buck* suggest short-term orientation.

You can also look to behaviors. Does the company rely unusually on
litigation and contract enforcement to manage supplier relationships
or employee terminations? Does it show an interest in its suppliers'
health, or is it primarily concerned about getting the lowest costs from
its suppliers? Is there an unusually strong culture of short-term performance indicators such as quarterly sales quotas or earnings performance? None of these guarantees an inability to trust, but they are all
directional signals.

Personal Drivers of Trustingness

The former Speaker of the U.S. House of Representatives, Thomas P.
"Tip" O'Neill, famously said, "All politics is local." He could have been
talking about trust; all trust is, at the end of the day, offered and experienced primarily in personal terms. No matter how favorable the industry or corporate indicators might be, if an individual client doesn't rate
highly in trusting, you're less likely to be trusted by that client.

I don't mean to be fatalistic; all but the pathological can be touched
by trust, if the one seeking to be trusted is diligent and caring enough.
But for some, if other opportunities are at hand, it just takes too much
effort to be worth it. The personal characteristics that help assess the
ability to trust include age, experience with general management, and
personal ego strength.

Age

We may bemoan the fact, but people are more trusting of those within
their age group or slightly older than they are of people outside their
age range—especially younger. If a 26-year-old consultant is matched

up against a 54-year-old client, there is usually tension. Worse yet, both are likely to feel guilty about those tensions, leading them to act out, to behave in passive-aggressive manners, or to overly seek out or avoid confrontations.

All of this is unproductive. Managers of professionals should be open and candid with their clients about the tensions age-difference pairings may generate.

Generalist Management Experience

A person who has been a general manager has learned several lessons in business, including the importance of a holistic perspective and the necessity of cooperation. These are traits that can be valued in a trusted seller by an experienced manager more than by a manager whose experience has been dominated by a functional or technical excellence.

Industry Experience

If the managers have experience in several industries, then the news is even better. Those people appreciate industry expertise for its own sake and not as simply a badge or credential. And they know the limitations of industry expertise. They are the most suitable to appreciate the value of an industry-knowledgeable outsider who can bring an informed perspective.

This sort of customer will value outside experts even if they have not honed their trustworthiness skills, because the client can extract value. If the provider is also trustworthy, this sort of client provides the opportunity for both parties to develop a valuable partnership.

Personal Ego Security

At the end of the day, the ability to trust is highly correlated with the ability to feel secure in the face of another's beliefs. One of the greatest challenges facing sellers is the challenge of getting clients to accept advice, even when the advice is correct. Correctness has little to do with acceptance.

If clients are personally secure enough to hear advice without judging automatically against their preset beliefs and opinions—to hear it as if for the first time, and as if no risks are at stake—then the clients have the ability to accept advice. They are valuable clients, not only for the trusted salesperson, but also for the relationship.

Industries, companies, individuals: looking at these dimensions will tell you where you are more likely to find customers willing to trust. But what do you do with them? Should you add them to your firm's formal processes of target account evaluation? Should you qualify prospects on the basis of trust?

After the Trust Evaluation

The business you are in determines which of the three areas over which you have the most control—the industry, the company, or the person. If you are selling semiconductor chips, the decision about your customer industries is determined by your product. And within a company, you're not likely to have a choice about with which buyer you will work.

The reinsurance business, by contrast, offers dozens of segments and hundreds of potential customers in many segments. A salesperson there has more control over both the industry and the company variables.

Remember one thing: the *fact* of trustingness happens *only* at the *individual* level. You may target industries and companies for greater trustingness, but it is not a guarantee. If you run across an untrusting customer, then you need to consider your options. You are better off spending time with other potential customers, if they are available—not because it means more money for you, but because you can generate more value with trusting customers..

A trusting customer in a low-trust industry and a low-trust company is always worth more than a nontrusting customer in a high-trust industry and a high-trust company. Trust is personal.

Should you then walk away from a lead that looks attractive on other more conventional dimensions but that you judge to have no possibility of forming a trusting relationship at the individual level? Yes.

Would you screen out a potential customer based on factors like growth, profitability, market share, share of their purchase order? Of course you would. You do it all the time. But if the presence of a trust-based relationship dwarfs all those other factors in terms of satisfaction, efficiency, and profitability, why would you not make a decision based on that factor above all?

Let me offer one caution. You can factor company and industry-based criteria into your qualification processes. You can even factor in things like buyer personality types—though I don't recommend it. But

I really don't recommend trying to analyze and formalize an individual-level screen for being able to trust. Trust takes two. It's a personal kind of thing. A trusting buyer plus a trustworthy seller as measured on some profile don't automatically translate into a perfect relationship. Instead, when in doubt, follow your gut.

Putting Targeting into Perspective

In golf, a hole in one is a rare event and a cause for celebration. But it is not the object of the game. Pros practice their swing not to get more holes in one but to improve their overall consistency and score. So it is with targeting customers on trust. The point of targeting is not to "ace" a customer, but to improve the overall quality of and value you add to relationships.

Trust is earned, not stumbled across. Those who would be trusted must shoulder most of the burden themselves. For sellers, perfection is an aspiration, a target—not a realistic goal. The same is true for clients: there are no perfect ones out there. As salespeople we must remember that customer selection or targeting ability to trust can help us in our search. But raising the average ability to trust of our prospect pool can never substitute for the hard and rewarding work of enhancing our own professional trustworthiness. Given an extra hour of time, spend it on improving your own trustworthiness, not on finding more trusting customers.

CHAPTER 17

ANSWERING THE SIX TOUGHEST SALES QUESTIONS

This Chapter at a Glance

The trust perspective highlights specific right and wrong answers to some major questions:

Why should we choose you? What makes you different from your competitors? How much experience have you had doing XYZ? We don't need what you're selling right now, so why should we spend time with you? We're happy with our present supplier, so why should we spend time talking? Why are you so much more expensive?

No matter what business you're in, you've probably encountered every one of the following six "toughest" questions customers ask:

- Why should we choose you?
- What makes you different from your competitors?
- What experience have you had doing XYZ in our business?
- We don't need what you're selling right now, so why should we spend time with you?
- We're happy with our present supplier, so why should we change?
- Why are you so much more expensive?

Compare the following trust-based answers with what you've been using. Decide for yourself which is the better to use.

Why Should We Choose You?

Here's how *not* to answer:

> *We are confident that XYZ can do the best job for you. We have the best/most accumulated/relevant experience, and we have the best/most experienced/most capable team. We are committed. We want to win. We have skin in the game, and we have the desire. We want this job more than the others do. That's why you should choose us.*

In answering this question, resist the temptation to list reasons why you are the best choice; don't give in to the desire to say how much you can help them.

If you haven't had experience doing this kind of business with these kinds of customers, then it is presumptuous of you to tell them why they should hire you. And if you haven't done *precisely* this kind of work with *precisely* these kinds of customers, *they* will think it's presumptuous even if you know it isn't.

And even if you *have* done precisely this kind of work with precisely these kinds of customers, they'll more than likely come up with a reason why that work and those customers were entirely different.

You don't win, and you don't get to help your customer by answering this question that way. Instead, say:

> *I don't know for sure that you* should *choose us. Not just yet, anyway. Given what I still don't know about your situation, it would be presumptuous of me to tell you flatly that you should hire us.*
>
> *But we are often the very best choice for many clients. It depends on your situation. I would suggest, if I may, that in your case it will particularly depend on A, B, and maybe C. So what we should do, together, is to focus on A, B, and C. Depending on what comes out of that discussion, the answer should be as clear to you as it will be to us.*
>
> *We are committed to helping you figure out just who you should choose. The last thing we want is a customer who hires us incorrectly, for the wrong reasons. It will do you no good, and make us look bad. No one wins. If we do our best to help you make the right choice—*

regardless of who that is—then I'm confident we'll get at least our share of wins, because we are the best choice for a number of customers.

So let's talk about A, B, and C. I'll let you know when I think I have an answer to your question—or maybe you'll let us know if you get there first. But I suspect we'll both know together.

What Makes You Different from Your Competitors?

Here's how *not* to answer:

> *The unique/defining/distinctive characteristic of XYZ is that we are the only firm who focuses on/specializes in/uses the approach of blah blah. This creates exceptional value for our customers, motivates our employees, and creates distinctive competitive advantage for XYZ.*

Resist the temptation to repeat your mission statement, your corporate advertising tagline, or your recruiting literature. First, the prospect client has probably read it. Second, most such literature usually sounds the same.

But most importantly, *that's all about you.* While yes, they did ask about you, that doesn't mean it's what they really want to hear. Answer the question directly and move it back to something of relevance and importance to the client. Say something like:

> *In talking to our customers, the distinctive characteristic they most often point out about us is our service network [or other true statement]. However, that's not always the most important reason people select us.*
>
> *The way we see it, the distinctive characteristic of competitor A is its size. For competitor B, it's their product design. But while these are the differences people most frequently point out or notice, they're not necessarily the differences on which people end up basing their decisions. Everyone buys for his own reasons.*
>
> *In your case, you've mentioned service integration [or other true statement] as a key issue for you. Could we talk more about that? Maybe*

that way we can see if there are differences between competitors that are important to you in your business.

How Much Experience Have You Had Doing XYZ in Our Business?

Here's a typical answer that won't do much to build trust:

We've had considerable experience across a number of dimensions. In your industry, we've had clients in the X and Y sectors. In this product/ service category, we have offerings in the P and Q lines of business. And we have some extremely experienced people we can draw from in our company. We're highly confident we have the experience to make this a truly winning initiative.

As a general rule, watch out for the overuse of personal pronouns (I, we) and of adverbs modifying adjectives (extremely, highly, truly).

Questions like this are credibility traps. The customer doesn't mean them to be, but they are. They invite you to inflate your experience, without ever speaking to your limitations. Unfortunately, such answers lead to cynicism.

Instead, try this:

Let me try and answer that specifically. XYZ is 23 percent of our business—it's our third biggest line of business, so we have depth on the product side.

On the industry side, we've never worked with your company before, so obviously we're not directly experienced with you. Nor have we done business with your competitors, except for some small sales two years ago to Competitor B. However, 12 percent of our sales across all lines go to your biggest customer segments—so we have experience with and understand your markets.

In terms of team capabilities, Joe here ran both customer service and engineering for the XYZ line for us. He is one of our three team leaders in the XYZ business. And Mary has sold for seven years into your key customer segment. The team therefore highlights our firm experience.

Does that help answer your question?

We Don't Need What You're Selling Right Now, So Why Should We Spend Time with You?

The temptation here is to get a foot in the door through guilt. It's often an effective way to get in, but you pay a price in trust. And when it doesn't work, you leave a door closed even more firmly behind you.

Try not to say:

> *Ah, I'll be fast. Won't take more than three minutes of your time, I promise you that. You never know when you're going to need [our offering] again. You can't be too careful. Would you like to take that critical three minutes now, or should I come back next Tuesday at 11:00?*

In Trust-based Selling you hardly expect a sale from an early meeting anyway. Your objective is to build a relationship and do the right thing for the client. So it's hardly a disappointment that you don't get a sale from an early meeting. Instead, try saying:

> *Well, thanks for managing my expectations. No sales today—I hear you, loud and clear.*
>
> *If you wouldn't mind, though, I'd like to understand your situation better. You will of course buy [what I have to offer] again sometime in the future and, when you do, I'd like to have something useful to tell you. I don't want to come here with just an order sheet.*
>
> *Would you mind taking 10 minutes to talk with me about XYZ's business? In particular, the quality ratings issue at XYZ written about in* BusinessWeek *last month? Was that a fair article?*
>
> *You may or may not ever buy from us, I know that. But I guarantee that I'll be able to help you make a better decision if I know more about your business. Could we take a little time to do that?*

We're Happy with Our Present Supplier, So Why Should We Change?

This isn't as tough a comment as it sounds. If a potential client really has a trust-based relationship with another supplier, you might as well walk away—the relationship is impregnable. However, in such cases the client is open. He'll say things like, "ABC frankly owns this relationship. We've been with them for X years, and we love them. We're not even interested enough to take the time to talk about the possibility of other alternatives."

In this case the word "happy" isn't as strong as it could be, and "why should we change?" could be a meaningful request for help, not just a rhetorical shrug.

Try not to say:

I'm glad you're happy; that's really great. I don't want to bad-mouth anyone in this business, but we do have a really compelling story to tell.

Ever have problems with ___ or ___? Sure, we all have. But XYX has focused on that problem and our clients almost never have it happen.

We have one of the best packages in the business for __ and __. With our special promotional package, good only until February 15, we are competitive with anyone.

And, to top it all off, we have a no-obligation satisfaction program. If you don't like it, you can cash in within the first 30 days, and we refund all your money; you're responsible only for ____.

The key here is to be respectful. Try this instead:

Thanks for that information. Most happy customers don't change, because they don't have any good reason to change. So I don't know that you should either.

In my experience, 90 percent of people change for one of only four reasons: dissatisfaction with the areas of price, service, quality, or value.

You probably have an opinion as to how happy you are on each of those four areas. And I of course don't know what that opinion is.

If you're interested, we can pretty quickly go through which of the four areas you think offers the most room for improvement. I can tell you how we approach that particular area, and you can decide if you like it or not.

You may get some good ideas to improve the situation with your existing supplier. I don't mind taking that risk. If I can be useful to you, then someday you may be in a position to reconsider me or refer me to someone else. That's a good enough reason for me to take more time exploring issues with you. What about you?

Why Are You So Much More Expensive?

There are two meanings of this question. If you hear it after having quoted price for the first time late in a discussion or series of discussions, it could very well mean, "Oh goodness, I had no idea it was going to be so big, and we really don't have the budget to do this. I'm sorry to have taken your time."

If this is the meaning, shame on you; this is a "learning opportunity." You're better off quoting a wide range of prices very early on, not just to qualify the prospect but to avoid embarrassment on both sides.

But suppose you already quoted a range earlier on. Now, "That's too expensive" can have at least four other specific meanings—requiring very different responses.

Price is almost everyone's least favorite subject. But viewed through the lens of trust, it's an opportunity. The usual tendency is to view such statements as challenging, a threat. And of course they're sometimes meant that way. But they don't have to be answered in kind.

Try not to say:

> *I may be able to come down a bit, but really it's a very fair price. You may be able to get it a little bit cheaper from other places, but not with the kind of ancillary benefits you get dealing with a reputable seller like us. Maybe I didn't explain the value of this proposition well enough; shall we go back over the benefits you get? This is not a cost; this is an investment that will pay for itself many times over.*

The key here is to not to assume the comment is an attack, or even that you know what the buyer means by the question. The key is to *find out* what the buyer means. Here's an example:

> *"Too expensive? Could you help me understand what you mean by that? [prompt if necessary]. For example, do you mean it doesn't feel worth it to you given that price? Or do you mean that you're surprised at the level of the price relative to what you had expected? Or is your concern that you feel it's uncompetitive? Or is it that you're worried you're getting a bad deal? Help me understand what your concern is here." [then listen, paraphrase, and empathize.]*

"Well, given that's your concern—what can I do that would be useful to you in thinking this through?"

- *If the answer is "value," then re-explore benefits (this is not unique to Trust-based Selling).*
- *If the answer is "the level of price," explore components and ways to redesign to lower the cost.*
- *If the answer is "uncompetitive," share competitive data.*
- *If the answer is "concern about getting a bad deal," then share the prices that other buyers paid (within legal parameters, of course).*

CHAPTER 18

WALKING THE WALK—
SMALL THINGS ADD UP

This Chapter at a Glance

What you choose to talk about—and not talk about—with your customers is not only an indicator of trust or its absence but also a driver or destroyer of trust as well. Assume a client hears everything you say internally.

When you are responding to questions, always give the direct answer first; then follow up with modifications or broader responses you need to make. Invite customers to sales meetings. When you rehearse sales meetings, rehearse improvisation in addition to scripting.

In selling, as in life, people watch your daily behaviors more than they watch your infrequent proclamations. We get judged by what we do, not by what we say. Therefore, as Aristotle said, "Excellence is a habit." So is Trust-based Selling. Here are a few areas of habit you can cultivate.

Watch Your Language

The head of sales at a major technology company told me, "We have two strategies: one is to be customer-centric; the other is to increase our share of customer wallet."

This sounds reasonable enough. But if it were your company, would you, or would you not, tell your *customers* both of those strategies?

If you do, you may offend them. Equating customers at the strategic level with their wallets objectifies them, and people tend to dislike being treated as objects, as a means to your own ends. Yet, if you don't mention that second strategy, then you are hiding a key strategy from a customer. And that violates the value of transparency.

If you wouldn't want it printed on the front page of the customer's in-house newspaper, then don't say it.

I heard a global head of sales of a major company start off his presentation at the company's annual sales meeting. It was after drinks and before dinner, after a long afternoon of presentations. "Let me just remind all of us here, in the middle of this event, the definition of 'sales'—the fine art of separating the customer from his wallet."

Do you think the head of sales would appreciate having his joke videotaped and sent to his customer base? While many of his customers would doubtless "get it" and share a chuckle over it, many would roll their eyes and take some offense. And all would on some level know that he wasn't just being funny, he was being serious too; and it's a joke that doesn't make a customer feel good.

The lesson? Unless you think you can hold 500 salespeople at cocktail hour to an oath of secrecy about a joke—don't tell it.

If you're a salesperson and your manager suggests you stretch the truth, I suggest you ask her directly, "Let me just be clear here; you're not asking me to lie, are you?"

And if you're a sales manager, do you want your salespeople to stretch the truth on occasion? If so, then how do you answer a salesperson who comes to you and says, "Let me just be clear here; you're not asking me to lie, are you?"

You could say, indignantly, "Of course not, I just want you to make sure we come off in a favorable light," which amounts to dodging the question. Better you think about it and say, "No I'm not, and I'm sorry I phrased it in such a way that it sounded like an option. Let's back up and make sure we're being completely aboveboard here. I want you to feel comfortable about being truthful."

First, Answer the Customer's Question

Most of the time, buyers ask questions of sellers. And the questions buyers ask are rarely the questions the seller would have preferred. There is a great temptation for us as sellers to reframe, rephrase, and restate the question so it sounds similar, but is in fact a more flattering question for us to answer. This is especially tempting when the buyer phrases a question in a challenging, "gotcha" kind of a way. Don't give in to the temptation.

Your question may indeed be the better question, one that is more useful to the customer. But the customer won't be listening for the answer to *your* question—only for the answer to the question *she* asked. Any sign of reticence on your part to answer the question will be interpreted as proof that you're avoiding something. If she were suspicious of you before, trying to rejigger the question will double her suspicion.

Instead, simply answer the question straightforwardly and directly. Pause. Then suggest another question.

Here are some examples of how *not* to answer and how to answer correctly:

Bad Answer 1

BUYER: "One of the criteria we agreed to look at was size or market share of the agency. In this market segment, how big are you? Where do you rank?"

SELLER: "Well, size or market share is certainly one important variable; we find that there are others that can be equally important depending on various . . ."

Bad Answer 2

BUYER: "One of the criteria we agreed to look at was size or market share of the agency. In this market segment, how big are you? Where do you rank?"

SELLER: "Our market presence in some segments is number one; in others, it's far less. The same is true for our competitors. Depending on how you define . . ."

Bad Answer 3

BUYER: "One of the criteria we agreed to look at was size or market share of the agency. In this market segment, how big are you? Where do you rank?"

SELLER: "I'll be touching on market share data in just a few minutes after I . . ."

Right Answer

> BUYER: "One of the criteria we agreed to look at was size or market share of the agency. In this market segment, how big are you? Where do you rank?"

> SELLER: "In the New York metro, in this category, we ranked number three last year according to the trade magazine, with about 15 percent share. The top two were ABC and XYZ, with 55 percent share between them. What else can I help you with?"

If you answer the question directly and forthrightly, several things happen. First, it becomes clear you're not hiding anything. Second, it invites more questions ("Well, do *you* think market share is an issue? What do you think distinguishes you from the two market leaders? How do you compete with larger market-share players? How do you suggest we think about size and share?").

Most importantly, it shows the customer that you're not trying to manipulate her agenda. You will respect her questions and give her the answers to the questions she asked. You take the customer's questions seriously, at face value, not as something to be manipulated.

Invite Customers to Your Sales Meetings

I have on several occasions spoken at meetings to which customers were invited. They were always among the more productive of meetings. Yet management was often nervous about inviting them.

"We can have them here for the panel presentation, but not for the discussion before or after—we need to be able to speak honestly." Or, "I'd be embarrassed to have them here. We can be frank among ourselves."

Clearly there are some parts of a company sales meeting that are not appropriate for customers to attend, and other parts where it is simply not useful to either party.

Still, you should consider inviting customers on a regular basis to sales meetings and to more, not less, of the event. Furthermore, having two or three customers in attendance makes for a more energizing session than having just one. If you have a two-day offsite meeting, consider an agenda item of two hours or so built around some aspect of customer relationships. Invite your customers to speak as a panel and then to respond to questions from the audience.

And if you do, invite them to the plenary, or the session beforehand, so that they have some feel for the group they're walking into. Invite them to stay for dinner.

Why be so open? The following box gives 11 reasons.

REASONS TO INVITE CUSTOMERS TO YOUR MEETINGS

1. You will generate great amounts of goodwill from the customers.
2. Your customers will work hard to articulate their ideas for you.
3. You will learn about major trends in the market.
4. Your salespeople will be role-modeling listening to a client.
5. Your salespeople will feel much closer to their own customers as a result.
6. Your salespeople will see that customers are "just folks."
7. You'll learn something about your competition.
8. You'll learn something about how you're perceived.
9. Your salespeople will learn that all customers agree on some things, and that they disagree on some other things—both of which may be surprises.
10. The customers can tell you some ugly truths you would otherwise deny.
11. Being invited to a provider's meeting has a positive effect on customers' likelihood of buying in the future, although you should not invite them for that reason alone.

Rehearse Improvisation

Do you rehearse too much? Do you prepare PowerPoint decks keeping three times as many slides in reserve as you'll need? Do you practice delivery—arm gestures, vocal tones, eye contact? Do you rehearse to decide which arguments precede or follow other arguments?

Most likely, the one thing you don't rehearse is how to handle unexpected client interactions. The usual approach is, "Let's imagine all the things clients might say so we can have answers for them." It's good to envision questions. But if that's all a team does, you will create a sense that any client interaction is either a win ("yay, we anticipated question 3B") or a loss ("darn, we didn't see that one coming").

But the point is not to *guess* what clients *will* say. The point is to *hear* what they *do* say. Client questions are golden opportunities for creating relationships. Relationships are not forged by dredging up preplanned responses, but by engaging in a dialogue and being willing to go wherever they go.

Next time your sales team rehearses a presentation, make sure they practice listening, engaging, reacting, forming true connections—not just guessing the answers in advance.

PART III

BARRIERS AND CHALLENGES

CHAPTER 19

THE HIGH COST OF WINNING

This Chapter at a Glance

Business in the last few decades has become focused more on competition and less on commercial interaction. This focus is embedded in the way we think and in the very language we use to talk business. It is endemic and pervasive.

The competitive perspective has permeated the customer relationship. In many ways, businesses view their customers as objects and even as competitors, which is destructive to trust relationships and to systemic efficiencies and profitability.

The competitive mindset focuses on getting the sale and extracting value from the customer. The Trust-based Selling mindset focuses on building long-term mutually profitable relationships. It is more profitable, and it begins with attitudes, not business processes.

The culture of Western business in the last 30 years has celebrated the idea of competition. Like many great ideas, competition can be overdone. And it has been. This chapter touches on the high cost of our obsession with winning.

The Cult of Competition

Whether you've been in sales for 3 months or for 30 years, you know that one of the strongest beliefs out there has to do with winning.

You've got to be a winner; second place is for losers. Only the lead dog gets a good view. Winning isn't everything, it's the only thing. No pain, no gain, and so on.

You are exhorted to "suck it up," to get out there and try some more. Don't take rejection personally (though it never seems to go away completely). Sales conventions celebrate athletic metaphors; coaches or star athletes are the most popular speakers at sales events.

You may participate in sales contests, some of which pit you against your fellow salespeople, some of which pit all of you against your competitors. You may enjoy sports yourself. A big element of selling in some businesses is time on the golf course or tickets to professional sports events.

Don't think you're immune because you're not a jock. Many people are intensively competitive, despite never setting foot in a stadium or on a golf course. They simply compete against the competition, their peers, and the industry standard. Business in the twenty-first century in the Western world is very much about competition, which is all about winning.

The most common metaphors used in sales today are probably related to sports. Here are just a few sports phrases that we encounter frequently in business—and these are only from American sports.

Let me quarterback this one
Last of the ninth, two down
It's shots on goal that count
The best defense is a good offense
Swinging for the fences
Monday morning quarterbacking
Threw him a curve ball
No holds barred
We'd better punt
We just need a level playing field
Just do blocking and tackling
They've got a really deep bench.

Notice that in all those sports metaphors, *there is no customer.* They are all about relationships with competitors. No customer or client to be found in them.

Probably the second most common metaphor used in (American) business is war. Business people sign up for courses on the relevance of Machiavelli, Sun Tzu, von Clausewitz and other military strategists.

Again, there is no customer in the war metaphor. It's all only about competition.

We have come to believe that somehow the final objective, the reason we're doing all this, the height of achievement—is to win.

We pay a price for those beliefs. Look at these quotes about Ford and Toyota.[1]

> *"In my opinion, [Ford] seems to send its people to 'hate school' so that they learn how to hate suppliers. The company is extremely confrontational. After dealing with Ford, I decided not to buy its cars."*
>
> —SENIOR EXECUTIVE, SUPPLIER TO FORD,
> OCTOBER 2002

> *"Toyota helped us dramatically improve our production system. We started by making one component, and as we improved, [Toyota] rewarded us with orders for more components. Toyota is our best customer."*
>
> —SENIOR EXECUTIVE, SUPPLIER TO FORD,
> GM, CHRYSLER, AND TOYOTA, JULY 2001

It's no accident that Toyota has been more successful than Ford for many years.

The hypercompetitive ethic is hardly limited to Detroit.

In a speech to a small group in a Wall Street firm, I told a story about admitting to a customer that you don't know something. After the talk, someone asked if I had been serious about recommending that you admit you don't know something if indeed you don't know it. Somewhat flabbergasted by the question, I said yes, I was quite serious, that being honest was pretty central to the idea of trust. And in that moment, as he folded his arms, shook his head, and sat back in his seat, he clearly concluded I obviously didn't know how things "really work."

One enemy of trust is cynicism. Certain circles—Wall Street being one—have more than their share of cynics, who believe it's a dog-eat-dog world out there and the idea of trust-based relationships is naïve.

It's hard to convince them otherwise, since cynicism is a self-fulfilling prophecy and there are enough examples of malfeasance to justify a belief that "it's a nasty world." For these people, "winning" is synonymous with "do unto them before they do unto you."

The poster child for this obsession with competition has to be Enron. Beginning as an energy company, it grew quickly to call itself "the greatest company in the world." That's pure, naked, competitive ambition, without reference to product, market, or customer.

When your only focus is to win, customers become objects, tools for achieving that goal. And customers don't care to be treated that way.

Ironically, true customer caring ends up being a more competitively successful strategy anyway. It's the paradox again: you will succeed competitively if you stop trying to succeed competitively. Just care about your clients.

Stop Competing with Your Customers

Economists since Adam Smith have pointed out that it's good to have competing alternatives in the marketplace—good for customers, good for society, and good for business. But competing alternatives are not exactly the same thing as competition. Business has come to focus obsessively on the idea of competition, and it has bled into our relationships with customers.

This is not an accident. A leading strategic thinker of our times, Michael Porter, says that business is *essentially* about competition, which is revealed in five critical business relationships—each of them competitive. Two of those five relationships—the firm's relationships with its buyers and its suppliers—are about buyer-seller competition. In other words, in his view, the nature of business is to compete with our customers.

This Hobbesian view of business isn't just locker-room talk; it's taught at the highest echelons of our business establishment. The problem is not our capitalist system or the idea of competition itself. It is a monolithic focus on nothing *but* competition, including competition with our customers, that has become the problem.

And so winning has come to have a double meaning in sales. All too often it slides into our relationships with our customers. We talk about "the pitch." We say, "You get what you negotiate," and we're talking about negotiating with our customers. We "win" or "lose" the sale. Our customer morphs into our competitor. The box that follows lists six indicators that you may be thinking of your customers as the enemy.

INDICATORS THAT SHOW YOU'RE THINKING OF YOUR CUSTOMERS AS THE ENEMY

1. You're trying to get the best price possible from them in your negotiations, no matter how high.
2. You try as hard to sell them your least valuable (to them) product as you try to sell them your most valuable (to them) product.
3. You're talking to one of their competitors and haven't told them.
4. You steer them to a higher-margin product that isn't as good for them as a lower-margin offering you have.
5. You don't mention a competitor's product that is clearly superior for this customer for this application at this time.
6. You keep information confidential from them.

The Point Is Not to Get the Sale

Nearly every sales book or training course I've seen assumes that the objective of selling is to get the sale. But this is exactly why people don't trust salespeople, why trust is so low in business, and why "trust" and "sales" rarely appear in the same sentence except as a joke.

In Trust-based Selling, the objective of selling is *to improve things for the client.* Think from the seller's perspective for a minute. If your objective really is to improve things for the client, then:

- You'd have to know a lot about the client's business.
- You'd have to know a lot about the client herself.
- You'd have to get very efficient about identifying the client's needs.

All these suggest you're far better off developing a long-term relationship with the client, rather than measuring the profitability of the relationship at every point in time, because the longer the relationship, the more you know.

You would also want the client to trust your advice when you know it is good advice; this means you had best give advice that is in the best interest of the client.

You would also want the client to involve you in decisions and discussions early rather than late; this means you had best be willing to work collaboratively, so that the client can be comfortable sharing information and decisions with you.

Finally, you would also want the client to understand your perspective too, so that he can approach issues knowing the impact of decisions on you, such as whether or not things are being done fairly or not. To achieve that relationship, you had better be willing to be transparent.

If you do all these things *and* there is profit to be made in the relationship for both parties, then the profit to be made will be maximized. If you do all these things and there is *no* profit to be made for both parties, then that fact will be abundantly clear to both parties and, at the least, you will have created a positive reference in the marketplace.

Look at it from a buyer's perspective. Imagine encountering a salesperson who:

- Clearly knows a lot but is willing to tell you what he doesn't know
- Comes to meetings prepared, but spends more time asking questions and listening than talking
- Has a point of view to offer, while acknowledging lack of information
- Appears willing to send you to a competitor if that's the right thing
- Is forthright about her company's costs and pricing policies
- Helps you in your decision process without seeming to be "closing" you
- Is clear about and makes no apologies for his firm's pricing and profit goals
- Is willing to invest time and attention on you

Whom would you rather see on your phone's caller ID? The number of that person? Or the number of one of the dozens of other salespeople whose objective is clearly, despite their efforts to hide it, to make the sale?

When a buyer encounters a salesperson who does the above, the instinct is to trust the seller. This is what all buyers really want deep-down, and what they justifiably fear they cannot get. But when they can get it, their strong inclination is to buy what they have to buy anyway from the one they trust. And that leads to relationships that are successful, profitable, and powerful for both parties.

Believing that the purpose of selling is to "win"—to close the deal—is to miss out on the powerful benefits, including profitability, that come from a trust-based relationship between buyer and seller.

Notes

1   Liker, Jeffrey K., and Thomas Y. Cho, "Building Deep Supplier Relationships." *Harvard Business Review*, December 2004.

CHAPTER **20**

ATTITUDE AND OTHER OBSTACLES TO TRUST IN SELLING

This Chapter at a Glance

You cannot become a trusted seller by mastering techniques or behaviors alone. Mindsets and attitudes are critical, both because trust is complex and because customers, who are very astute, evaluate the intentions behind our behaviors. Attitudes can be worked on and changed.

Some of the factors driving wrong attitudes are: fearing the seller, mistaking views of customers' intentions and of the role of expertise and knowledge, seeing trust as achievable through goals and incentives, blaming others, and lacking passion.

The cult of competition and the need to win, even against our customers, has to rank as the biggest set of obstacles to Trust-based Selling. But there are a few more.

Again, these obstacles are attitudes—mindsets, beliefs. Not lack of skills, not bad systems or procedures, but attitudes. Here are nine that really get in the way.

1. Being afraid of trust
2. Believing that customers mean what they say
3. Being tempted to say "trust me"
4. Believing you have to appear brilliant
5. Believing that a great track record sells itself
6. Seeing trust in terms of process and incentives

7. Believing that leads are scarce
8. Believing "the system won't let me"
9. Lacking passion

Before we can dig into them, you may be thinking, "attitudes, schmattitudes—just tell me some tips and tricks and techniques for dealing with them and the attitudes will follow. Well—not exactly. Let's talk about the power of attitudes.

Changing Your Attitude

There is a deeply held belief in business today that the way you change things is through behaviors. Fake it 'til you make it; put the incentives in place, and the mindsets will follow; do a needs assessment and train for the missing skillsets. Maybe you've heard the phrase, "You can act your way into right thinking better than you can think your way into right acting."

It depends on what you're talking about.

This kind of thinking is rooted in behavioralism. You can see why it's attractive to business—it focuses on actions, results. Things you can plan, write down, and above all, measure.

But it is not the only way to get things done.

The actor Luke Perry decided to do his own stunt work in the movie *8 Seconds*, about the life of Lane Frost, the famous rodeo bull rider. He hired Gary Leffew, bull-riding champion and film consultant to such shows as HBO's *Deadwood*. The catch was— Perry was not to be allowed on a bull until the last day of shooting. All his training had to be done without touching a bull. (The producers wanted to be sure their investment wasn't lost in case of an accident).

Leffew used only mental training, meditation, and drills for Perry. And, as he put it, "The first bull that [Perry] got on, he made the most beautiful ride you've ever seen, unbelievable. It kind of shows you the power of the mind. All I did was teach him concepts that've been around for thousands of years."[1]

If you want to know how to become more effective at selling, there are plenty of people who have magic phrases, closing techniques, surefire phone scripts, and strategic processes. That's the behavioral route. And of course some of it works, to some extent.

But when it comes to deeper issues—dealing with human emotions like fear, trust, respect, envy, or ambition—you can't get by with clever lines.

Sometimes, there is no substitute for changing your attitude.

This is not so far-fetched. The field of acting in the mid-twentieth century was revolutionized by moving from the old English approach of mimicking, to the "method" school of acting of trying to understand the character's motivation.

Many approaches to psychotherapy are rooted in trying to understand from where one's feelings came. Top sports psychologists routinely tell their famous athletes to "envision" success as a means to achieving it. Athletes themselves know the vital role of attitude before going into their critical moments.

Physicians tell us that happy people are healthier people. There is wisdom behind common sayings like, "Walk in with a smile on your face," or, "Don't let them see you sweat." There's a reason that motivational speakers have been so popular in the sales field—sales managers and salespeople know that attitudes matter.

The preferred treatment for alcoholism and drug addiction is, increasingly, 12-Step programs, which are as mindset-oriented as they are behavioral. You probably know the difference between approaching a strange dog in the park with fear as opposed to approaching it with curiosity and a smile—certainly the dog does. Small children respond to our emotions and emotional tones, not our words.

A Harvard Medical School study in 2002 uncovered a shocking finding—shocking, that is, to doctors, particularly surgeons.[2] Surgeons are probably the medical specialty most frequently sued for malpractice.

The study took two 10-second audio clips from surgeons' conversations with their patients. Those audio clips were then rated on a blinded basis by coders to characterize each surgeon's levels of certain emotional qualities in their tone of voice. Those ratings were cross-referenced to the surgeons' malpractice claims history.

> The results? As the study put it, "Ratings of higher dominance and lower concern or anxiety in their voice tones significantly identified surgeons with previous claims compared with those who had no claims."
>
> In other words, strangers can predict a surgeon's malpractice record on the basis of hearing 20 seconds of patient interactions. The likely implication: the way a surgeon talks to his or her patient is not only a significant predictor, but most likely a significant cause, of lawsuits. Your attitude bleeds out. Your tone of voice can get you sued.

If attitude can get a doctor sued (or not), help someone kick a heroin habit, bring an Olympian a gold medal, and help Luke Perry learn how to ride a bull without ever having touched one—maybe there's something in it for you.

How you go about changing your attitude is beyond the scope of this book, which tries to show you what you should change your attitude *to* or *from*. But whatever you do, it begins with *noticing*.

The rest of this chapter examines the nine beliefs you should be on the lookout for.

One: Being Afraid of Trust

You would think that, with all the benefits of trust-based relationships, we would all be in a major hurry to do what it takes to become trustworthy. But we aren't. Why is that?

The root negative human emotion is probably fear. When someone acts in ways that appear dysfunctional or irrational, a good rule of thumb is to ask, "What are they afraid of?" And becoming trustworthy can often feel scary. The trick is to get over it.

Most salespeople are happy to work hard to get better at technical skills, at product knowledge, and at presenting to audiences. But to be worthy of someone's trust—particularly if you're asking them to buy something from you—a customer demands more.

To consider you trustworthy, customers demand that you not lie to them. Lying doesn't just mean flat-out untruths—it means white lies and lies of omission too. If you knowingly let customers believe that your product is better for them and it isn't, you just violated a trustworthiness principle. And it's scary to tell that much truth.

To consider you trustworthy, a customer demands that you acknowledge your weaknesses. And that's scary.

To consider you trustworthy, a customer demands that you care about the relationship, not just the next transaction. That's scary too, because sometimes we have that quarterly or annual target coming up, and we sure would like that sale.

To consider you trustworthy, customers would want you to have their best interests at heart. That means that, if it ever came down to it, you'd be willing to recommend a competitor's service, if the competitor was clearly the right option for the customer. And that's scary.

To consider you trustworthy, you have to believe that, if you continually behave in a trustworthy way, the economics will take care of themselves—but that you might not get this particular sale! And that's scary.

That's the paradox of trust. To be trusted, customers have to believe you're not trying to control them for your own benefit, but instead are focused on their long-term needs together with yours.

That means you have to give up control.

And that's what's *really* scary.

Two: Believing That Customers Mean What They Say

We all believe it's important to know what our customers want. And the most obvious way to find that out is to ask them.

Customers will usually tell you what they want. They will say they want just this kind of result, done in such and such a way, using these and those protocols and procedures, and that timing is critical and price needs to be very competitive. Such customers sound like they know what they want.

Sometimes they do. Often they don't. Particularly when they insist that they do.

If clients knew what they wanted, they could (and they sometimes do) draft their own wills, design their own information systems, manage their own financial portfolios, build their own routers. But the daily stock in trade of a provider of complex intangible services generally looks like a black art to the client. We all know the basics about shirts and hamburgers, but not about probate or XTML or media buys or wraparound industrial leases.

Clients are also victims of sales myths. They are afraid of being conned by salespeople and respond by tightly bounding the problem statement. Fear is one motivation for using request for proposal (RFP) processes. Only the most self-confident clients admit that they themselves don't fully understand the problem, which is precisely why they seek out experts. A well-defined problem makes the answer look easy. Real expertise and art lie in defining the problem.

You don't have to doubt customers or challenge them or confront them. Nor do you have to think of them as willfully deceiving you. Simply get rid of the belief that everything you hear from a customer is the truth. Cultivate an attitude of curiosity without blame.

When you think you're not getting the whole story, what can you do? You can use extremely open-ended questions to encourage clients to be frank and further explore their own concerns. Examples:

1. "What's behind that?" Use this as a socially acceptable manner of getting one level deeper or clarifying the situation when you're really not sure of what is being said. It is also a good phrase to use when you're feeling very judgmental—if you're tempted to say, "How can you possibly believe such a thing!" try instead, "What's behind that . . .?"
2. "Help me understand." The subtext in this question is that you, the questioner, are taking on full responsibility for any lack of understanding. Further, you are asking a favor of the speaker— the favor of helping you out of a jam.
3. "Tell me more." The single best extreme open-ended question. It lets the customer define the agenda to be talked about; it is simply a statement of interest, of willingness to go where the customer wants to go, and of your intent to follow along.

Three: Being Tempted to Say "Trust Me"

The two most trust-destroying words you can say may well be "trust me." They guarantee that the listener won't trust you.

The urge to say "trust me" runs deep. Often it comes from a good place; we really are being trustworthy, we really do want people to recognize our good intentions, and we want to convey to them that they can trust us. But they still won't. Saying "trust me" just makes it worse.

Trust is earned, not given on demand. Trustworthiness is perceived through your actions and based in your character. Talking about your actions isn't the same as acting; and insisting on your character only cheapens it.

Trust, like ethics, is something you live, not preach. Let others say it about you; it's far more convincing than saying it about yourself.

Ultimately, "trust me" is a negative for the same reason as other statements, like, "We really want this job," or, "We're willing to work really hard on this," or, "We really have skin in the game on this one," or, "We really want your business." All those statements are about the seller—not about the buyer. They all betray the high self-orientation behind them.

The only thing worse than saying "trust me" is, "I want you to trust me." That's a double dose of self-orientation. Leave the trust testimonials to others; leave your litany of what you want behind at the train station. When you're with the client, focus first on the client, not on yourself.

Four: Believing You Have to Appear Brilliant

What are the three words we try the hardest to avoid saying? Probably they are, "I don't know."

Yet ironically those may well be the most believable three words you can say. You have no reason to say them unless they are true. And if they are true and if you are willing to admit it, the customer immediately knows he is dealing with someone who is honest and direct, with high integrity—someone he can trust.

The desire to pretend we know something about every question runs very deep. But the minor embarrassment of having to say, "I don't know" on occasion is nothing compared to the pain and misery caused by someone lying about her capabilities or those of her company—and then having to sustain the lie or get caught.

Brilliance is a seductive attribute for many in business. We may be tempted to fudge a bit about our golf score or our child's accomplishments or about how well we know someone. But the big temptation is to nod our head wisely in front of the boss or the client when we don't really understand what was just said, to be the one in the know. It is easy to overstate what we know, because we rarely get caught at it.

But being untruthful, noncredible, or in any way striving to be what you are not is the biggest relationship sin you can commit. It destroys the basis for trust, because if you are not what you present yourself as being, then everything you say or do becomes suspect.

Be clear about what you know; be equally clear about what you don't know. You are not supposed to be a genius, and your customers don't expect you to be. What they really want to know is, can they trust you? Defining the boundaries of your knowledge helps customers do just that.

Change your attitude about brilliance. You are what you are. Brilliance is overrated and is trumped by credibility. If you are credibly you, you trump someone who is more brilliant. And your brilliance won't get you past someone who is more believable.

If you make a habit of trying to appear brilliant, you may find it a difficult habit to break. To make it easier, try incorporating some self-effacing humor and some direct responses.

- "I guess I'm going to have to ask a dumb question here; probably not the last one, either. Could you go over again how that process works?"
- "Ah, sorry to interrupt—I realize I really do need to understand this well, and I'm afraid I don't. Can you tell me a little more?"
- "At the risk of repetition, would you mind going over the XYZ situation again?"
- "I'm sorry—could you back it all up about one level? I'm not sure I understand the context of this."

Five: Believing That a Great Track Record Sells Itself

Do you believe that "good work sells itself" or "build a better mousetrap, and the world will beat a path to your door"? Unfortunately, these beliefs often amount to a strategy of aggressively waiting for the phone to ring. It just doesn't work very well.

The main reason waiting to be called doesn't work is that customers tag you with the image of the last sale. In their minds, that was very specific, and a very long time ago (even if it was just last week). When a new need arises, just having done the last job doesn't guarantee that they'll think of you for the next one, particularly if the service or product is even slightly different.

You can't depend on customers to figure out what you can do—only what you have done. If you sell a customer relationship management (CRM) system successfully to a new customer, that customer will probably look to you the next time she needs to know something about CRM. But what about some help with some other systems or other customer-related need? The perception of you is limited by the customer's experience of you.

A top lawyer in his field told me that the secret of success in law was to be among the top two or three lawyers in the country in your particular area of expertise. I asked him, "How many areas of expertise do you think there are?" He said, "About 50 to 60 in total." This suggests there are at most only 180 successful lawyers in the United States. Which, given the population of about a million lawyers in the United States, would come as a surprise to a great many.

Relying on ringing phones is reactive, not proactive. It doesn't involve reaching out and getting to know the client or the client organization. It presumes the client problem definition is right. It shows no interest in finding out what other issues might arise or where the next problem might come from. It demonstrates no attempt to find patterns in the problems. It shows no sense of personal connection. Worst of all, the strategy of "do excellent work to get more work" shows no interest in the client beyond representing a source of new sales for the seller.

Contrast that with a salesperson who is curious and proactive. She listens for what's behind the customer's concerns. She asks questions; she is willing to take risks by hypothesizing and brainstorming with the customer. She looks for patterns and tries to understand the customer industry. She talks about the customer as an individual and how he is affected by the issue at hand. She does not hesitate to offer observations outside the scope of the job at hand if they are valid and useful to the customer. And she is very direct about difficult issues like pricing, quality, scope creep or staffing, because she handles them in a larger relationship context.

Most clients never meet an expert who cares. Most experts stop at problem solving. This is a huge competitive opportunity because clients can tell if you really care about *them*, not just about their work, and the difference can matter hugely.

Many, whose fields—service or product—require great levels of technical skill are inclined to believe that technical mastery is the secret to their success. It makes sense, from their perspective. If you work many hours per week, over years, and nearly all that work is focused on mastering and maintaining cutting-edge expertise or technology, it will feel like your success is due to what you have spent your time on. It ain't necessarily so.

Insecure salespeople—which is to say, most of us—are also susceptible to this myth. We like to think we are recognized for our talents and good work; we don't like to think of ourselves as manipulative. Most of us don't like the self-image of a "used car salesman." So it becomes tempting to think, "They like me for me and my expertise, not because of my mastery of techniques I might not always like." Only the most cynical, untrustworthy salesperson takes delight in "putting one over on" his customers through pure "salesmanship" unaided by true benefits to the customer.

In the customer's mind, you are what you were—until you help her to figure out how you might be something else. Obviously, moving up the ladder from product-based selling to needs-based selling helps; moving further up to relationship-based selling helps more. But Trust-based Selling helps the most—by multiples.

Six: Seeing Trust in Terms of Process and Incentives

It's true that organizations affect people's behaviors. It's also true that people have considerable control over their own beliefs and actions. The business world in the past few decades has focused heavily on the former.

Process solutions to business problems were all the rage in the 1980s and early 1990s—think business process reengineering. Today we hear a lot about business process outsourcing. Plenty of consultants can talk to you about how to design your lead tracking system, change your incentive system or your supply chain management process or your process for reskilling human resources.

Much of business has come to believe that, to manage well, you just have to identify what you want people to do, design processes to best produce the results, and then reward people for the outcomes. With all the emphasis on process, we have forgotten that people are capable of doing more than responding like rats to cheese.

The process approach—rooted in a behavioralist view of people— works for certain things: training your dog, learning a golf swing, and incenting higher-margin product sales, for example. It's a belief system that B. F. Skinner (famed for studies with rats and pigeons) would have loved.

The problem comes when trying to apply the process approach to a higher order of human functions—like trust. Suppose I want my salespeople to be more trusted by their customers. Following the Skinnerian-dominant management approach (figure out goals, then apply incentives), I might:

- Design a customer-satisfaction measurement process to assess trust
- Design a customer-interface process to maximize trustworthy interactions
- Design scripts to optimize trustworthy behavior
- Give salespeople rewards for scoring highest on trust measurements

But notice how this thinking plays out. The 17-year-old ticket-taker at your local movie theater house chants a meaningless, "Welcome to XYZ theaters, enjoy your show" with as much enthusiasm as reciting the answers to his math test. The sales force at ABC Widgets complains about why measurement 2a for credibility is given less weight than measurement 4c for intimacy in determining its bonus. And, in the ultimate absurdity, you get moments like this:

> *I called a telecom service provider with a problem. After waits and switches, I got to a customer service rep who at first seemed to be knowledgeable. After five minutes, he determined that he didn't know the answer and wasn't sure who would know but that I should try another department, to which he would transfer me. "Before I transfer you," he said, "may I ask you if you received excellent customer service from me today?"*
>
> *"No." I replied. "You were nice enough, but you didn't solve my problem."*
>
> *"But—" he spluttered, "surely I gave you excellent customer service!"*
>
> *"No." I repeated, "My problem is not any closer to being resolved. So, by my definition, I did not get excellent customer service, or even half-good."*
>
> *"But sir," the CSR stammered, "my ratings depend on this!"*

It's hard to begin cataloging how many sins the company has committed in this case. But let's try.

- It's manipulative to ask customers point blank if you have given them excellent service; it is embarrassing, self-serving, and highly self-oriented.
- The transparent use of customer-service ratings as behavioral indicators reduces on the spot the feeling of any genuineness.
- The company is blatantly relying on coerced ratings to determine compensation.
- Worst of all is the CSR himself, who has reduced himself to begging a customer to respond to psychological coercion—so that the CSR can get more money! It is like the famous *National Lampoon* magazine cover that showed a man holding a cute dog and pointing a gun at the dog's head and demanding, "Buy this magazine—or we'll shoot this dog!"

Trust is a deeply personal human trait. Reducing it to the same techniques we use for supply chain optimization or process quality control is to dehumanize it—which makes it absurd. Don't be absurd—be human.

Seven: Believing That Leads Are Scarce

Two comanagers of an American consulting firm had a disagreement about entry into the South African market. One said, "We are resource-constrained. We have just been through a merger; we are in the midst of a changing market; some of our senior people have come in from outside, and we are experiencing relatively high growth. We simply cannot afford to devote scarce resources to a relatively small market that is geographically distant and that presents some unique challenges."

The other manager said, "For this firm to be successful, we have to continue growing our people to adapt to the ever-changing market and to stay fresh and excited. The biggest motivation for them is the opportunity to continue growing, learning, and having an impact on clients. Those opportunities are hard to come by, and we must seize them whey they arise. The opportunity to move people between Europe, the United States, Asia, and Africa is an unparalleled chance for them to grow and be motivated. We are not resource-constrained, we are opportunity-constrained."

Perceived scarcity can drive us to self-oriented behavior. But if we focus on growing capabilities, being outward- and opportunity-focused, not self-oriented, we find that the opportunies suddenly show up.

The world is a vastly imperfect place. Every one of your customers has dozens of opportunities to work better. You probably know quite a few of them yourself. In many cases, you can even articulate a good case for why your product or service might be part of the solution for your customer.

If you can see opportunities for improvement in your customers' businesses, ask them about it. They don't have to be opportunities related to your product or service; in fact, you get credits for curiosity and client-orientation if you notice things outside your own narrow range. The point is to develop meaningful conversations with your clients about issues relevant to them—not to sell your product. That happens naturally, from the context of conversations.

There is no shortage of leads, because there is no shortage of problems. There is a shortage of trust-driven conversations about needs that lead to solutions to real problems. The issue isn't lead shortage, it's personal courage and creativity.

Eight: Believing "The System Won't Let Me"

A lot of people say, "Charlie, I agree with your point of view and find it makes a lot of sense in general. But you don't know my sales manager (or my company, or my industry). I'd love to do it, but *they* should attend your seminar, because they hold me to the latest contest or margin levels or targeted offerings." (Often the sales manager *has* attended the seminar and is trying to get the salespeople to change).

One business unit leader in a technology company told me, somewhat ruefully, "You know, if we had a choice between a one-time product sale with a 60 percent margin and a multiple-year annuity services sale with a 40 percent margin, we'd take the product sale any day."

For the salespeople who feel locked in by the system, try the following.

Have a talk with your sales manager to make sure he is not inalterably opposed. Say that you're going to do your best to abide by the principles in this book. Explain that you'll be directing more efforts into long-term potential clients. You may be investing more time at some accounts for no immediate payoff; at the same time, you'll probably be bidding on less price-based business. You may even walk away from some RFP types of opportunities. Your volume may suffer, though your margins may increase. Tell your manager that, for 12 months, you're not going to shoot for the Hawaii trip (though you may win it, and if so of course you'll go). For 12 months, you're going to seek a reputation as a straight shooter. For 12 months, you're going to be customer-centric, not seller-cenric, go where your clients lead you in conversations, cultivate your curiosity, focus on the long term, be open with your customers about what you are doing and why, and ask them to be straight with you in return.

At the end of 12 months—sooner for some businesses, longer for very few—you should have, relative to your fellow salespeople:

- A higher repeat purchase rate
- Higher margins on sold business
- Better word-of-mouth and referral business
- Higher hit rates on new business
- Fewer dry holes

Ask your sales manager if he's willing to make that relatively small investment along with you. Then get to work.

"The system" is given as an excuse far more often than it merits. Unless you are 24 months from retirement or from totally shifting companies and industries, you will see benefits *within* that 12-month time frame, and most sales managers will be able to see the merits of the case and the wisdom of making that small investment.

Nine: Lacking Passion

Most of the attitudes up to this point inhibit trust. But a lack of passion suggests a vacancy, a hole where something ought to be. Customers definitely don't like it. A lack of passion in a salesperson is an emotional trigger—why should I want to buy from you if even you don't seem charged up about the product or service—or about me the buyer?

Have you ever felt, or been told, that you're not passionate about what you're selling? What was your reaction?

If you didn't think it was true, then you have some investigating to do. First of all, if your passion doesn't lie in the product or service, don't despair—you're better off being passionate about the customer than the product anyway. Great relationships result in great sales as long as the product is competitive. Make it a point to exercise your curiosity about the customer.

Some people who can't get passionate about the customer are passionate about the product, and this can be a good thing too. Enthusiasm inspires confidence in the buyer and helps creativity in applications.

But if you thought there was some truth to the assessment that you lacked passion, then perhaps you need to look seriously at why you're continuing to do what you're doing. Most jobs, if not done with some passion, are deadly dull, and that's especially true for selling. This is something deeper than you can solve with "motivational" speeches or even a desire to win constantly.

Buyers read passion as a close proxy for caring. They want to do business with someone who cares, preferably about them and acceptably about her product or service. They are not comfortable working with someone who's apathetic. Nor should you be comfortable with that view of yourself. Life's too short!

Notes

1   Interview with Gary Leffew, Fresh Air program from WHYY and National Public Radio, aired Monday April 18, 2005.

2   Ambady, et al., "Surgeons' Tone of Voice: A Clue to Malpractice History," *Surgery*, Volume 132, No. 1, 2002.

CHAPTER 21

TEACH PRODUCT PEOPLE SALES OR TEACH SALESPEOPLE PRODUCT?

This Chapter at a Glance

All else being equal, the level of product complexity determines whether you're better off training technical people to sell or teaching salespeople technology. But all else is not always equal. The best indicator is the ability to be customer-focused. Some engineers have that and some salespeople don't. The ability to care trumps both, and defines the "hire versus train" debate.

If you're in the complex businesses we're speaking of in this book— particularly those that are more driven by intangibles—then you have faced a key question: Who should your salespeople be?

This question gets raised the wrong way in many organizations. For example, some companies might say, "We need more of a sales orientation in this company. We're too technical. We need to bring in some sales blood to shake up the engineers."

But it isn't just about the mix between salespeople and technical people because often, the one who must sell and the one who must have expertise are the same person. Even when you have a mix of pure salespeople and pure technical experts, the customer will want to know that the salesperson understands the expert and that the technical expert appreciates the customer's issues.

So a better way to phrase the question is:

Should you hire technical people and train them to sell—or should you hire salespeople and train them in the technical aspects of your product?

Here are the rules:

1. The more complex and intangible your business, the more you should concentrate on hiring technical people and training them to sell.
2. The less complex and intangible your business, the more you should concentrate on hiring salespeople and teaching them about the product.
3. Caring trumps both.

This relationship is shown in Figure 21.1.

Rules One and Two are based on pure efficiency. An English major just isn't likely to have the science and engineering perspective to discuss the value of gallium arsenide in semiconductors. And most firms aren't willing to invest in the equivalent of another university degree to train her to get there.

Similarly, a distributor handling candies had better be very good at the nuts and bolts of sales; and it's probably easier to teach him the required science regarding chocolate than it might be to teach him semiconductors.

Figure 21.1   Teach Sales to Technicians, or Product to Salespeople?

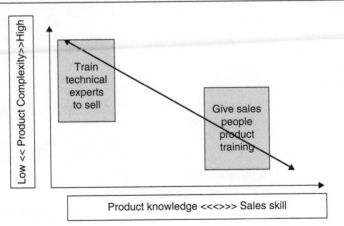

But what if you're in the middle? What if you're selling products that don't require a degree in rocket science but aren't too simple either? That's where the third rule comes into play, and it operates mainly at the company level.

Some companies hire and grow salespeople with the cynical, compete-with-your-customer, point-is-to-close-the-sale worldview. They are often Type A personalities whose aggressive and competitive view of the world is deeply baked into their psyches. Even if you could train them technically, those are not the most successful attitudes and belief systems for succeeding with customers in complex product and intangible services businesses. They don't really care about the customer.

There are also some companies in which most technical people are introverted, for whom problem solving is only of academic interest, and for whom customers are simply opportunities to play with toys, ideas, and methodologies. They are not any more customer-focused or less self-oriented than the negative stereotype salesperson. They, too, don't really care.

Sometimes the two backgrounds can coexist. The accounting and consulting professions employ with some success specialized business development executives whose sole job is new client business development. The key is that it is understood up front by all parties—especially the prospective client—what these people can be expected to know and do, and what they cannot. If and when they uncover a valid need, it's understood there will be a handoff to someone with deeper technical knowledge. It is the clarity of roles that makes this OK; no expectations are being violated.

But Rule Three—caring—trumps both the other rules. There's an endless debate about whether companies should hire or train for certain attributes. I personally don't know whether it's easier to train an adult in particle physics or in emotional intelligence—but it seems clear it's easier to hire either one rather than to train.

The talents required for Trust-based Selling match up with the four trust principles—that is, the abilities to be other-focused, transparent, collaborative, and to delay gratification. If you have hired intense introverts or people with strong control needs, you're not likely to be able to retrain them to fit the profile required for selling this way. This suggests the importance of hiring, rather than training, for sales programs intended to be built on trust.

But there is a counterargument. There is an enormous gap between having a psychological makeup consistent with trust principles and being able to sell using those principles. Trustworthiness isn't susceptible to Six Sigma kinds of programs. In particular, there is no upper limit to how trustworthy one can become; there's no such thing as perfection, and there is always room for improvement.

There are some skillsets that can be acquired—better listening, Name It and Claim It, conversation-structuring. And there is a great deal more that can be done to change unexamined beliefs, unproductive habits, and nonoptimal mindsets. This book is an attempt to point out many such opportunities.

At some level, if you don't care about your customer, training won't help you. But at another level, those who care can get better at it by remembering and noticing when to care, communicating that care to the customer, learning how to focus that caring in useful directions, seeking out opportunities for caring, and so on. If you hire the right people, there is still an enormous upside to be gained by developing them.

CHAPTER 22

DIFFERENTIATION BY SELLING, NOT BRANDING

This Chapter at a Glance

For consumer goods companies, the brand image of a company affects not only the first (screening) phase of the buying process, but the second (selection) as well. In intangible services businesses, the brand differentiates mainly at the first phase—not in the second. Differentiation at the selection stage is very much a function of the salesperson-client interaction. Selling plays a key role in competitive differentiation for these kinds of businesses.

You may see your job as limited to sales results, revenue. But you are also responsible to a great extent for your company's differentiation in the market. You—not the marketing department or the advertising manager.

How does Coke differentiate itself from Pepsi? Ford from Toyota? *Time* from *Newsweek?* Largely through branding and related product or service differences. Advertising plays a big role, and other elements of the marketing and product mix are tuned to provide an integrated and consistent image of the brand in question. Differentiation is a function of branding and of the design of the offering itself.

Is it any different when it comes to Citibank versus JPMorgan Chase or BCG versus Booz Allen? PricewaterhouseCoopers versus Ernst & Young or Oracle versus SAP? Jones, Day versus Shearman & Sterling? Do the same rules of differentiation apply when it comes to sellers of complex goods and services?

Many marketers and brand mavens see them as identical cases. But they're not.

For many consumer products, the two steps of buying—screening and selection—are very closely related. The ad for Cheerios ready-to-eat cereal serves both to make us aware of Cheerios *and* to motivate us to choose it when we are next in the supermarket.

But that's not true when it comes to buying blade servers or reinsurance or selecting a commercial Realtor. In those cases, a strong branded presence serves to get you on the short list. It does affect the screening process. But it does very little to affect the selection process.

In complex goods and services businesses, branding differentiates you at the screening stage. But it is selling that often differentiates you at the selection stage.

What are the implications?

- Many firms spend too much money, time, and energy on branding, believing that greater brand differentiation will affect selection as well as screening.
- For this reason, marketing is often overrated and selling is underrated.
- If you are not getting invited to bid, you have a visibility problem and need to invest in market awareness.
- If you are losing competitive bids, look to invest in your sales process, not your brand image.
- Your best opportunity to differentiate in the selection process lies in reframing the sales process.

Branding and the Buying Process

Branding is one thing that gets you on the screening list in the first place. If customers haven't heard of you or don't think of you when a certain issue arises, then it's going to be hard to get on their short list for screening. Branding can be particularly important in businesses in which relative market share is low and there are many names to know (consider the market share of the top five law firms or consulting firms, compared to the top two soft drinks).

Once in the door, however, the trust evaluation dynamic takes over. Differentiation at a brand level may have existed when the short list was put together, but another more powerful form of differentiation begins to take over in an actual sales meeting, rapidly overtaking brand impressions.

Some businesses have two levels of customer—take Intel, for example. Its "Buy Intel" strategy helps it differentiate itself at the end-user retail consumer level, as well as offers its direct customers—PC makers— an additional level of branding. But its differentiation at the direct-customer level—buyers of semiconductors—also comes heavily from the way it interacts with those customers.

Differentiation in the Selling Process

If you are in a complex intangible services business, you know that the low bidder very frequently does *not* get the business. The winner is the firm that manages to create the highest level of confidence in the buyer.

Most firms try to increase buyer confidence by stressing the differentiation of their particular product or service. They talk on and on about office locations, unique methodologies, and the like.

What they forget is the biggest differentiator of all—the increased level of confidence that comes through trust, which is created through the experience of work done on a real client's real issues—selling by doing. Buyers of complex goods and services want the confidence that comes from trust, and that trust comes from direct experience.

This is good news, because it's a lot easier to differentiate human beings deployed against unique problems and individual clients than it is to differentiate dozens of complex abstract intangible services firms.

Here's some more good news. Differentiation by trust at the selection level is more powerful than differentiation by qualifications. It travels over time to be effective with the same buyer in the future. It travels across customers, through referrals. It even travels through lost sales, because potential future buyers see you and form an impression of you, even if they judge that the particular job in question is not right for you.

CHAPTER 23

TALKING STRAIGHT ABOUT PRICE

This Chapter at a Glance

For most approaches to sales, price is at the heart of the zero-sum part of the relationship—the seller wants it higher, the buyer wants it lower. Most sales approaches recommend not talking price until value has been established.

In Trust-based Selling, talking about price—and price itself—are important parts of the development of the relationship. Transparency can change fear-based and suspicious price negotiations into an opportunity to build trust in the relationship.

Price is also at the heart of many psychological fears for buyer and seller alike. Getting price out in the open early to discuss it, far from being dangerous, is a valuable tool for increasing trust.

Trust can transform pricing discussions. Talking price doesn't have to be about power and control. Talking about pricing affects trust through two of the trust values—long-term relationships and transparency. Talking about price also raises credibility and intimacy, two of the factors in the trust equation.

Pricing, Trust, and Long-term Relationships

In most approaches to sales, price is the thing that the seller wants to get higher and the buyer wants to get lower. From that perspective, the best price for the seller is the highest price possible; the best price for the buyer is the lowest price possible.

In Trust-based Selling, the best pricing is that which builds the relationship. There is no easy formula to define just what that is, and it may vary by transaction. Sometimes what builds the relationship is related to market conditions or to the profitability of both buyer and seller. Other times there has to be a sense of fairness—admittedly itself hard to define.

That means a powerful seller looking to create trust-based relationships shouldn't use its power to extract excessive profitability from its customers. Of course, a lot of companies with powerful market positions decide not to care about building trust-based customer relationships and settle for getting the maximum out of their leveraged position. They pay a price in customer loyalty, but there are examples of such price pressure-based sellers continuing successfully for long periods of time. Egregious behavior, when you have excessive power, can be profitable.

But if you want to pursue a trust-based strategy, you probably won't use "all the market will bear" as a sole pricing consideration. Similarly, customers shouldn't assume that a weak seller should subsidize them in the name of trust.

Buyers or sellers shouldn't allow self-indulgent or unprofitable behavior on the part of the other to drag down their own profit models in the name of trust. Nor should one party or the other have an obligation to subsidize the other continually. Hostage-taking violates trust. Sellers have the right to raise prices, and customers have the right to go away. Trust doesn't change that.

What trusting relationships do is allow parties to discuss the long-term implications of pricing behavior. If a relationship is to be based on trust, both parties must be around to enjoy the benefits of that relationship in the future.

The best arbiter of pricing policies is to ask, "What if we priced that way in all our future dealings? What would be the effect on both our positions vis-à-vis our own industries? What would be the sum total of the benefits accruing to each of us?"

Price Negotiations and Transparency

One reason pricing is a problem is that most buyers and sellers consider it to be a zero-sum game—what one wins, the other loses.

Therefore, they both try to hold back information from the other. From that position you get "opening bids" and "initial positions," and the game is on.

When partners don't trust each other and withhold information, fear comes into play—the fears of not getting the best deal or of not getting a "fair" deal. The antidote to these fears is a healthy dose of transparency.

Consider this statement:

> *A long-standing client came to us and said our price was too high for a job we quoted. They said one competitor was priced 20 percent below us, and another 30 percent below. We're seeing this a lot; word is we're the high-priced firm in this market, and we've lost a few big jobs. It seems to be pretty much a question of price. This business is getting commoditized. Particularly in this economy, we need to consider cutting prices. But our margins are already low.*

Have you heard those words lately? Perhaps spoken them? Before you act, make sure you investigate the situation. This chapter gives you a structured approach to doing so, asking you to look at causes, solutions, and handling discussions.

Before you respond to demands for lowering price, it is useful to understand what lies behind such demands. Three things drive the vast majority of client demands:

1. *Fear—the simple fear of being taken advantage of.* If clients perceive that someone else is getting a better deal, they can feel abused and may react negatively. Clients who feel abused become very creative about attributing the causes—your rates, your profits, your margins, for example.
2. *Miscommunication—usually around scope and design issues.* The "apples and oranges" problem can arise from many project design issues, including the scope of issues addressed, the leverage of your team, the depth to which issues are explored, timing, and choices about staffing, materials, or subassemblies. If the customer thinks orange and you price apples, he may think you are charging absurd margins on fruit.
3. *Quality—misaligned assumptions about the quality required.* Many service providers make an implicit assumption about the quality required for a certain kind of work. Often the client doesn't

perceive the need for the Cadillac/Mercedes solution. She thinks a Chevrolet/Volkswagen will do just fine. And often, it will.

Customers demanding price concessions do not present the issue in these neat terms. They simply say, "Your price is too high, and you need to cut it." This does *not* necessarily mean that your price is too high or that you need to take drastic action. But it does mean you'd better investigate what's going on. Here's how.

1. Suggest a series of price drivers—from scope and quality concerns to economic drivers—and commit to exploring each in turn.
   - *Start* with *scope and design* issues. Ask the client to compare in detail your project design with the competitor's. That means nailing down modules, scope of research, design tolerances, support and staffing levels, and everything that might be different. Then compare. More than half the time, discussion will stop right there. Most fears are simply misunderstandings of design.
   - Move on to *quality* issues. Determine whether quality in your proposal is higher than that proposed by a competitor. Are you putting more senior people on the job? Doing double due diligence? Designing in more redundancy? Going for extremely low sample errors? If so, then ask whether the customer is willing to pay for extra quality. If he is not, be ready to scale back or walk. Your "standards" may be costing you business.
   - If the issue is not yet settled, then explain your economic structure. Tell the client your rates and pricing policies, costs, discounting structures, compensation structures, leverage model, target margins, overhead, utilization rates, recovery rates. Explain why these numbers add up to a fair profit model for you and why they probably don't vary much by competitor—certainly not by 30 percent.
2. Now you can face the competitor's 30 percent discount head on. Confirm the project design is comparable. Say to the client, "I believe their economic model is similar to ours—and we could not sustain a 30 percent discount. How long do you believe you will continue to get that discount? And are you willing to switch again if and when they move to sustainable prices?"

The box shows how a law firm might handle that conversation.

CLIENT: We are getting quotes from competitors of yours at 25 percent below what you're charging us. That is simply way out of range. If you want to keep this business, you will have got to come down significantly in price. I want to know what you intend to do to keep this business.

LAW FIRM: Well, I certainly don't want to lose your business. Let's dig in and see what I can do. First of all—do you have a specific proposal from a competitor that is comparable to the work we're doing?

CLIENT: Well, not entirely. Some is in the proposal; some is just in general approach and discussions.

LAW FIRM: OK; first let's talk about scope. If you went with them, would you envision them handling all your trademark and copyright issues, the same as we do?

CLIENT: No, we'd talked about keeping the small ones in-house and their firm doing the larger ones. It's cheaper for us to do the little ones. And I suppose we could do the same with you. I see your point. It's not quite apples and oranges. But still, their bid is much lower.

LAW FIRM: Well, let's continue. Are there other scope issues—same geography? Same industry scope?

CLIENT: Yes, no difference there.

LAW FIRM: Then let's talk about acceptable quality. Do you want the same ratio of senior to junior people that we assign on this work? Do you want the same 95 percent confidence levels we talked about maintaining?

CLIENT: Yes, the same caliber of people. Though we could talk about reducing our aversion to risk. That can get expensive.

LAW FIRM: So that may be another area to make adjustments in comparisons between us and the other firm.

CLIENT: True enough. But it's still a big difference.

LAW FIRM: OK, right. Now, I want you to see what we pay our various levels of professional staff; here's our utilization data; here's our per square foot rent; and here's some basics on our systems and overhead. Now let me ask you—how different do you think our people's salaries are from theirs? Do they have cheaper people?

CLIENT: Probably not. They're pretty good too. Probably went to the same schools.

LAW FIRM: I agree. I doubt the 25 percent discount is there. You know where their offices are; do you think their rent is lower than ours? Do you have any knowledge that their systems are cheaper than ours?

CLIENT: No, they're probably much the same.

LAW FIRM: Well, that's the bulk of our income statement—and theirs too. Their economics look a lot like ours.

So let's reduce their 25 percent discount by taking away the small trademark/copyright issues; by, say, 5 percent? And perhaps another 5 percent for the lowered risk levels? That leaves 15 percent.

I will tell you, we could not sustain an ongoing 15 percent discount from our economic model; that's a big chunk of our profit and bonus pool. And I'm sure that's true for them too.

CLIENT: Well, they're still offering us that rate, regardless of why.

LAW FIRM: Yes, but look what it means. That level of discount is unsustainable. It is clearly a promotional price, aimed at giving you a price break to try them. Unless you believe you are unique among their clients, they will have to raise their rates to you at some point. How long do you think that would be?

CLIENT: I don't know.

LAW FIRM: I don't either, of course, but let's say it's 6 or 12 months. You now have a real choice. You can either switch law firms every 6 to 12 months to gain a 15 percent discount—and I'm sure you can always find someone ready to discount—or you can pay a higher rate and gain the benefits of a relationship.

CLIENT: Well, some of those benefits include efficiency and knowledge, so we do get some of the savings back anyway.

LAW FIRM: You said it, not me. But yes, that's true. It's not a false choice; some firms will take the low-cost side, though most will take the relationship option. Which will it be for you?

If the client would be willing to switch yet again to find yet another dis-counter, then you probably should walk away and find a relationship buyer. If so, walk away smiling. Your competitor just lost money and you didn't.

Conversations like that shown in the box can't be scripted; each is unique. They will flow naturally *if* you drive them from the trust—principles in particular, a commitment to discover the right solution *for thecustomer*, regardless of what it means for you and a willingness to be completely transparent.

Should you ever cut price? Yes, in two cases. The first is for a volume discount, including existing-customer discounts. In these situations, your cost of sales is genuinely reduced; that's real money, and it can be shared.

The second reason is to buy your way into a new business or client. Don't do it lightly. Eventually you will have to raise rates to sustainable levels; and remember: a client who switched to you on price is prone to switching on price once again.

Why Talking Price Is Hard

Most salespeople don't enjoy talking about price. Before we can feel good about talking about price, we will have to face the reasons we don't like doing it; otherwise we'll never be comfortable with it.

The following box lists 10 reasons we don't like talking price: Which ones apply to you?

REASONS WE DON'T LIKE TALKING ABOUT PRICE

1. It is largely out of our control.
2. We are likely to get challenged on it.
3. Talking about price never results in higher prices, only in reductions.
4. We think customers put the highest weight on price.
5. It reduces everything to just one number.
6. It doesn't let us talk about all the other parts of value.
7. It makes it more difficult to differentiate ourselves from competitors.
8. We don't always have the lowest price.
9. Price-driven buyers are no fun and, in addition, unprofitable.
10. It feels final, like the last step, from which there is no appeal.

The fears listed in the box are why most salespeople delay talking about price as long as possible. They hope that by talking first about features, benefits, and value, they will build up a positive perception that "outweighs" the price.

But delaying price discussions lowers trust. If a customer asks a question, you should answer the question, not resist it. Customers perceive resistance to questions as being disrespectful. Worse yet, they interpret it to mean you are hiding something, either to trick them or because you are ashamed of something. Your credibility is lowered, and your perceived self-orientation heightened.

Why Customers Resist Talking about Price

Talking about price is complicated even further because buyers share our reluctance to discuss it.

Buyers are hesitant because:

1. They are afraid of being manipulated.
2. They are afraid of being made a fool of.
3. They are afraid the price will be higher than they thought.
4. They don't know what to talk about after price is mentioned.
5. They are afraid of bargaining.
6. They are afraid of being told "no."
7. Talking about price can feel crass or rude.

So customers also often buy the idea that pricing has to be the last item in a conversation. On top of that, customers have very little perspective on how prices are set from the seller's perspective. They see price only in their own context.

This is a recipe for gridlock: neither seller nor buyer wants to talk about price until the last minute possible. That means both parties are holding back important truths. That means neither is being transparent; that together they are being noncollaborative; and that neither trusts the other.

The gridlock is unnecessary. Not only that, but you can *create* trust by reframing the way pricing conversations are handled.

Salespeople Overstate the Importance of Price

Research generally suggests that salespeople themselves think price is more important to the customer than it really is. One of the findings of the Gallup Organization's exhaustive study of salespeople over the years is that "price in most cases was not a significant driver of repurchase intentions."[1] The Gallup study and others show that strong trust relationships far outweigh price in customer decision making.

Notice what that doesn't mean. It doesn't mean customers don't *tell you* that price is critical; often they do. It also doesn't mean price is irrelevant; it's not. But price in general is a second-order issue for most buyers. It has to be in a certain range, and price may get used as an excuse.

But that doesn't change the truth. Customers who trust their buyers will rank price lower down the list—much lower.

Pricing Talk Doesn't Have to Happen Last

Some salespeople recommend delaying the discussion about price until value can be calculated. That means no price-talk until all the benefits are discussed.

But if you avoid talking price, many customers will think about nothing else. The longer you delay discussing price, the more you give the impression that you're trying to hide something. That makes you look devious (high self-orientation), and it takes away the ability of your customer to hear you, and you them.

It's not necessary. All you have to do is to state that value can't be fairly determined without seeing all benefits. Most customers will grant the reasonableness of that statement. That means you can mention price and still go back and discuss other value components.

For one thing, buyers are perfectly capable of changing their minds about price if they learn about some benefit they had not previously understood. They are also capable of appreciating price differences if they understand pricing from a perspective other than their own.

The scenario in the box that follows shows how it might sound.

CUSTOMER: I'm interested in the XP-27 series. Can you quote me prices on it?

SELLER: You want to go straight to prices?

CUSTOMER: Yes; we can come back to features later.

SELLER: All right. Unit prices on the XP-27 start at $8.50; we have two sliding scales for volume that go as low as $6.25 at the 5K unit level;

and the enhanced XP-27a series generally maps out at 8 percent higher. Does that answer your question?

CUSTOMER: That sounds kind of expensive.

SELLER: It depends on what it's worth to you. I have a five-point checklist of value components for the XP-27 that lets you break down the value. Would it be useful to go through that? Then we can come back and assess whether that price is worth it to you.

CUSTOMER: Well, let me see the list.

SELLER: OK. The first item is floating point arithmetic speed. I've got price performance statistics, but why don't we start with your telling me how important that feature is to you?

Why Facing Up to Price Is Good

The fact that both buyers and sellers are afraid to talk about price is the very reason it is useful to talk about it. Getting it out in the open gets rid of the fear, reduces barriers between buyer and seller, and lets each get more honest about the issue at hand. The conversation increases transparency and intimacy and, therefore, trust.

Sellers often think buyers have a fixed number in mind. Talking about price early helps sellers realize that buyers may have flexible ideas about pricing.

For their part, buyers have little sense of sellers' costs. If buyers come to see that a seller's cost structure is different from what they had thought it to be, buyers are capable of modifying their price triggers.

Mutual ignorance is a recipe for mistrust. Facing up to price early reduces mistrust.

And finally, an obvious reason for early discussions of price is because it is a good way to qualify a lead. Here is language that works to set an early pricing discussion for lead qualification purposes:

"I wouldn't want either of us to be embarrassed by going too far down the road and then discovering something we hadn't noticed, so it might help to talk broadly about price. Of course we'll have to dig deeper, but this feels to me like a mid-seven-digit number. Does that sound surprising to you, or was that the range you were thinking too?"

When to Talk about Price

Trust-based Selling suggests that you talk about price much earlier in the conversation and do not resist if the customer asks questions about price.

If asked, tell them and tell them directly. Do not hesitate, do not add more answer to the question until you've answered it, and do not hedge.

For example:

CUSTOMER: I notice XYZ's lowest price on the A52x is lower than your lowest XP-27 cost of $6.25. Why is that?

SELLER: Let's check for an apples-to-apples comparison. First, make sure the volume level price point is the same for us and for them.

CUSTOMER: It is; I got quotes on 10,000 units in both cases.

SELLER: Good. The main reason the A52x is priced lower than the XP-27 is that it's only 40 percent as fast on floating point arithmetic as the XP-27. It's critical to know how important that is to your application. If floating point arithmetic isn't all that important to you, I'd suggest you compare XYZ's A52x to our XP-25, not to the XP-27. Would it be OK to spend some time looking at your application for these kinds of issues? It may be that yet another chip is best for you.

CUSTOMER: OK, let's do that.

Price and Fear of Rejection

I don't know of any salesperson who enjoys rejection. I don't know any who are truly neutral. It is natural to feel bad about being rejected.

Pricing plays several roles in the fear of rejection. On the one hand, we'd prefer to be rejected on price rather than almost any other reason. It's impersonal; it's not about us and, in most cases, we don't have full control over pricing anyway. It lets us off the hook.

It also lets buyers off the hook. They don't have to get personal when they use price as a reason for rejecting a seller. So everyone wins—or pretends to—because no one has to face the real truth. The truth is that the seller failed to make a relationship connection, much less a trust-based one.

Price is also the first refuge when we are afraid of losing a sale we want. Every sales manager knows what to expect when she asks the sales force, "What could we do to improve sales?" Cut the price, of course, the salespeople say.

If you don't see this fear for what it is, it will destroy you. Not only will you destroy your profitability, but you will also erode trust and not even make that many sales.

When I was a project manager in consulting, I frequently team-sold with Scott, a senior vice president. Scott was known for great work but for impulsively discounting prices as well. Since project managers had to "eat" overruns in that system, I rapidly figured out that his psychological need to cut prices was hurting my own bonuses. We had a heart-to-heart, and he agreed that in the future we would jointly decide prices.

At our next major sales call, we had decided to price a job at $230,000. "Under no circumstances can we go below $210,000," I said, and Scott willingly agreed. The final presentation meeting was going fine. The client liked the approach, milestones, and design. Then it came time to quote the price, and—out of the blue—Scott said "$180,000." I practically choked.

Sitting next to Scott, I elbowed him sharply. Scott shushed me; I elbowed him again, and he changed the subject as the client, sitting across the table from us, looked with growing curiosity at the obvious discord between the two of us.

Finally I said, "I'm sorry, but Scott you know we agreed this project priced out at $230,000, and the very lowest we could commit to was $210,000." Scott frowned at me, the client looked incredulous that we would dare to argue in front of him, and the meeting lurched along. After the client left, Scott and I had further words.

That night, the client left a message to both of us: "You've got the job—and you've got it at the full price of $230,000. That's because it was clear you had worked that price out and it was genuine. And it's also because I want your butts on the line with no excuses. I look forward to working together."

How many clients would react that way? I don't know, I only did this once. The moral is not to argue price in front of the customer, but simply to point out that transparency in all matters—including pricing—beats control and manipulation.

Judy, an HR consultant, described to me her fear of an upcoming sales call. "They are a new potential client for us, and have the reputation of being somewhat price sensitive. I know one competitor that is involved is known for price cutting. Also, they sound like they're interested in fairly base-level services, and our strengths lie more in value-adding areas. I'm afraid if we're not very competitive on price, we're just not going to get this one."

As we talked about it, it became clear that her company didn't particularly need this sale. The client might be problematic, and her company was trying to find higher-margin clients in general. Judy's assumption that the client was interested in only base-level services wasn't very data based as probably no one had explained higher-value services to this potential client.

We agreed Judy should adopt an advisory stance with this client. She would go in and help them understand their options, being quite willing to live with the implications of their desires. If, after she had explained the client's options, the client wanted higher-value services, Judy's company would charge full rates for them; if the client wanted lower-value services, Judy's company would not expect to get the business. Either outcome would be fine. One would result in full-margin business; the other, in a satisfied company, grateful that someone had been willing to educate its people and point out alternative options.

Notes

1   Smith, Benson, and Tony Rutigliano, *Discover Your Sales Strengths*, New York: Warner Books, 2003.

CHAPTER 24

DEALING WITH RFPs AND PURCHASING AGENTS

This Chapter at a Glance

For many reasons, the use of RFPs (requests for proposal), specialized purchasing departments, and third-party buying specialists seems to be on the increase and is viewed by most sellers as a threat. A common response to the threat is to seek ways to go around the process or the specialized purchaser.

There is an opportunity to form trust with the intermediary. Since most other sellers are trying to do the opposite, this approach is more distinctive than usual. Accept the new process and become a trusted advisor to your new customer.

Have you been told by a client that your services will henceforth be purchased through an RFP process? Or that your service offering is now lumped together with those categories covered by the purchasing department? Or that your client has engaged the services of a consultant to help manage the services buying process?

You are not alone. For a number of reasons, the phenomenon is rapidly increasing. Doing something about it requires at least some understanding of why it is happening. There are several reasons, including:

- Declining half-life of intellectual capital, leading to more competition
- Increased comfort with outsourcing and ubiquitous opportunities to do so

- Increased professional mobility and solo practitioners
- Increased economic pressure on client value chains
- Increased buyer mistrust and cynicism

The last reason may be the greatest. And sellers have largely themselves to blame. Buyers don't become cynical without reason. They have a desire to trust, unless their trust is abused—as it too often is.

Buyers resort to RFPs and other formalized processes because they are afraid. (I explicitly exclude governmental and some nonprofit organizations, which have legitimate public trust reasons for using transparent processes.) They are either directly afraid (of being duped) or indirectly afraid (of being accused of being duped or of being too closely allied to sellers). Formalized buying processes are the socially acceptable tools for reducing risk—both real business risk and political cover-your-behind risk. They are all fear-based, they all result in higher transaction costs, and they all decrease trust.

Ironically, the greatest value for clients comes when they *do* work with a service provider in order to shape the best outcome. And clients can't possibly stipulate all their needs through a third party. Yet absent trust, buyers will forgo that value. The rise of formalized buying processes is a systemic failure of trust—one that costs all parties.

How *Not* to Approach Formalized Buying Processes

The stated purpose of formalized buying processes is to optimize services and prices through fair and open competition. But their unstated, real purpose is to cope with sellers that are neither trusted nor seen as trustworthy. The resort to a formalized buying process is a late-stage indication of systemic trust failure. The worst thing to do is further feed the mistrust. Refer to the following box for eight things not to do.

**EIGHT THINGS *NOT* TO DO WHEN
FACING FORMALIZED BUYING PROCESSES**

1. Quibble with the design of the process
2. Hint at ways to end-run the process
3. Seek special favors based on past relationships

4. Withhold any part of the responses required by the process
5. Challenge the validity of formalized buying processes
6. Tell your client how much the work means to you
7. Snipe at the process in a passive-aggressive manner
8. Include pot shots at your competitors

The approaches listed in the box all have one thing in common—they are clearly aimed at improving the seller's situation. But the very impetus for new processes comes from a perception (often valid) that sellers are "in it for themselves." More of the same, particularly when a company has already taken the strong step of adopting formalized buying processes, is simply adding nails to the relationship coffin.

If formalized buying processes are a result of fear, then the only antidote is a massive dose of trustworthiness—*collaboration, transparency, client focus,* and a *long-term perspective.* Applying those principles to a client who has initiated formalized buying processes requires certain mindsets and certain specific actions. Here are eight steps you can take—assuming you still have *some* measure of contact with the client.

1. *Comply fully with the process.* Fill out all forms, meet with all requested people, and don't talk to those who are put out of bounds. Put your emphasis on compliance, not on getting credit for complying. The customer will notice.
2. *Accept the client perspective.* If the client gets a better job for a better price from a competitor, then you should expect that the client will accept that proposal. Deal with it.
3. *Make major client-helpful suggestions.* But be honest. *Only* make process suggestions that clearly benefit the customer and be very direct. If you can't find suggestions that help the customer much more than they help you, don't mention them.
4. *Accept competitor parity.* If you suggest a process interaction with the client, then suggest that the client have exactly the same interaction with your competitors.
5. *Ask for permission, not forgiveness.* Before sending extra data or answering unasked questions or providing additional references, ask permission. Assumptions in this situation are seen not as helpful but as arrogant. Now is the time to show respect.

6. *Think and talk long term.* This transaction is ideally just one of many. Talk to the client about which RFPs or bids you think best suit you. If you think this bid is a long shot, say so. It shows you value the relationship, not the transaction, and that you can be objective about your capabilities.

7. *Suggest a post-decision process debrief.* Offer the client a chance to hear your views about how to improve the process *after* the decision has been made. And make sure you suggest that the client hear from your competitors as well.

8. *Offer total transparency.* Offer customers the chance to sit in with you on all discussions about project design, staffing, and price. If they accept, tell them that you assume they will ask other bidders for the same transparency and that you accept the buyer's professionalism in dealing with confidentiality. Then do not abuse that professionalism by picking at the edges for advantage.

Clients resort to formalized buying processes out of fear. Fear is defeated only by trust, and that doesn't happen over night. If you believe in client relationships, then, by definition, you're in it for the long haul. Behave accordingly.

CHAPTER 25

KILLING TRUST WITH MEASUREMENTS AND REWARDS

This Chapter at a Glance

The current trend toward micromeasurement of the customer inter-face processes threatens trust. By making customers into objects of study, much like raw materials in a supply chain, we can reduce trust.

The idea that if you can't measure it, you can't manage it is wrong. In fact, over-measurement can threaten the measurer's trust-worthiness. The pharmaceutical industry is one example of what an excess of measurement can do.

We have all heard the phrase *if you can't measure it, you can't man-age it.* Most managers accept it uncritically, and many believe it passionately.

But it's not true. There are lots of ways to manage—values, personal example, praise, fear, threats, inspiration, team creation, message align-ment—which don't require measurement to be effective.

Worse yet, when it comes to trust, a mania for measurement isn't just benign; it can be positively trust-destroying. This is true of measuring both the business impact of trust and the trustworthiness itself. Let's explore an example to see why and then talk about what can be done.

An Example: Pharmaceutical Reps

In the pharmaceutical business, the key salesperson is the rep, or detailer. His or her job is to visit doctors and hospitals. The reps' objective, as most firms define it, is to influence the doctor or hospital to prescribe (write "script" for) the drugs their firm represents. Lacking direct data because reps don't walk out with an order, the industry is understandably very interested in tracking the effectiveness of reps' calls on physicians.

The industry has developed sophisticated metrics for tracking and analyzing the effect on physician script writing of the number of reps' visits, their precise message, the success of particular rep demographics and psychographics, and the complex incentive pay schemes for reps. A typical rep gets a quarterly report describing the calculation of his or her compensation. It includes factors for market share, growth, and performance against target across all products, with different weightings and margins for different products, weighted by one's team's performance, all customized to the particular rep's geographic area, which in turn is given an assessment of potential by a corporate unit. The industry is well beyond a simple system of unit volume times commission rate.

Why does the industry do this? Because it is desperate to address some depressing statistics:

- From 1995 to 2001, the number of pharmaceutical reps doubled to 80,000.[1]
- In 1996, the average representative had 808 meetings with doctors; by 2001, that number declined to only 529 doctor meetings per rep.[2]
- Only 8 of 100 rep visits end with the physician meeting the rep and remembering what was said.[3]
- The length of sales calls varies widely, from as little as 20 to 30 seconds, to a few minutes, with the average somewhere between 1 and 2 minutes.[4]
- 40 percent of doctors' offices now limit the number of reps they admit each day.[5]
- 82 percent of doctors feel that reps have changed over the last five years—and not for the better. Doctors describe their current reps as "younger," "more aggressive," "less informed," and "more rushed" than in the past.[6]

So pharmaceutical firms measure, collect, and analyze the data seeking answers. The radical hypothesis—that the measurement system is itself a *cause* of the results—does not seem to have been considered.

Just imagine you're a physician. Five or more reps per day want your time. They call you a *target*. They have data on prescriptions you write (although they don't like to talk about it), and they want you to prescribe their drug more often. You know their compensation is affected by their success in so doing. You know their company has spent millions on figuring out just what kind of reps and what message will influence you the most. You know your responses will be measured and fed into a database; and the next time you see a rep, he or she may ask you why you didn't take his or her advice.

In that scenario, how much do you trust the rep?

Physicians increasingly see reps as out to increase their firms' sales, while they see themselves as focused on patient health. Most physicians feel they must get beneath the hype to figure out the truth.

The market has gotten tougher. Yet the pharmaceutical industry's response has been exactly wrong. Faced with an indirect sales situation, with very little face time with physicians, and with intense competition for time, the industry's response has generally been to do *even more* of the very things that caused customer cynicism in the first place: hiring more and younger reps, more training on the sales message, and more measurement systems to assess the profit impact on every dimension of the physician interaction.

This response generates feedback noise. More reps means less time per rep; younger reps means that they have less technical experience and less emotional maturity; more emphasis on message not product training means less credibility. Sophisticated measurement systems and marketing tell the physician that, as far as the pharmaceutical company is concerned, he or she is simply a wallet in a white coat.

The message the physician takes away from such high-powered marketing programs is that the company's interest in her is somewhere between little and none. Why should she trust a rep? Would you?

It's ironic that an industry so filled with people whose motivation for joining it was to help people has come to be perceived as so untrustworthy. One hypothesis is that the pharmaceutical industry has been so highly profitable over the decades that it has been a leading purchaser of cutting-edge management thinking, which has tended to emphasize competition and to micromeasure and analyze the front-end, customer-interacting parts of business processes.

Those systems often treat people like objects. The idea of highly refining measurements so that every aspect of every process can link directly to the bottom line was developed in talking about supply chains and distribution systems. Containers don't care if you count them. Raw materials don't care if you calibrate the effect on profitability of their time in inventory.

But people do. People react negatively when you measure them the same way you measure silicon or iron. Humans resent being treated like objects.

The pharmaceutical industry's dilemma will get worse until it figures out that measurement, behaviors, and processes aren't the problem—attitudes are. If I, as a customer, believe that your objective is first, last, and foremost to maximize my profitability to you, then I feel no different from a supply chain or a raw material. To you, I am merely an object to be managed, cost-reduced, and revenue-enhanced.

In such a case, highly refined measurements of the system's effectiveness don't make me feel better. They simply compound the fact that you view me as an object.

Half-measures compound the problem. Pharmaceutical firms are hardly alone in telling their customers things like, "We want your loyalty," "We want to be your trusted advisor," or, "We are customer-focused." Meanwhile, they work to ensure that every customer interaction maximizes the impact on the seller's bottom line.

The pharmaceutical industry's issues come from habits and values that are deeply ingrained; they won't change easily. But they can change, and the industry is increasingly aware of the problem.

Solutions will emerge. They might include, at least directionally, some of the following themes:

- Not just allowing, but urging, reps—within regulatory guidelines—to comment on competitor products when those products are better, based on contraindications or on clinical studies.
- Serious creative investigation into the real business needs of physicians (who are so accustomed to the existing system that it's difficult for them to be creative about solutions).
- More focus on treatments and on patient health than on prescribing.

- Deeper rep training in medical issues beyond those directly affecting the drug being sold.
- A willingness to evaluate physician value-adding programs over a longer term and with less direct "prescription ROI payback."
- Serious revamp of rep training programs, moving them away from micromeasuring scripted phrases and their effect on quarterly prescription rates to a trust-based model of ongoing relationships. *Note: this doesn't require changing the quarterly compensation system; it does require that reps recognize the greater economic power of cultivating trusted advisor relationships when measured over a period longer than a quarter or two.*

The Problem with Trust Measurement

The problem with measurement isn't limited to linking customers to profits. It also arises in measuring trust directly.

In Chapter 10 I talked about "the Heisenberg principle of trust." At a subatomic level in physics, certain metrics are affected by the act of measurement itself—the more precisely you measure position, the less precisely you can know momentum, and vice versa. With people, at the interpersonal level, the level of trust is affected by the attempt to measure it. In other words, getting too precise about measuring trust destroys it.

I once got a phone call from someone who had developed a four-page list of indicators of trustworthiness—multiple metrics for each of the trust equation variables of credibility, reliability, intimacy, and self-orientation.

He proposed to implement them as part of his firm's core skillset, complete with a needs analysis package and skills development program. Central to it all was measuring the performance of his firm's people on their trustworthiness and, of course, rewarding them on the basis of how effectively they performed against the trust metrics he developed.

In other words, he was proposing a system centered on skills measurement, training, and rewards for being trustworthy. This is a classic knee-jerk model of change used in many companies these days—define the desired behaviors, measure the gap, then align the rewards system with the desired behaviors. It sounds self-evident.

But suppose you were a client of that firm. How much would you trust an employee whose "trustworthiness" depends on how much he gets paid for being "trustworthy?" How intimate would you feel about some- one who is measured and rewarded on objective indicators of "intimacy"?

Most absurd of all—how self-oriented, noncredible, and untrustworthy is someone whose outward appearance of low self-orientation is in fact motivated by a *highly* self-oriented desire to be rewarded for *pretending* to be low in self-orientation?

I found it hard to explain the problem to him.

"After all," he said, "If you can't measure it, how can you manage it?"

Notes

1   Elling, Martin E., Holly J. Fogle, Charles S. McKhann, and Chris Simon, "Making More of Pharma's Sales Force," *The McKinsey Quarterly*, 3 (2002).

2   McKinnell, Hank, *A Call to Action*, New York: McGraw-Hill, 2005, p. 55.

3   *The McKinsey Quarterly*, op cit.

4   Rowe, Kim, "Physician Access and the Future," *HBA Bulletin*, September/October 2004.

5   *The McKinsey Quarterly*, op. cit.

6   Accel Health study.

POSTSCRIPT

Very simply, the only way to be trusted is to *be* trustworthy. The only way to be trustworthy is to have your customers' best interests at heart. If you *are* trustworthy, you will come to be seen as trustworthy. And if you are seen as trustworthy, you will also become very profitable.

The paradox is, you can't *set out to be* profitable by being trustworthy—it destroys the concept. You actually have to care. Profitability is a by-product; it disappears if you treat it as the sole goal.

You can measure the effect of trust and profitability in the long run, and you should. But you can't manage to it in the short run without destroying it. The measure of trusted relationships is at the relationship level, not the transaction level. The right measure of customer profitability is the lifetime, not the quarterly, time frame. The right focus of customer profitability is systemic, not customer-by-customer.

The most influence comes when you stop trying to influence and just help. The best measurements come when you stop trying to measure everything and just do the right thing. The best relationships come from acting from our humanity, not from our spreadsheets. In the long run, spreadsheets will tell the tale; in the short run, act from your humanness.

It may be obvious that to trust someone, you have to take a certain amount of risk. There are no guarantees in trusting; that's the nature of the thing.

But it's also risky for the seller, the one aspiring to be trustworthy. It requires that you give up control over the short term of your secrets and your belief in tit-for-tat competitive economic models. It takes a bit of courage to behave in a trustworthy manner with no guarantee that every action will be met with an equally positive reaction.

And individually, they won't. But in aggregate, they will. What you put out in trustworthiness gets more than repaid. You just don't know exactly when or from whom.

The ultimate risk—and return—lies in giving up control over your customers and clients. For your customers to trust you, you must trust them as well.

APPENDIX:
A COMPILATION
OF LISTS

This appendix duplicates the lists contained in the book. You can use this "list of lists" to:

- Get a quick feel for the book and what it's about
- Identify a topic of interest for more in-depth reading
- Review for reminders or as a checklist before certain events

The More Your Customers Trust You, the *Less* They Will:

(Chapter 3)

- Challenge your ideas indiscriminately
- Use multiple vendors
- Second-guess your advice
- Rely solely on narrowly written RFPs (requests for proposal)
- Challenge you on pricing
- Double-check things you do or say
- Force you to adhere to a rigid purchasing process where unjustified

The More Your Customers Trust You, the *More* They Will:

(Chapter 3)

- Be willing to listen to you
- Share information that might be useful to you

- Take your phone calls
- Make exceptions to standard procedures as appropriate
- Expedite, fast-track, and move things quickly
- Sole-source business to you
- Allow you to influence or interpret RFP specs
- Give you preferred status
- Forgive you the occasional mistake
- Share important information with you
- Seek out and take your advice

22 Benefits of Trust-based Relationships for Buyers

(Chapter 3)

1. Lower cost of purchasing
2. Lowered risk exposure to the good or service being purchased
3. Shorter time to market
4. Availability of expertise
5. Advance warnings of problems with goods or services
6. Input early on in product design and development decisions
7. Early access to relevant market information
8. Economies of information sharing
9. Ability to be flexible regarding processes, timing
10. Ability to ask a special favor
11. A supplier who understands the buyer's objectives
12. A supplier who understands the buyer's language, processes, terminology
13. Someone who will be honest and direct with you about problems
14. Greater ability to design-in features for the buyer's product line
15. Access to greater knowledge in components' areas
16. Knowledge of other uses or applications
17. Lower legal expenses
18. Less risk of legal exposure
19. Faster, shorter contracts
20. Managerial solutions to what were previously legal problems
21. Speed in resolving minor disputes, for example, payables terms
22. Ability to bring expertise to bear on the customer's customers

The Four Trust Principles

(Chapter 4)

1. A focus on the customer for the customer's sake, not just the seller's sake
2. A style of selling that is consistently collaborative
3. A perspective centered on the medium to long term
4. A habit of being transparent in all your dealings with the customer.

Why Client Focus Is Critical

(Chapter 4)

1. Client focus improves problem definition for customers who deal in complex problems.
2. Client focus allows constant learning on the part of the seller who can't know all the answers.
3. Customers won't let you *earn the right* to offer solutions until they feel you've understood their situation—and that comes about from truly paying attention.
4. True client focus works *competitively*—because few people really practice it.
5. Customer focus encourages the customer to *share more*, open up, and allow more access.
6. Client focus leads to *collaboration* by the client.
7. Customer focus fosters *acceptance* of recommendations.
8. An outsider's perspective often brings new insights that help all involved.
9. Focusing on another enriches our own lives.

Unconscious Destroyers of Customer Focus

(Chapter 4)

1. Seeking to control the agenda or outcome of a meeting or phone call
2. Focusing on one's own "share of client wallet"
3. Waiting too long to talk about money issues
4. An inability to confront customers on difficult issues

5. A belief that problems will get better if they are just left alone
6. Focusing on beating the competition
7. Cross-selling for its own sake, not the sake of the client
8. Pushing for a job when another firm is more qualified
9. Focusing on credentials, rather than customer issues, in the selling process
10. Seeing selling as unrelated to adding value
11. Being motivated by fears of how a client will perceive us as individuals
12. A preference for working "back at the office" rather than on the client site
13. Attachment to "winning" an argument
14. The belief that there are trade-offs between customers' interests and our own

Benefits of Collaboration

(Chapter 4)

1. Shared perspectives
2. Enhanced creativity
3. Efficiency through division of labor
4. Efficiency through enhanced communication
5. Efficiency through shortcutting where mutually agreeable
6. More buy-in on the part of the customer
7. Fewer misunderstandings
8. Less elapsed time
9. Greater honesty
10. Better working relationships
11. Improved understanding of each others' business
12. Greater understanding of motives behind words and actions
13. Staff development on the part of buyer and seller

Reasons We Resist Collaboration with Customers

(Chapter 4)

1. A belief that we compete with our customers
2. Ego—wanting to be seen as able to do everything

3. An inability to constructively confront difficult issues—especially emotional ones
4. Fear of sharing corporate secrets
5. Fear of being found out to have stretched the truth in the past
6. Lack of common goals
7. Fear of being seen as not knowing enough
8. Fear of sharing our economic model
9. Discomfort with speaking openly with customers
10. Fear they'll use knowledge learned to bring in a competitor
11. Fear they'll use knowledge learned to push for lower prices

Why a Medium- to Long-term Perspective Is Critical

(Chapter 4)

1. It gives you room to invest in the relationship.
2. It provides better return-on-investment data.
3. Both sellers and buyers can make a few bad short-term decisions.
4. The consequences of trust-creating behaviors—and trust-destroying behaviors—become clear.
5. It often takes a while to develop a relationship.
6. Beyond the transaction, the economics of scale and of relationships take hold.
7. Over time, buyers and sellers learn about each other's businesses.
8. In the short term, relationships can look like win-lose or lose-win; in the medium to longer term, they all become clearly win-win or lose-lose.
9. Time allows multiple relationships to develop across buyer and seller organizations.
10. The value of trust relationships isn't just additive; it fosters more trust relationships. Time helps trust become scalable.

Pressures against Adopting a Medium- to Long-term Perspective

(Chapter 4)

1. Quarterly earnings targets (for public companies)
2. Quarterly (or monthly) sales targets (if allowed to contradict longer-term good)

3. The desire to look good among one's peers—"the President's Inner Circle"
4. The lure of sales contests—"the trip to Hawaii"
5. Promotional pricing or other short-term incentives
6. The competitive sense between salespeople
7. The desire to help the team—"win one for the Gipper"
8. A fear of being taken advantage of by the buyer
9. A fear of establishing a precedent
10. A desire to get the maximum now, in case it doesn't come up again

Benefits of Operating Transparently
(Chapter 4)

1. Your customers have no doubt about your motives.
2. Your clients have the data to know you're telling the truth.
3. Little time is wasted in arguing about what the truth is.
4. You get a reputation for truth-telling.
5. Since your flaws as well as your strengths are evident, people can make sensible judgments about you.
6. For the same reason, people don't think you exaggerate.
7. Customers feel fairly treated by you.
8. Buyers are not suspicious of you.
9. Clients reciprocate by being open and aboveboard with you.
10. Buyers can see what is a fair profit for both of you.
11. You gain credibility—people believe what you say.

Reasons People Don't Practice Transparency
(Chapter 4)

1. A belief that, "They'll find me out and reject me—I'm not good enough"
2. Fear that we'll lose control of the sale
3. Fear that we'll have no value to add after all the information is out
4. Fear that we will be manipulated
5. Fear that the buyer will "cherry-pick" us for free ideas and then buy from a competitor
6. Fear that the buyer will use information to his or her advantage against us

7. Embarrassment or shame over our policies, products, organization, or ourselves
8. Belief that to be transparent is to give up advantage, therefore profits
9. Belief that transparency will help our competitors more than our customers

The Trust Creation Process

(Chapter 4)

1. *Engage*—understand what your customer values and be well-prepared to discuss one of those issues.
2. *Listen*—to the themes and issues that are important and real *to the customer.*
3. *Frame*—the true root issue, problem statement or opportunity statement in terms that both of you agree to.
4. *Envision*—jointly, an alternate end-state—how things will look if the issue was resolved.
5. *Action*—offer up specific actionable steps that are agreed upon by both parties.

23 Ways to Get and Stay Client-Focused

(Chapter 6)

1. Before you meet with a client, do whatever it is that you know helps calm you down. If you don't know how to calm down, go ask someone. If you don't know whom to ask, then try deep breathing, or sitting still with your eyes closed for 60 seconds.
2. Go into customer meetings well prepared. Then be prepared to drop all your plans. The point is to be ready to meet reality, not to try to control it.
3. Go into customer meetings with an objective. If the objective turns out to be wrong, then ditch it.
4. When the client is describing something, first let him describe it in his words. If the description is about something that happened, let him describe it chronologically. Just ask, "Then what happened?"

5. Start all customer interactions with agenda checking; "I want to make sure we get done what you want today. I thought we might start with X and Y; does that meet your goals?"

6. Don't try to take notes while you're listening. Either get another person to take notes, or write them as soon as you leave the meeting. Or stop occasionally and say, "Oh I'm sorry, just give me a second. I want to make sure I get this, let me just make a note." Then do so. Then put the pencil (or the keyboard) down.

7. Let the conversation go where the client drives it.

8. If the client is drawing diagrams, ask her to draw it in your notes, rather attempting to copy her drawings.

9. If you think you're in a negotiating situation with the customer, define before the meeting just what you think it is the customer wants. And why. And what's behind that. Then check the "why" and the "what's behind that" with the customer.

10. Be curious. About everything. All the time.

11. Open-ended questions are almost always better. You knew that, of course. But here are four of the best open-ended questions:
    What's behind that?
    Help me understand [why] [how] . . .
    Please tell me more . . .
    That must have [been] [felt] . . .

12. Instead of thinking "What an idiot" (or worse yet saying it), say, "Help me understand how it is you see it that way? It's not clear to me."

13. Make a list of the four top issues that keep your customer awake nights. (Even if you're meeting that customer for the first time). Then ask him to review and correct your list for accuracy.

14. Restudy listening 101. Sign up for listening 201. Demand listening 301. And read Chapter Eight in this book.

15. Don't multitask. When you're with the customer, turn off your phones and mobile devices of all types, and look away from your e-mail. Sit with your back to the glass hallway door or to the window with the great view. The customer is view enough.

16. When you feel angry at your client, stop and ask why she is doing what she is doing. From her perspective, not yours.

17. Make a list of five things you wish you knew about your customer (see Chapter Nine for some ideas). Find them out. Every time you find out one thing, add one more question to the rolling list of five.

18. Pregnant pauses are your friend, not your enemy. Hold them just a bit longer. If the client isn't filling two-thirds of the pregnant pauses, you're talking too much.

19. What percent of the time should the customer be talking versus the salesperson? You'd probably say 70/30. But have you ever timed it? Try it sometime.

20. If you don't understand something—ask about it.

21. What was your client's last job? What's her next one likely to be?

22. If the buyer doesn't buy from you, what's likely going to be the reason?

23. Try role-playing your customer with someone.

How to Know When You're Being Truly Collaborative
(Chapter 6)

1. You write the proposal *with* the client.
2. You are willing to think out loud.
3. You run a sales meeting like an early phase project meeting.
4. You openly discuss prices, fees, rates, and discounts with the client.
5. You're perfectly willing to discuss personalities with the customer.
6. You aren't afraid to say, "I don't know" when you don't—which is often.
7. Both you and your client have strong points of view and express them freely.
8. You're willing to say what concerns you about this potential sale.
9. You're willing to work with the customer's staff instead of your own.
10. You can name three times when the client changed your mind on a point.
11. When you have a client relationship problem, the first call you make is to the client.

Ten Ways to Adopt a Medium- to Long-term Perspective
(Chapter 6)

1. Remember that sales and earnings targets may be monthly or quarterly; but your career is long term. Sprinters don't win marathons—in fact, they lose them.

2. For any given issue—price, terms, timing—imagine doing the same deal 100 times. Ask yourself whether you would take that deal 100 times. Ask yourself whether the client would take that deal 100 times. If you both would, congratulations. If only one of you would, then talk about when and how the imbalance will be redressed.

3. If you think the prospect is taking advantage of you, be clear about your time horizon. Say, "This has to work for both of us in the long run; this price [or these terms] aren't sustainable for us. If we do this, it's a one-off."

4. Don't be greedy. Be willing to offer phased, partial, or incremental sales, rather than insisting on "the big contract" where it isn't necessary.

5. Accept that you have total control over your sales effectiveness— and very little control over its timing. Sales closed on trust are sales closed on the customer's calendar, not yours.

6. Be willing to push back on internal short-term pressures like sales goals and contests. I'm not recommending career suicide; but most sales managers will recognize the wisdom of choosing steadily growing sales over a few years versus pushing for the maximum every quarter until the balloon deflates, if you explain it well.

7. Learn to like deferred gratification. The benefits of trust usually outweigh the benefits of competition—you just have to increase slightly the measurement period to prove it.

8. Don't hesitate to say how this sale will lay the groundwork for X, Y, and Z initiatives that have to happen down the road, and how you might help. Say you'll bring it up again in three months. Then don't mention it again until the three months are up. In other words, be forthright about your intent to think long term, then don't sneak it into every conversation.

9. In your benefits discussions, don't settle for short-term definitions of value, like payback time. Make sure you talk about longer terms as well; *annual* savings, *compound* growth rates, *cumulative* reductions and increases.

10. Be willing to cut price, but be completely open about why and when you do it, and how you expect to recoup the investment over what time frame. (And don't cut price very often.)

13 Things You Can Do to Be More Transparent

(Chapter 6)

1. Talk about price early on. If clients ask about it, tell them. If they don't ask about it, tell them anyway: "So that neither of us runs the risk of embarrassing ourselves, perhaps we should initially touch on price. This feels to me like a medium six-digit kind of price range we're talking about; is that the kind of range that you were expecting?"

2. Answer direct questions directly, with no spin control. All of them.

3. Be prepared to candidly discuss the relative merits of your company's offering with those of your competitors. Honestly.

4. Introduce all the customer-facing people on your team to the customer. Make people's e-mails and phone numbers available. Their pictures too, in the case of relationships like call centers or support staff.

5. If you're worried about your competitors getting the information you share with your client, say, "This is the kind of information we of course want to keep confidential with you, our customer." Look the customer in the eye when you say it, and say it seriously. But *don't* then follow it up with a legal confidentiality or nondisclosure agreement.

6. If you *must* use legal agreements, get them vetted by a literate nonlawyer. In such cases, say, "This is one of those things we need to have written agreements on, I hope you'll understand."

7. Don't think about "opening bid" positions with customers; be straight about what you need.

8. Within legal boundaries, answer questions about pricing to other customers.

9. Invite the client to your offices—on your nickel.

10. Invite the customer to speak at an offsite sales meeting.

11. Let your customers know your profit model; their profitability to you; and where they stand vis-à-vis your other customers' profitability to you.

12. When you don't know, say so.

13. Don't ever lie. Ever. Nope. Not once. Ever.

Reasons a Customer Asks about Qualifications and Experience

(Chapter 9)

1. Fear of dealing with other more psychological and scary issues
2. Desire to find some chink in your armor
3. Desire to become expert quickly in your area so he can defend himself
4. Desire to buy time while she figures out what to say
5. Desire to see if you can connect with him
6. Trying to see if you understand her business
7. Desire to check off the box on what he is supposed to do
8. Collect information on what you've said so she can relate it to others
9. Desire to see if there is a basis for connection, common geographic or educational experience or leisure interests
10. Protecting himself by covering all the bases
11. Comparing her own understanding of issues with yours

Fears That Keep Salespeople from Being Authentic

(Chapter 9)

1. Fear that we haven't got what the buyer is looking for
2. Fear of being found out for not having done our homework
3. Fear that defects in our product or service will be found out
4. Fear that we have to exaggerate to get the job and will be found out
5. Fear that we'll disappoint customers
6. Fear that we'll have to cut price to get the business
7. Fear that our personality won't fit
8. Fear that we're not as good as we think we have to be

A Beginning List of Curiosity Questions

(Chapter 9)

1. How many organizational levels are there between your client and the CEO?

2. How is your customer's business organized differently from its chief competitors?

3. Where did your client go to high school?

4. What percent of total cost does your product represent for your customer?

5. What percent of cost does your product represent for your customer's customer?

6. How many of your customer's sales force do you know?

7. Does your client's organization do 360 feedback? Why or why not?

8. About whom does your client use the term "vendor?"

9. Which of your client's competitors has the highest return on equity?

10. Which purchase—from you or others—did your customer feel best about last year?

11. Who is your client's boss's trusted advisor?

12. When it comes to your customer's competitors, how much of what you do is outsourced versus done internally?

13. What do your client's customers like best about your client?

14. What's the biggest threat to your client's business as known by the client?

15. What does your customer spend annually on advertising?

16. Is your client's company the highest or lowest priced in its industry?

17. When was the last time your customer significantly altered his or her main product?

18. What's your client's go-to-market time for new offerings?

19. How do your client's salespeople approach selling?

20. How else might your client consider organizing the sales function?

21. What functions might your customer conceivably consider outsourcing?

22. Why is your client's company headquartered where it is?

23. Who are your customer's biggest customers?

24. How long has the company's CEO been in the job? Where was that person before?

25. What are your client's kids' names?

26. Why isn't your customer's office in [name that city] or in [name another city]?

27. When was the last time your client got promoted?

28. What's the level of staff turnover in your client's business?

Implications of Principles for Buyer/Seller Negotiations

(Chapter 12)

1. *Agree that if there is a fair solution, it'll be clear to each party.* Lack of perceived fairness by either party is a fact in itself. It says one of the two of you doesn't feel good about this. Perceived unfairness is prima facie evidence that the negotiation hasn't succeeded. Aim higher.

2. *Be willing to share 100 percent of your economic model—and all information.* How can the other party know what you want if you don't honestly tell him or her? Not sharing information decreases trust. Further, if previously withheld information ever comes out, you will appear to have lied. By contrast, if you behave transparently, your customer has the information on which to make sure that you feel fairly treated and knows you haven't behaved in an untrustworthy manner.

3. *Have a principle-based rationale for when you do or don't give discounts.* Many buyer-seller negotiations are over money. Arguments can be prevented by having a very logical and transparent pricing policy that you adhere to. This goes to the sense of perceived "fairness." Many clients aren't so much upset by a price as they are by the possibility that someone else might be getting a better deal.

4. *Project this transaction times 100 and assess the impact on each party.* Trust-based negotiation is about the relationship. So presume the relationship and envision each particular settlement multiplied a hundred times. Is it fair? If not, what is required to offset it—if not in this negotiation, then in future dealings?

5. *Never lie, withhold the truth, or even knowingly mislead the other.* Even just leading the other party to believe something that isn't true destroys trust. It puts your motives into question; it destroys your credibility; and it makes you look like you'll sacrifice the long-term relationship for short-term gain.

6. *Assume agreement; then try to justify the agreement to each party.* The competitive approach to negotiation keeps focusing on you, your needs, what you will do. But if you can each approach negotiation from the other's perspective, you lower your self-orientation, help yourself see the other side, and generally improve the overall offering.

The Six Toughest Sales Questions Customers Ask
(Chapter 17)

- Why should we choose you?
- What makes you different from your competitors?
- What experience have you had doing XYZ in our business?
- We don't need what you're selling right now, so why should we spend time with you?
- We're happy with our present supplier, so why should we change?
- Why are you so much more expensive?

Reasons to Invite Customers to Your Meetings
(Chapter 18)

1. You will generate great amounts of goodwill from the customers.
2. Your customers will work hard to articulate their ideas for you.
3. You will learn about major trends in the market.
4. Your salespeople will be role-modeling listening to a client.
5. Your salespeople will feel much closer to their own customers as a result.
6. Your salespeople will see that customers are "just folks."
7. You'll learn something about your competition.
8. You'll learn something about how you're perceived.
9. Your salespeople will learn that all customers agree on some things, and that they disagree on some other things—both of which may be surprises.
10. The customers can tell you some ugly truths you would otherwise deny.
11. Being invited to a provider's meeting has a positive effect on customers' likelihood of buying in the future, although you should not invite them for that reason alone.

Indicators That Show You're Thinking of Your Customers as the Enemy
(Chapter 19)

1. You're trying to get the best price possible from them in your negotiations, no matter how high.

2. You try as hard to sell them your least valuable (to them) product as you try to sell them your most valuable (to them) product.

3. You're talking to one of their competitors and haven't told them.

4. You steer them to a higher-margin product that isn't as good for them as a lower-margin offering you have.

5. You don't mention a competitor's product that is clearly superior for this customer for this application at this time.

6. You keep information confidential from them.

Nine Attitudes and Other Obstacles to Trust

(Chapter 20)

1. Being afraid of trust
2. Believing that customers mean what they say
3. Being tempted to say "trust me"
4. Believing you have to appear brilliant
5. Believing that a great track record sells itself
6. Seeing trust in terms of process and incentives
7. Believing that leads are scarce
8. Believing "the system won't let me"
9. Lacking passion

Reasons We Don't Like Talking about Price

(Chapter 23)

1. It is largely out of our control.
2. We are likely to get challenged on it.
3. Talking about price never results in higher prices, only in reductions.
4. We think customers put the highest weight on price.
5. It reduces everything to just one number.
6. It doesn't let us talk about all the other parts of value.
7. It makes it more difficult to differentiate ourselves from competitors.
8. We don't always have the lowest price.
9. Price-driven buyers are no fun and, in addition, unprofitable.
10. It feels final, like the last step, from which there is no appeal.

Why Customers Resist Talking about Price

(Chapter 23)

1. They are afraid of being manipulated.
2. They are afraid of being made a fool of.
3. They are afraid the price will be higher than they thought.
4. They don't know what to talk about after price is mentioned.
5. They are afraid of bargaining.
6. They are afraid of being told "no."
7. Talking about price can feel crass or rude.

Eight Things *Not* to Do When Facing Formalized Buying Processes

(Chapter 24)

1. Quibble with the design of the process
2. Hint at ways to end-run the process
3. Seek special favors based on past relationships
4. Withhold any part of the responses required by the process
5. Challenge the validity of formalized buying processes
6. Tell your client how much the work means to you
7. Snipe at the process in a passive-aggressive manner
8. Include pot shots at your competitors

Eight Steps to Take in Selling to Formalized Buying Processes

(Chapter 24)

1. *Comply fully with the process.* Fill out all forms, meet with all requested people, and don't talk to those who are put out of bounds. Put your emphasis on compliance, not on getting credit for complying. The customer will notice.
2. *Accept the client perspective.* If the client gets a better job for a better price from a competitor, then you should expect that the client will accept that proposal. Deal with it.
3. *Make major client-helpful suggestions.* But be honest. *Only* make process suggestions that clearly benefit the customer and be very

direct. If you can't find suggestions that help the customer much more than they help you, don't mention them.

4. *Accept competitor parity.* If you suggest a process interaction with the client, then suggest that the client have exactly the same interaction with your competitors.

5. *Ask for permission, not forgiveness.* Before sending extra data or answering unasked questions or providing additional references, ask permission. Assumptions in this situation are seen not as helpful but as arrogant. Now is the time to show respect.

6. *Think and talk long term.* This transaction is ideally just one of many. Talk to the client about which RFPs or bids you think best suit you. If you think this bid is a long shot, say so. It shows you value the relationship, not the transaction, and that you can be objective about your capabilities.

7. *Suggest a post-decision process debrief.* Offer the client a chance to hear your views about how to improve the process *after* the decision has been made. And make sure you suggest that the client hear from your competitors as well.

8. *Offer total transparency.* Offer customers the chance to sit in with you on all discussions about project design, staffing, and price. If they accept, tell them that you assume they will ask other bidders for the same transparency and that you accept the buyer's professionalism in dealing with confidentiality. Then do not abuse that professionalism by picking at the edges for advantage.

INDEX

objections and, 87, 113
problems of focus on, 112–113
in sales process, 57, 58
theory and reality of, 111–112
Collaborative style, 38–40, 64–66,
assessing how things are going,
emotions as facts in, 150–152
focus on process in, 148–150
in formalized buying processes,
writing proposals with customers,
cult of, 183–186, 190
with customers, 186–187, 207
measurements and rewards in,
price pressure and, 214–218
questions concerning, 168–173
in transaction focus, 104–109,
Conflict of interest, 32
Contacting, in sales process, 57, 58
Corporate buyer (*see* Customer)
experience and, 95–97, 167–169
in trust equation, 45

Curiosity, 100–103, 195, 198, 202
Customer, 3–12
    advantages of trust-based selling
        for, 21–23, 28–29
    building trust with (*see* Trust
        creation process)
    competing with, 186–187, 207
    differentiation and, 209–211
    levels of selling and, 19–20
    relationship as, 23–26
    reluctance to trust sellers, 34–36
    as term, xv
    two-step process for, 3, 6–8,
        71–72
    wants of, 4–5, 10–11, 194–195
    writing proposals with, 147–148,
        227–228
    (*See also* Customer focus;
        Customer selection)
Customer focus, 36–38, 61–63,
        86–103, 205–208
    achieving, 62–63
    authenticity and, 97–99
    channeling information in,
        99–100
    curiosity in, 100–103, 195, 198,
        202
    customer profitability and,
        108–109
    defined, 37
    doing the next right thing,
        93–95
    elevator question and, 91–93
    in formalized buying processes,
        147–148, 227–228
    importance of, 37, 90–91
    irritated customers, 88, 89–90
    nature of, 20–21
    polite customers, 87, 89

ABOUT THE AUTHOR

Charles H. Green is a consultant, author, speaker, and educator, focusing on the nature of trust in business relationships. Besides *Trust-based Selling*, he is the coauthor (with David Maister and Rob Galford) of *The Trusted Advisor* (Free Press, 2000).

Charles has spoken before companies in a variety of industries. An engaging and content-rich speaker, he has taught in executive education programs for the Kellogg Graduate School of Business at Northwestern and for Columbia University Graduate School of Business, as well as through his own firm, Trusted Advisor Associates. He focuses on businesses with complex customer relationships and buying processes.

Charles is a graduate of Columbia College (BA Philosophy, 1972) and of the Harvard Business School (MBA, 1976). He spent the first 20 years of his career with the MAC Group and its successor, Gemini Consulting, where his roles included strategy consulting (in Europe and the United States), VP Strategic Planning, and a variety of other firm leadership positions.

Charles's clientele includes leading companies in technology, accounting, consulting, financial services, commercial real estate, health care, and energy, as well as internal consultative functions like IT, HR, and legal.

Charles has published articles in *Harvard Business Review*, *Management Horizons*, and *Directorship Magazine*; a collection of articles are available at www.trust-basedselling.com.

He resides in Morristown, New Jersey, and may be reached at:
cgreen@trustedadvisor.com
www.trustedadvisor.com
(01) (973) 898-1579